Workforce Development Politics

Civic Capacity and Performance

Workforce Development Politics

Civic Capacity and Performance

EDITED BY
ROBERT P. GILOTH

TEMPLE UNIVERSITY PRESS
Philadelphia

Temple University Press, Philadelphia 19122
Copyright © 2004 by Temple University
All rights reserved
Published 2004
Printed in the United States of America

⊛ The paper used in this publication meets the requirements of the American
National Standard for Information Sciences—Permanence of Paper for Printed
Library Materials, ANSI Z39.48-1984

Library of Congress Cataloging-in-Publication Data

Workforce development politics : civic capacity and performance / edited by Robert P. Giloth
    p. cm.
    Includes bibliographical references and index.
    ISBN 1-59213-228-6 (cloth : alk. paper) — ISBN 1-59213-229-4 (pbk. : alk. paper)
    1. Hard-core unemployed—Government policy—United States. 2. Urban
poor—Employment—Government policy—United States. 3. Job creation—Government
policy—United States. 4. Occupational training—Government policy—United States.
5. Full employment policies—United States. 6. Community development, Urban—
United States. 7. Economic development projects—United States. 8. Local government—
United States. I. Giloth, Robert.

HD5708.85.U6W669 2004
331.12'042'0973—dc22

                                                                    2003064589

2 4 6 8 9 7 5 3 1

Contents

Acknowledgments

THIS BOOK was made possible because of the commitment of the Annie E. Casey Foundation to make multiyear investments to improve the long-term performance of workforce development. As a part of these investments, the Foundation has encouraged thoughtful reflection about how to make workforce systems more responsive to the needs and aspirations of low-income, low-skilled families. Participants in the six Jobs Initiative sites deserve thanks for their implementation of innovative workforce strategies while researchers looked over their shoulders.

I want to thank David Imbroscio for suggesting that I contact Clarence Stone of the University of Maryland about this effort to deepen our understanding of the politics of workforce development. Clarence has given generously of his time, insights, and encouragement at all stages of this project. He also co-authored (with Donn Worgs) Chapter 8 of this book. Their chapter raises provocative and important questions about the workforce development enterprise.

All of the authors have been enthusiastic about this project, and have brought their particular theoretical orientations to bear on improving our understanding of workforce development. Two papers commissioned as a part of the Annie E. Casey Foundation's Job Initiative could not be included in this book. I want to thank the authors of those papers: Peter Plastrik, Marlene Seltzer, and Judith Combes Taylor, and Robert Whelan, David Gladstone, and Tricia Hirth.

Kristin Coffey, Susan Gewirtz, Sheryl Lewis, and Georgianna Skarlatos have provided essential support along the way in commissioning these papers, convening author conferences, and preparing the manuscript.

Finally, I thank Kari, Emma, Lian, and Jack for supporting, in their own unique ways, my extracurricular writing projects.

ROBERT P. GILOTH

1   The "Local" in Workforce Development Politics
An Introduction

EVERY YEAR in many inner-city high schools half of the students who started out four years earlier as freshmen graduate. Although high school dropout rates declined in the 1990s, there are now more than 3.1 million 14- to 24-year-olds who have not graduated but are no longer attending school (Halperin, 1998). These young people are in more economic jeopardy than they would have been in the past. More broadly, there are 4.5 million working poor families with more than 10 million children who have insufficient skills and incomes (Annie E. Casey Foundation, 2002).

What has changed for these young people and families is the complexity of skills demanded by employers for jobs that promise family-supporting wages and careers. Not surprisingly, young adults who graduate from high school and obtain some post-secondary education experience steadier work and higher earnings and income than those who drop out or those who only receive a high school diploma (Judy and D'Amico, 1997; Pines, 2000).

The failure of schools is a central reason behind the emergence of "second chance" employment and training programs. This fragmented, hodgepodge of programs—high school equivalency degrees (i.e., GEDs), basic skills remediation, English as a second language, short-term training, long-term training, on-the-job work experience, dislocated worker and reemployment programs, and upgrade training for incumbent workers—tries to supply the education and training that the "first chance" system of schools, colleges, and employer training failed to deliver. Although there is much variation in their design, target groups, quality, and availability, second chance programs typically fail to provide a leg up on the economic ladder for low-wage, low-skilled, frequently minority, workers.

This book is about the politics of second chance employment and training systems and their relation to first chance systems. We define politics

1

as the ways in which we collectively organize and interact to solve problems, in this case trying to make second chance systems more coordinated, effective, and linked to the mainstream. A guiding question of this book is "why" ineffective training programs, largely serving communities of color, are tolerated.

What is distinctive about this book is that it focuses exclusively on the politics of local and regional—rather than national—workforce development. Although little has been written about local workforce development politics, except for occasional implementation studies related to the latest federal legislation, this topic is important because labor markets are largely regional; they are not based in central cities alone, nor are they simply the reflection of national economic trends and policies.

This book is not about developing a blueprint for new federal workforce legislation; it is not about identifying a pathway for U.S. workforce systems to become more like those in northern Europe; it is not about arguing that more good jobs need to be created, particularly in areas suffering high unemployment. These goals are important, particularly given the recent economic slowdown, however, this book shows that without attention to local politics, these reforms will ultimately fail.

High dropout rates and second chance employment and training systems are affected by a fluctuating and changing economy, shifting demographics and immigration, and poor program implementation. They reflect a deep confusion in America about how to best help people obtain jobs that lead to family self-sufficiency.

Public opinion polls, for example, show that 88 percent of Americans believe that education and training resources should be available for the jobless (Jobs for the Future, 1999). Eighty-one percent of Americans believe that the working poor should receive public benefits (Draut, 2002). Annual surveys by the National Association of Manufacturing (NAM) and the United States Chamber of Commerce demonstrate that 68–78 percent of employers have identified workforce and skills shortages as top priorities. These surveys contrast to issues given priority in the past, such as local economic development, which usually is focused on business climate issues and business attractions (Manufacturing Institute, 1998; Center for Workforce Preparation, 2001).

Conversely, although some evidence shows that increased investment in skills offers economic benefits and is the only sustainable pathway to economic prosperity for the working poor, evaluation studies cast doubt on how successful job training is in raising the incomes of low-income, working families (Lerman, McKernan, and Riegg, 1999; Smith, et al., 2002).

Public expenditures, primarily from the federal Department of Labor, for training and retraining low-skilled workers have diminished from a peak of $24 billion in 1978 to $7 billion in 1998, and a little over $6 billion in 2000. These expenditures lag behind public training investments in many other countries (National Center on Education and the Economy, 1990). Employers in the United States invest approximately 2 percent of payroll expenses in training, mostly for higher-level workers, in contrast to a 6 percent investment by employers in other advanced economies (Carnevale and Jacobson, 1997; Berg, 1996).

As we have seen, public opinion and employer priorities do not guarantee federal legislation that promotes substantial public commitments to workforce training and advancement (Martin, 2000). President Clinton's ambitious economic stimulus and employer training package was defeated in 1994; however, welfare reform passed in 1997 and reauthorization debates occurred in 2002–2003, emphasizing time limits, "work first," and some recognition of career advancement challenges. The Workforce Investment Act of 1998 (WIA) replaced the Job Training Partnership Act (JTPA) of 1982 and resulted in a cut in overall resources while attempting to consolidate programs, introduce competition, impose performance measures, and more fully engage employers (Buck, 2002; O'Shea and King, 2001).

Under the guidance of President George W. Bush, the Department of Labor and its myriad programs have become, according to some observers, the willing object of budget cuts. Nevertheless, work-based social policies, such as the $30 billion Earned Income Tax Credit (EITC), have bolstered the incomes of lower-income, working families, and won widespread congressional support. However, even the EITC has not been immune to "welfare bashing."

The constituencies of employment and training interventions—workers/job seekers and employers—experience today's labor market and workforce development systems in different ways. For the working poor or unemployed, family self-sufficiency represents much more than a minimum wage job. It requires a family budget that amounts to 200 percent of the federal poverty level, or about $37,000 for a single mother with two children in the Philadelphia region (Pearce and Brooks, 2001). Few jobs requiring modest levels of training exist today that pay these wages (Northwest Policy Center and Northwest Federation of Community Organizations, 1999; Bartik, 2002).

Moving up the economic ladder requires as much as 1,000 hours of basic education and training if you are a low-skilled worker (Carnevale and Reich, 2000). Ethnographies of low-skilled workers show that this is not a short-term process; many workers never choose to move in this direction because they are not confident about the job and wage benefits that will result from improving their skills and they lack the time and resources necessary to make these improvements (Iversen, 2002).

Alternatively, businesses, particularly small businesses, face a global marketplace driven by incentives to pursue "low-road" investment in workers and technology, contingent or temporary workers, or to simply relocate to the periphery. These firms frequently do not see their labor force as an asset deserving of investment. Firms underinvest in the training of entry-level workers because of "lean and mean" management strategies or because they fear that other firms will reap the benefits of their training investments by luring away newly trained workers with promises of slightly higher wages. However, employee turnover, retiring workers, and skill shortages impose real costs on many businesses, frequently constraining their ability to expand and grow. These challenges are likely to grow as baby boomers retire. It is not surprising that many businesses turn to the contingent or the immigrant workforce as short-term human resource solutions (Osterman, 1999).

The ability of employment and training investments to address these challenges has fallen short of expectations, and, in fact, has engendered serious skepticism. Despite the best of intentions, our reforms have either made employment issues worse or have contributed to the reduction of public commitment to human capital investment. We have, however, learned a great deal about what combinations of training, work supports, industry targeting, and human service supports deliver results for both workers and employers (Giloth, 2000). There exists a political problem: How do we translate what we have learned into collective action to produce scale impacts?

The impetus for organizing this book is the multi-city Jobs Initiative demonstration of the Annie E. Casey Foundation. The Jobs Initiative (JI) is an eight-year, $30 million effort launched in 1995 to change the ways in which second chance systems perform in connecting inner-city young adults with good jobs in regional economies. Ineffective training programs perpetuate the problem while good jobs go unfilled. The JI has not only invested in specific jobs projects that connect job seekers to jobs, it also has aspired to build local coalitions of businesses and other stakeholders to change the scale and sustainability of public and private investments in effective and coordinated workforce development.

The Foundation chose six diverse, large- and medium-sized cities—Denver, Milwaukee, New Orleans, Philadelphia, St. Louis, and Seattle. Within these cities, it chose an eclectic group of intermediary organizations—ranging from a city government to a union/employer partnership—to organize the JI in their city and region.

The JI embraced a set of principles for jobs projects and system reform investments that changed the thresholds for good practice and definitions of success.

- Outcomes for low-income workers should be related to higher wages, labor market retention, and career advancement

- Jobs investments should be customized to job seekers and workers who have different workforce experiences, basic skills, barriers, assets, and aspirations
- Diverse resources and partners should be integrated

Since 1995, the JI has placed 6,000 entry-level and hard-to-place workers in jobs with an average wage of $9.10 an hour. A follow-up survey of participants concluded that the JI had helped workers increase their earnings by $4,000 annually. These results, for a harder-to-employ population, compare favorably to the results of other welfare-to-work and workforce programs (Fleischer, 2001). The prolonged economic downturn, unfortunately, has undermined the sustainability of some of these positive employment effects.

All JI sites adopted the same principles for developing strategies to address the question: How can local workforce development systems become "performance driven," that is, organizationally focused and committed to promoting access to higher-wage careers for low-income job seekers and workers? Consequently, JI sites have pursued ways to foster systemic change by investing in "high-leverage" strategies that change the underlying forces that shape the way labor markets function. A good example of such a strategy is helping businesses to become more organized in relation to fulfilling their workforce needs (Jobs for the Future and On Purpose Associates, 1999).

JI sites have pursued and achieved a variety of workforce system reforms, even as they implemented short-term jobs projects. These reforms include creating flexible funding for job seekers, increasing employer voice in key policy forums, changing in-state policy rules and resources for education and training, and implementing standards of practice and organization for workforce providers. In order to accomplish these reforms, JI sites mobilized and expanded their relationships with a wide variety of stakeholders (Mueller and Schwartz, 2002).

As a part of the knowledge development needed to accomplish this system reform, the Foundation commissioned a number of background papers to advance the knowledge and theory about the politics of workforce development. This book is based on these papers.

These papers were not intended as substitutes for the ongoing evaluation of the JI, nor were they intended to be exhaustive examinations of the landscape and dynamics of workforce systems in particular cities and regions. Rather, authors were asked to combine case study material with relevant theories about local politics, system building, implementation, public policy, and economic change and development.

A simple question about "public will" motivated the JI. Why couldn't a local coalition of civic leaders be assembled to transform lackluster second chance programs into high-performing workforce development investments just as they mobilized, time and again, to build a new sports stadium, or make a bid to host the Olympics? Economic prosperity, tight labor markets, and long-term labor shortages in skilled occupations seemed the perfect setting to explore such a coalition. The payoffs for creating a competitive workforce seem obvious: Competitive firms, productive workers, a higher tax base, and more attractive and competitive regions. Why did such coalitions not form?

At the outset of the demonstration, the JI searched for sites with the "civic infrastructure" that could serve as the platform for such an ambitious agenda (Giloth and John, 1995). Yet, the selection of JI sites and local organizers was based on only modest knowledge of their civic potential and their willingness to pursue workforce development reform.

This Chapter discusses five background issues as a way of introducing the local politics of workforce development:

- Definitions of workforce development
- Approaches to workforce system reform
- The national and local contexts of workforce development politics
- Key ideas that chapter authors use in their case studies of local workforce politics
- The major themes and questions raised by authors that are addressed in the book's comparative chapter (Chapter 7)

The relative failure of second chance employment and training systems has usually been attributed to a failure of public commitment, design, and execution. Most of the attention has focused on the roles of Congress and the federal government. Also, it must be acknowledged that a failure of national public will is evident in our toleration of underfunded, fragmented, and poorly performing second chance programs.

This book, however, offers a different approach. It begins with the question: How have local politics contributed to the failure of workforce development systems on behalf of low-skilled, low-wage workers and job seekers? Secondly, it asks: If local politics played a different role, could it help make workforce development more coordinated and effective?

WORKFORCE DEVELOPMENT, REGIONAL LABOR MARKETS, AND SYSTEMS CHANGE

Second chance employment and training systems are not islands, although they are isolated in many respects. This is especially true because many workforce experts argue that workforce development must engage businesses as well as workers and integrate resources across a number of institutions, such as community colleges. The commitment to workforce development involves engaging businesses and making programs responsive to them, defining success as job placement and retention rather than graduation, and gaining a better understanding of how job seekers and workers are embedded in informal networks (Giloth, 2000; Harrison and Weiss, 1998).

To understand the politics and policies of second chance systems, it is important to understand the larger environment of which workforce development is a part, including the public, private, and nonprofit sectors. Moreover, it is also useful to understand some of the approaches that advocates have used to improve and, in some cases, reform the performance of these employment and training programs. These reform approaches give an indication of possible strategies for encouraging local politics to support workforce change.

Second chance workforce development programs and institutions are part of largely private, voluntary regional labor markets made up of millions of individual and business decisions about occupations, skills and qualifications, wages, and hiring, firing, and promotions. These business decisions are influenced by macro factors related to economic growth, structural economic change, and technology, as well as micro factors related to external and internal labor markets, labor supply, geography, labor market intermediaries, informal networks, and unionization. Many factors related to industry structure, race, ethnicity, gender, and public policy also affect these decisions.

Today's regional labor markets are characterized by technological change, geographic dispersion, service-sector growth, growth of small firms, contingent work, and decline in union density. Changes in labor markets and the structure of firms have produced economic incentives for the development of new workforce efforts to bridge supply and demand, city and suburb, neighborhood and sector. The structure of firms has dramatically changed the prospects of workers and workforce development because of the collapse of internal labor markets and career ladders, lean- and high-performance workplace designs, nontraditional work arrangements—such as temporary work—and heightened insecurity among employees and job seekers (Osterman, 1999). Many firms now lack the organizational capacity to find and keep workers.

Employment and training efforts overlap with, as well as depend upon, first chance education and training systems. For many communities, the failure of the public school system relegates its young people to lower-paying jobs and a remedial system of education and training.

The first chance system, however, extends beyond high schools, including vocational education, community colleges and technical schools, four-year colleges, proprietary schools, nonprofit training providers, private-sector training institutions, and on-the-job employer investments. There are 1,000 two-year colleges, 2,000 four-year schools, and 4,000 propri-etary schools nationally (Carnevale and Jacobson, 1997). The second chance system depends upon these institutions as training partners. How-ever, these first chance institutions frequently are reluctant to invest in entry-level workers or in unprepared entrants except in times of labor shortages and environments flush with public subsidies.

Three images illuminate the roles and dynamics of first and second chance employment and training programs in regional labor markets. Together these images represent a composite of organizations and activities.

The first image is a market. Workforce programs enhance the human capital of individuals seeking work, improving their competitiveness and chance of moving to the head of the hiring queue. In the best of cases, these programs serve as credentialing intermediaries that link the job-ready with employers, help employers define jobs and job qualifications, and provide an alternative to the informal hiring networks that operate through internal labor markets. Billions of dollars in federal grants and loans, such as Pell grants, have enabled welfare recipients, dislocated workers, and low-skilled workers to improve their skills and compete in the marketplace (Carnevale and Jacobson, 1997).

The second image is an industry. In this case, first and second chance employment and training programs represent a cluster of cooperating and competitive organizations that share common or related goals, standards, technologies, human resources, and outcomes. Sometimes these similar programs are referred to as a field. The industry image calls attention to the capacities, human resources, and common practices of organizations with similar goals and policy agendas. In a number of cities, trade asso-ciations or coalitions of these workforce providers have formed for the purposes of sharing knowledge and promoting beneficial policies. More broadly, these industries are organized nationally as associations of com-munity colleges, workforce boards, or sectoral employment programs. In turn, these national networks create their own specialized intermediaries for policy, financing, and technical assistance purposes.

Finally, the third image is a system. This image more comprehensively identifies the policies, regulations, and financing resources—many of which are federal in origin—that shape and reinforce the capacities and behaviors of individual and networks of employment and training orga-nizations. These environmental and institutional constraints shape the basic functions and strategies of workforce development providers. What kinds of job training are allowed, and for whom? Who qualifies for spe-cific types of training programs and economic supports? Who are the implementers of workforce development and how are they financed? Again, the employment and training components are related, but in this image the accumulation and weight of various policies and their administrative rules are a key determinant of their shape and behavior.

The Regional Workforce Partnership of Philadelphia, for example, recently produced an organizational map of what workforce development systems look like in Pennsylvania. Its complexity fairly represents what would be found in all other states (Regional Workforce Partnership, 2002). The map shows five state agencies, twenty-two local workforce investment boards, and forty-nine job training and education programs. This institutional map represents close to $1.3 billion in federal and state investment; there is an additional $48 million in new programs for 2002.

Nevertheless, this map only captures a part of the complete picture of state workforce systems. It does not include, for example, the investments of many federal agencies such as the Department of Housing and Urban Development or of state agencies that invest in local school districts. Nor does the map show the hundreds of for-profit and nonprofit workforce providers who operate at the ground level, preparing, training, placing, and supporting workers and employers.

Changing how labor markets and workforce development systems are organized and function can help promote the scale, sustainability, and structural changes needed to improve access to good jobs and career ladders for large numbers of low-income job seekers. Workforce system reform means changing how public and private resources and actions support long-term job retention, career advancement, and neighborhood employment change. The systems reform route, however, is not without peril; it requires a conceptual framework that identifies opportunities for change in labor markets, the capacity to build political alliances around change strategies, access to significant public and private resources, and a commitment to produce measurable results for low-income job seekers.

Labor market complexity makes reshaping workforce development policies extremely difficult. Reform strategies range from comprehensive and detailed lists to highly targeted investments. One approach contrasts administrative exceptions and flexibility, specific policies, such as living wage ordinances, and comprehensive reforms containing multiple aspects of labor markets (Okigaki, 1997). A second approach identifies a limited number of strategic leverage points for change in labor markets, such as the cooperative organization of employers, credentialing and standards, and community policy mechanisms (Jobs for the Future and On Purpose Associates, 1999). A third approach promotes improvements in job quality, career ladders, internal labor markets, and labor market coordination and benefits (Bernhardt and Bailey, 1998). A fourth approach recognizes the new and powerful role that workforce intermediaries play in bridging supply and demand, job seekers and employers, neighborhoods, sectors, and occupations (Evans and Kazis, 2000; Mt. Auburn Associates, 1996).

Examining these proposed reform strategies and many others suggests a surprising consensus among workforce experts about how a changed workforce system should function and what it should look like (Grubb, 1996; Halperin, 1998). This consensus is not, however, about the realism of such a vision, how to bring about such change, or who should do it.

Workforce system change requires, first of all, exceptional public commitment and resources to integrate first and second chance systems to create ongoing opportunities for training and advancement. Workforce system reform should produce:

- Job retention and career advancement as driving outcomes
- Creation of and investment in good jobs and career ladders
- Workforce and education programs that are "vertically linked" to high school graduation, career training, post-secondary education, and skills upgrading
- Support services that are vocationally oriented and connected to training and jobs
- Opportunities, careers, and pathways that are visible, coherent, and interconnected
- Business engagement at every stage of workforce development

Workforce development is not just about public investments in programs and incentives. Workforce development is a part of regional labor markets in which business investments and behaviors are critical for the success of all workers. But there is a dilemma: A complicated and frequently disconnected set of funding silos and programs has developed that performs as much to secure its ongoing existence as to solve real labor market problems. Although there are a number of strategies for reforming these workforce development systems, any discussion about workforce development politics must begin by discussing the federal policy landscape.

FEDERAL POLICY AND WORKFORCE DEVELOPMENT

Second chance systems of employment and training have grown dramatically during the past fifty years due to federal policy and local implementation, although their history extends back to the last century. As a part of their recent evolution, the local- and state-funded first chance systems received additional federal dollars, even as parallel institutions emerged to serve new or redefined target populations. Federal workforce policies and politics establish a baseline of public commitments, institutional designs, strategies, and performance criteria that severely limit the possibilities of local workforce development politics.

The storyline of federal labor market policies since World War II shows an overall narrowing in the ambition, ideas, target populations, and funding. Although the Works Projects Administration (WPA) and Civilian Conservation Corps (CCC) of the Great Depression Era involved public job creation and national economic planning, the final Full Employment Bill of 1946 signaled the direction and shape of workforce policy for decades—more concern with small-scale, human capital investments rather than active labor market policies (Harvey, 1989). The original ambition and rhetoric of this bill was kept alive, however, in the Humphrey Hawkins Full Employment Bill of the 1970s.

Five characteristics distinguish the U.S. workforce policy paradigm that emerged during this fifty-year period (Mucciaroni, 1990; Weir, 1992; King, 1995; Martin, 2000). First, the final version of the 1946 Full Employment Act separated active labor market policies, including workforce training, from national economic management. By the 1950s, economic management emphasized commercial Keynesianism—the stabilizing of aggregate demand rather than more directive or adaptive approaches to economic structural change and its effects on labor markets. This meant that labor market policies became secondary in the policy thinking and action toward U.S. economic growth.

Second, employment and training policies developed throughout the 1960s targeted the poor, as evidenced in the Manpower Demonstration and Training Act (MDTA) of 1963 and the War on Poverty of 1964. Specialized workforce investments became limited rather than universal, severely constricting the constituency for these policies. This also became the case with the United States Employment Service, established under the Wagner Peyser Act of 1933, which tended to connect the unemployed with low-end jobs (King, 1995).

Third, workforce legislation and policies favored human capital investment, or supply-side strategies, rather than public job creation or sectoral strategies that sought to affect employer or industry decisions and behaviors. Nevertheless, public job creation strategies reappeared in the 1960s and 1970s as a part of Office of Economic Opportunity's (OEO) New Careers, the Comprehensive Employment and Training Act (CETA), and in the 1990s, now called "transitional jobs," as a part of "welfare reform."

Fourth, federal legislation and budget allocations have committed only a small portion of the resources required to address the employment and training needs of even the narrow target populations. The Job Training Partnership Act (JTPA), for example, reached as few as 5 percent of the population in need of—and eligible for—workforce services (Lafer, 1994, 2002). This paucity of resources not only limits the impact of these employment training programs, but again circumscribes the constituencies that benefited from them and had reason to care about their performance.

Fifth, the rapid development of employment and training policies and programs in the 1960s created fragmented programs and funding, so-called "silos." By 1995, there were still 163 workforce programs administered across a wide array of federal agencies that totaled $20.4 billion (Grubb, 1996).

Since the 1960s, Congress has mounted repeated efforts to consolidate, coordinate, and devolve decision-making about these programs to local and state governments. Although these administrative reform efforts have had positive impacts, employment and training systems remain a maze of institutions, regulations, and mandates.

A parallel track of first chance education and training evolved at the same time as programs devoted to targeting the low skilled and poor or unemployed. The G.I. Bill of Rights (1944), for example, supported the education and training of WWII veterans in a time of surging labor demand for skilled workers. Post-secondary education in the postwar era expanded and contracted depending upon demography, labor demand, and the relative value of college education. Today, the value of post-secondary education is rising again because of the relatively low value of high school diplomas and the increasing demand for skilled workers (Carnevale and Jacobson, 1997).

The politics associated with these federal workforce policies has ranged from conflict about ideas and ideology to questions of who gets what, how best to calm civil unrest, and the devolution of authority and resources to states and localities. Interests and priorities have shifted over time. Employment and training versus public job creation is a recurrent theme. In general, business participation in workforce development has been sporadic and weak except in times of ideological contention over the scope of labor market policies or with firms that have developed an organizational commitment and "policy legacy" for workforce development (Martin, 2000).

Not surprisingly, business cycle and unemployment impacts have generated interest and opportunities, most clearly in the 1970s with the passage of public job creation. In a number of situations, unions have opposed employment training and public job creation because these programs typically are directed only at a narrow population group and, in some cases, would produce lower-paying jobs that could undermine existing union employees.

Today's national policy context for workforce development embodies policy, political, and institutional tensions that took shape in the 1980s, although strong continuities with the past are also present. In some sense, today's federal policy challenge is to recognize that old reform formulas have proven unworkable and no accepted vision exists for building a better system. Indeed, competing social policy ideas emphasize work rather than welfare, work first rather than training, and making work pay supports rather than investments in career development.

President Ronald Reagan's policies in the 1980s and the recession of 1979–1983 combined to produce cutbacks and devolution of social welfare programs and discussions about how to enhance economic productivity in the new context of global competitiveness. The Job Training Partnership Act (JTPA) of 1982 reduced the largesse and public service employment of CETA and introduced performance contracting and employer representation on local Private Industry Councils (PICs). JTPA contracted with many community-based organizations as providers, but its performance measures skewed service delivery to dislocated workers and those least in need of services.

From the mid-1980s until the early 1990s, there was growing bipartisan support for concerted policy attention to issues of skills and economic productivity. This began with *A Nation at Risk*, published in 1983, which called attention to lagging educational achievement in the United States. In 1987, *Workforce 2000* highlighted the coming workforce crisis in terms of skill requirements (Judy and D'Amico, 1987). Elizabeth Dole, Secretary of Labor, established the Secretary's Commission on Achieving Necessary Skills (SCANS) to explore national skills standards. In 1990, the publication of the widely influential *America's Choice: High Skills Low Wages* documented the crisis of human capital and global competitiveness in the United States (National Center on Education and the Economy, 1990). This publication would serve as a playbook for the early training proposals of the Clinton administration (Martin, 2000). Finally, the JOBS program of the Family Support Act of 1988 signaled a renewed attempt to transform our welfare system into a system promoting human capital investment and work.

In the early 1990s, two related events shaped workforce-related policy and practice for the decade to come. In 1993, Congress dramatically expanded the EITC, first established in 1975 as part of the Budget and Tax Reconciliation Act. This is a refundable tax credit for working poor families that by 2000 would amount to $30 billion a year, making it the largest antipoverty program in the United States. Later that same year, Abt Associates completed its evaluation of the JTPA, concluding that these employment and training investments had modest, if any, effects overall (Orr, Bloom, and Bell, 1995). One exception to their conclusion stood out: The Center for Employment Training (CET) achieved remarkably positive income impacts through a combination of employer-driven training, contextualized learning techniques, and community support (Melendez, 1996).

Additional data from the Riverside (Gain) project in 1994 reinforced the growing belief that investments in workforce development were not as productive as getting people into jobs—any jobs—and supporting them with work supports like the EITC (Strawn and Martinson, 2000).

President Clinton's administration attempted to connect workforce training to an ambitious economic stimulus package and employer training taxes. Although most of this ambitious plan was scuttled, skills standards and apprenticeships received endorsement in Goals 2000 and the School to Work Opportunity Act (Lafer, 1994; Martin, 2000).

In 1997, Congress passed and President Clinton signed welfare reform legislation, the Personal Responsibility and Work Opportunity Reconciliation Act (PRWORA) of 1996. PRWORA imposed time limits on welfare recipients, using a work first approach to connecting to the labor market and making work pay provisions. The overriding emphasis, however, was on reducing the welfare roles rather than eliminating poverty or investing in skills development and careers.

The Workforce Investment Act of 1998 also emphasized the work first approach, but embraced parts of the failed Workforce Security Act of 1993 and continued a long tradition of attempting to consolidate workforce programs, devolve authority, engage employers, integrate services into One-Stop Centers, introduce competition, and set more ambitious outcome standards.

National politics surrounding workforce and welfare policies continued to be schizophrenic. President Clinton was a New Democrat who sought ambitious new funding and taxing roles, but settled for "ending welfare as we know it" and a reinvented but shrinking employment and training system. The business community continued support for employment and training policies, but also became an advocate of welfare reform in the context of tight labor markets.

The election of George W. Bush as President coincided with the end of nine years of economic prosperity, new tax cuts, and public attention diverted from domestic policy to our "war on terrorism." The reauthorization debate for federal welfare legislation in 2002 kept the basic policy tenets and funding intact, while tinkering with work requirements and adding ideological commitments to promoting marriage. While much attention focused on the adequacy of and access to work supports, such as the EITC, renewed attention focused on how workforce development investments might contribute to helping working poor families move toward self-sufficiency.

The Workforce Investment, Carl D. Perkins Vocational Education, and the Higher Education Acts are up for reauthorization in 2003–2004, offering new opportunities to modify, and perhaps incrementally improve, our fragmented and shrinking workforce development systems. The possibility also exists for further budget cutting and devolution.

THE LOCAL POLITICS OF WORKFORCE DEVELOPMENT

This book explores collective problem solving related to second chance workforce development systems. As we have seen, these systems serve a relatively small number of low-wage, low-skilled people who have failed in the first chance system of education, although a much larger number of similarly situated people need human capital investment to move ahead. As many as 15 million to 50 million adults between the ages of 16 and 64 may need human capital investments because of lack of basic skills, English proficiency, high school degrees, or technical training (Carnevale and Desrochers, 2002).

Workforce systems are nested in regional labor markets, made up primarily of employer opportunities and constraints, but they also exist within a limited and shifting context of ideas, authority, and resources created and reinforced by fifty years of federal workforce development policy and insufficient local implementation.

To date, local workforce systems largely fail to satisfy the needs and aspirations of both job seekers/workers and businesses. Low-wage and low-skilled workers are not supported on career paths that help them reach economic self-sufficiency, and businesses do not obtain a sufficient number of job-ready employees who can perform productively, acquire needed skills, and reduce turnover rates by remaining on the job. Some of this problem involves how to coordinate and integrate the multiple silos and programs; another part is about how to create pathways to careers.

The "local" we are focused on refers primarily to older central cities and inner-ring suburbs where poverty and large numbers of working poor with lower skills are concentrated. In most cases, these populations are largely communities of color. Much of this discussion, however, is also relevant for rural areas and small towns, which frequently face more challenging economic development problems. Although embedded in regional economies, many inner-city urban neighborhoods, particularly those experiencing a legacy of racial exclusion, did not fully benefit from the prosperity of the 1990s and still suffer the effects of high unemployment (Kotkin, 2002).

Although the cities are similar, they are not the same. Some have experienced population increases and the pressures of gentrification; others continue to shrink and are part of declining or no-growth metropolitan areas. In some cities, the poor are moving to the suburbs. In all cases, however, manufacturing jobs have declined, and job growth has occurred in the suburbs or exurbs.

Although cities have limited powers to affect policy and economic changes, a growing number of cities have explored the connections between economic and human capital development in the 1990s (Clarke and Gaile, 1998).

The local dimension of workforce politics, policy, and implementation has been further complicated by the increased role of state government in the administration of welfare reform under the PRWORA and the WIA. For example, state policy has been critical in defining work requirements, time limits, work supports, and access to education and training resources for welfare-to-work programs. States have also established state workforce boards, and have had the opportunity to pursue unified plans that would bring some level of integration to welfare, workforce, and community colleges (Clymer, Roberts, and Strawn, 2002). Few states took advantage of this opportunity. Not surprising, many welfare and workforce advocates have developed conflicting state policy agendas (Clavel and Westmont, 1998).

Clarence Stone has conceptualized the political challenge of local human capital politics, including education and workforce, as the question of whether "employment regimes" can be transformed into "performance regimes" (Stone, 1998). This question is part of a larger theoretical effort, called regime theory, to understand why and how informal and formal arrangements are produced to support stable governing coalitions (Stoker, 1996). Such arrangements bridge state and market, city hall and civic leaders, and take on various forms under different economic and policy conditions. Stone argues that adequate financial resources, access to authority, and common ideas are necessary for durable coalitions to form and last around particular policy issues.

Employment regimes are those implementing institutions that are most concerned with perpetuating their own survival and the jobs they provide. They are bureaucracies more focused on survival, job protection, and deflecting change than with doing what it takes to transform ineffective training programs into high-performing investments.

In contrast, the normative meaning of performance regime is that this same set of institutions, now enmeshed in a broader civic context of relationships, networks, and leadership, can drive toward more ambitious results and outcomes—good jobs, careers, and productive employers.

This conception of local workforce development politics suggests that problem solving is highly influenced but not completely constrained by federal policies, economic competition, and institutional arrangements. In other words, there is room to arrange things differently, ideally on a performance basis. This is a different type of autonomy than is usually posited by regime theorists, who have been more concerned with the impacts of intermetropolitan economic competition on local politics and policies. Indeed, the balance of local urban political analysis has focused on the issues of economic development, and the evolving pattern of business, public sector, and civic arrangements that have advocated for local growth.

One of the most common metaphors for these arrangements is a "growth coalition" of land-based elites who single-mindedly pursue local economic growth, downtown expansions, new infrastructure investments, and mega projects (Logan and Molotch, 1987). Political analysts have described these growth coalitions at work and identified opportunities for limiting or redirecting the local growth pattern of politics to consider other populations and public needs.

There is some ambivalence about such growth coalitions. Although their efforts may ignore other economic development strategies or equity considerations, at best they provide opportunities and incentives for creating and sustaining focus, a rare asset in a local political and institutional environment often characterized by a fragmentation of interests and authority. Unfortunately, rarely has this civic ability to focus transferred to the realm of human capital or quality of life for the entire urban population. The question of focus, and how to work incrementally to get it and maintain it, is at the heart of thinking about local workforce politics.

Workforce or human capital politics face a number of challenges related to building focus and coalitions when compared with local economic development. An overwhelming challenge is that workforce or employment and training constitute a subsystem of local policymaking (Stone et al., 2001). A subsystem suggests that workforce issues are smaller and more self-contained than other policy issues.

Subsystem may be misleading, however, in that it still suggests a level of commonality in terms of ideas, priorities, organizations, and resources. Given funding silos, regional fragmentation, and multiple problem definitions, commonality at the subsystem level may be elusive as well. As a subsystem, workforce development may need to be connected to other issues and stakeholders in order to gain broader acceptance and priority, and at the same time, may require more investment to construct itself as a subsystem with comprehensible and related ideas, functions, and decision-making processes.

Achieving this level of organization and credibility will be difficult because the incentives at work in the workforce development arena are simply not as strong as those in the economic development arena, and authority is widely dispersed (Clarke and Gaile, 1998). Workforce development benefits are limited rather than universal and accrue over the long term. Of course, this presumes that workforce development is effective in producing benefits. Improvements in workforce development, for example, accrue to individual workers and firms, but do not as easily benefit key stakeholders, and cities and regions in a visible way.

Economic development, in contrast, generates a variety of multiplier effects, producing financial opportunities for banks, contractors, developers, lawyers, and politicians. The ongoing investment impact of new physical infrastructure, such as an airport or highway, is obvious. The strongest benefits created by workforce development may be those jobs and contracts of workforce institutions that make employment regimes impediments to the reform process.

The fragmentation and dispersal of authority in the workforce development arena make it extremely difficult to target and capture even these limited benefits. Workforce development comprises multiple systems with weak governance—welfare-to-work, workforce, school-to-work, community colleges, adult education, and vocational education. Indeed, the two central constituents of workforce development—employers and workers—are largely unorganized for collective action at the local or regional level. Only a small number of these constituents can even theoretically receive benefits from these systems. This problem is compounded when we consider regional labor markets—multiple jurisdictions and workforce development planning areas and a multitude of diverse employers (Hughes, 1996).

These authority and fragmentation problems are exacerbated by the increased role of state governments. The state has always been involved in workforce-related issues—welfare, unemployment insurance, employment service, community college, and vocational education. However, the state's role and importance has increased with recent federal legislation and because of the resources they invest. What this does in many states is to pit cities and older suburbs—which frequently have large minority populations—against mostly white suburban and rural legislative majorities, which have different policy beliefs and agendas (Orfield, 2002).

As a subsystem with limited, short-term benefits and dispersed authority, how can workforce development inspire a politics capable of pursuing and achieving a performance regime in which workers and employers obtain significant benefits? Stone et al., in their work on urban education reform, have concluded that a politics of education reform (and perhaps human capital politics more generally) must turn toward building civic capacity—the networks, relationships, and institutions connected and mobilized around a common set of ideas, issues, and objectives. Their research suggests that cities with civic capacity are more likely to achieve reform impacts (Stone et al., 2001). What this approach to building civic capacity suggests is that civic mobilization to overcome dispersed authority and small, long-term benefits to achieve workforce systems, change through incremental, systemic victories. Civic capacity is the sustained ability to overcome local divisions and fragmentation to pursue an accepted social purpose.

There is no single pathway for this civic capacity to emerge, or to become more transparent or viable. In some cities and time periods, workforce development may provide an organizing principle or opportunity. Educational reform has frequently provided such a starting point. In other situations, however, a broader "livelihood" agenda may be the banner under which to pursue workforce development objectives (e.g., social equity, affordable communities, or quality of life) (Evans, 2002).

No matter what the umbrella set of ideas and objectives, progress will not be made without "agents of reform"—intermediaries that are able to create and take advantage of local opportunities to build local civic capacity (Evans, 2002). These agents of reform can be quite diverse, but they must have the ability to use information, navigate and broker relationships, chart courses of action, identify concrete steps forward, and combine an entrepreneurial spirit with a realistic sense of the possible.

Finally, in the longer run, civic mobilization and capacity must contribute to a "systemic agenda" for change, in this case toward what we have characterized as a performance regime in workforce development. What will be needed is a sense of the interim steps and strategic levers that can achieve change and produce multiplier effects of additional change and civic capacity. It may be overly optimistic to suggest that this cycle of civic capacity building and systemic change can reach a turning point in the short run, but important steps toward performance regimes are possible.

Where is the civic capacity related to workforce development found in cities and regions? If found, how can it be mobilized and focused to support a systemic workforce development agenda for making progress from employment regimes to performance regimes? Who can make this happen?

Several contemporary examples show different forms of civic capacity, different approaches to systemic change, and different opportunities defined by timing and circumstances. In several cases, a "sectoral" approach to workforce development, building civic capacity and workforce programs with particular industries, has been adopted (Dresser and Rogers, 1998). None of these examples, however, demonstrates full-blown reform of workforce development systems; instead, they illustrate how small victories over time may accumulate into meaningful changes, increased credibility, and the development of more civic capacity.

Project QUEST

In 1992, after the Levi Strauss plant closed and laid off hundreds of workers, Project QUEST of San Antonio was founded by COPs/Metro, an Industrial Areas Foundation (IAF) church-based, community-organizing network (Lautsch and Osterman, 1998). After numerous house meetings with residents, and numerous research actions to identify powerful workforce models, COPs/Metro formed Project QUEST to provide pathways to family-supporting jobs. The QUEST model involves employer commitments for hiring, flexible funding to support families for up to two years, a church-based recruitment and mentoring system, and a redesign of community college courses to fit the needs of employers and job seekers.

Achieving employer commitments and flexible funding required major organizing efforts because they essentially refashioned the relationship between working poor families and the labor market and public systems. Since 2002, Project QUEST had trained and placed 1,400 people in jobs paying an average of $10 per hour, and achieved average income increases of $7,000 for each participant. Project QUEST has been replicated and adapted in Austin and El Paso, and has influenced the Better Jobs Initiative agenda of San Antonio's new mayor.

Seattle Jobs Initiative

The Seattle Jobs Initiative (SJI), a Casey Jobs Initiative site, was launched in 1995 under the leadership of Mayor Norm Rice (Smith and Davis, Chapter 5; Fleischer, 2001). Its impetus derived not only from the availability of foundation funds, but also from three converging forces:

- The social equity vision of the mayor in light of tremendous regional growth and downtown investment
- The first municipal budget surplus in decades
- Impending federal welfare reform and the perceived likely impacts on low-income residents

The mayor, city council, and other allies established SJI to change the way the workforce systems operated. SJI targeted higher-paying jobs, used community-based organizations for recruitment and support, organized employer brokers, marshaled flexible resources to support job seekers, and established human service and housing programs.

SJI has placed 2,692 people in jobs paying an average hourly wage of $9.69, and leveraged an additional $25 million for workforce investments. SJI also has pursued a systems reform agenda that has included developing case management standards for retention and advancement, collaborating with community colleges to develop more effective short-term training, and integrating human services and benefits into workforce efforts.

CLEVELAND JOBS AND WORKFORCE INITIATIVE

The Cleveland Jobs and Workforce Initiative is a project of the Cleveland Growth Association, one of the largest regional chambers of commerce with nearly 17,000 members, started by the former Associate Director of the George Gund Foundation. The role of the initiative is to make catalytic investments in making the workforce systems more focused, particularly from the employer's point of view (Berry, 1998). Its purpose as an intermediary is change, not operating programs, and identifying the public, private, and civic supports needed to sustain these changes. Accomplishments include setting up a successful CET program, promoting sectoral initiatives in health care and telecommunications, successful advocacy for new employer-based tax credits for training, and organizing a workforce consortium for manufacturing in Cleveland. These efforts have resulted in more than 1,000 people receiving skills training and jobs with starting hourly wages of $8.00–$9.50, 300 people obtaining basic skills training, and 150 people placed in jobs after job readiness training. Twenty-five million dollars in tax credits leveraged an additional $25 million, and supported skills upgrade training for 3,000 workers in 145 companies (Greater Cleveland Growth Association, 2002).

WISCONSIN REGIONAL TRAINING PARTNERSHIP

The Wisconsin Regional Training Partnership (WRTP) is an implementer of Casey's Milwaukee Jobs Initiative and was founded by employers and unions in 1992 to modernize manufacturing and provide incumbent worker training (Fung and Zdrazil, Chapter 3; Fleischer, 2001). Since 1992, this partnership has grown in membership to include more than 125 employers and unions, including 100,000 workers, and has expanded to many other sectors, such as hospitality, construction, health, and finance.

WRTP is one of the most mature examples of a sectoral initiative in the United States; it operates with deep knowledge of and cooperation with employers, unions, and training providers, and it targets pathways to higher-wage jobs. Supported by the regional Chief Executive Officer (CEO) organization, the Greater Milwaukee Committee, and the State of Wisconsin AFL-CIO, WRTP has expanded its scope over the years to include the training, placement, and support of inner-city workers. By 2002, 1,200 workers were placed at an average starting wage of $10 per hour. They have brokered or subcontracted training to over 6,000 existing workers, and employers have invested $25 million in education and training for their front-line workforce. Its system reform agenda includes helping employers adopt best practices for workplace learning, mentoring, and career ladders, as well as advocating for public policy changes. WRTP's civic resources and credibility made it a key player in helping set up a $20 million state fund to support career advancement as well as crafting a new partnership to set up a new career development center that combines case management and human-services support with employer-based training.

Each vignette of local workforce politics and systems change shows how civic capacity is grown and mobilized, whether deriving from church-based organizations, community organizing, political leadership, employer associations, or employer/union partnerships. What is evident is that intermediaries are essential as an expression of civic capacity and as vehicles for articulating and pursuing systemic agendas for change. Minimally, these agendas involve the collective organization of employers, major reallocation of financial and organizational resources, reconfiguration of community colleges, and integration of human services.

All of the examples above show that reform efforts have to move against the grain, and ultimately involve the acquisition of power, influence, and leadership. These stories, however, are still in the making, and are still small in the scheme of needs and aspirations. They do demonstrate, however, even now how stakeholders outside of normal workforce systems can build coalitions and partnerships that produce a different set of outcomes. How far these efforts, and others like them, can evolve is difficult to predict.

PERSPECTIVES ON LOCAL WORKFORCE DEVELOPMENT POLITICS

Second chance workforce systems are relatively limited efforts with a limited track record of effectiveness. The accumulation of federal policies and programs over the past fifty years has produced a fragmented set of projects, institutions, and systems that are not only disconnected from each other, but also are disconnected in many respects from regional labor markets and from first chance institutions, such as community colleges.

Reform efforts instigated at the federal level have helped in modest ways, although they seem to unwittingly have produced new variations of employment regimes with inevitably fewer resources.

The primary aim of a new local politics of workforce development must be to integrate and focus workforce development activities and institutions to be more performance oriented in connecting people with pathways to good jobs. Finding and building on the requisite civic capacity is necessary to support such a politics, but it is hard to find and challenging to build. When it is built and mobilized, it must be focused on a systemic agenda for change, however small at the outset.

The case study chapters in this book explore the opportunities and constraints of mobilizing civic capacity around a systemic workforce development agenda from a variety of perspectives. Each of these perspectives enriches our understanding of the components and dynamics of employment regimes and the factors and conditions that may contribute to mobilizing civic coalitions for change. In their case studies, the authors adopt different theoretical tools to explore the notion of performance regime, and not surprisingly, differ substantially in their optimism for making progress toward performance regimes in the arena of workforce development.

In Chapter 2, Susan E. Clarke's analysis of Denver focuses on how effective governing coalitions can be mobilized, sustained, and institutionalized in relation to workforce development. Although Denver demonstrates a number of environmental conditions favorable to performance regimes, such as economic change and public recognition, long-term change is constrained by competing problem definitions and agendas and competition for resources.

Archon Fung and Scott Zdrazil use Norton Long's metaphor of "ecology of games" to explore the largely privatized welfare and workforce landscape of Milwaukee in Chapter 3. They develop five ideal type ecologies, derived from the rules and behaviors engendered by public policies, and use them to explore several labor market intermediaries in Milwaukee. They find the "coordination ecology" of the WRTP to embody strong elements of performance related to good jobs and careers.

David W. Bartelt, in his chapter (Chapter 4) on Philadelphia, explores the "contested terrain" of performance-oriented programs and investments in what remains a "private city," dominated by individual "deals" rather than civic goals and strategies that motivate and direct change. Multiple and conflicting conversations about strategic workforce issues, such as soft skills, welfare, and employers, make it even more challenging to build a broader consensus about performance.

In Chapter 5, Steven Rathgeb Smith and Susan Davis, drawing from the literature on implementation failures, examine workforce development

24 ROBERT P. GILOTH

systems in Seattle/King County. They offer the most optimistic scenario of high-level political leadership, combined with broader civic capacity and available resources, creating a large-scale effort at workforce change.

Scott Cummings, Allan Tomey, and Robert Flack situate workforce development in the fragmented politics of St. Louis in the context of deindustrialization, racial polarization, and geographic sprawl in Chapter 6. Divisions among growth coalition members perpetuate and expand this fragmentation, undermining the potential for regional solutions.

The remaining two chapters (Chapters 7 and 8) compare and draw lessons and conclusions from a critical reading of all chapters. Chapters 7 and 8 seek to understand the strengths of the theoretical approaches adopted in the case study chapters in light of workforce development challenges and city and regional characteristics, and offer a typology of the case study cities and types of workforce systems change. This framing identifies the conditions under which systemic change of workforce development may occur. Chapter 7 draws upon two additional papers not included in this volume, a presentation of an approach to systemic reform of labor markets by Peter Plastrik, Judith Taylor, and Marlene Seltzer (2003), and a case study of New Orleans workforce systems by Robert Whelan, David Gladstone, and Trisha Hirth (2003). In the concluding chapter (Chapter 8), Clarence Stone and Donn Worgs argue that efforts must focus on fashioning a radically different relationship between isolated, disconnected young people and the mainstream economy. Such a refashioning is not just a matter of better workforce development programs, but of a community development agenda in the broadest sense.

Changing the career prospects of young people who drop out of high school or graduate with less than adequate skills is a daunting challenge for the so-called second chance workforce development projects and systems. To date, these workforce efforts have not lived up to this challenge, although there are many examples of good programs and underperformance is arguably a result of the public policies themselves. This book considers the idea that a new and more effective local politics of workforce development, one emphasizing performance, is one strategy for changing these outcomes.

However, there are other approaches that may be more effective or feasible given the fragmentation, dispersed authority, and relatively small scale of second chance workforce programs and systems.

What if, for example, the first chance, K-12 education system did not fail so many young people of color in our cities? What if school readiness became the mantra and reality across neighborhoods and the region? What if community development strategies contributed to a concentrated rebuilding of hope and capacity in inner cities to support children and adults? What if more jobs paying family-supporting wages were created through smart public and private investments? What if an expanded labor movement negotiated a new social contract with business that emphasized skills, productivity, higher wages, job security and reemployment, and career paths? What if families were able to build assets to overcome the wealth disparities that constrain each new generation? Such an effort might begin with citywide campaigns to make sure all eligible residents take advantage of the Earned Income and Child Tax Credits. What if society made a serious financial commitment to full employment and built a system of public job creation and education and training similar to what continues to exist in many European countries?

These are not simply theoretical possibilities. The mayors of Boston, Chicago, Denver, Milwaukee, New York, and Indianapolis, to name a few, are spearheading impressive EITC campaigns that connect with other public benefits and asset-building tools like bank accounts, savings programs, and homeownership. The mayor of San Antonio has signed on to the "Better Jobs Initiative" that calls for investments in lifelong learning from cradle to adulthood. A number of cities have passed living wage ordinances, established low-income housing trust funds, and fought the negative consequences of blight and predatory lending.

We may prefer one of these alternatives to our proposals for a new politics of workforce development. Each alternative presents its own set of challenges, some perhaps even more demanding than reforming workforce development systems. Many would argue that given the scope of need these approaches might not be alternatives, but instead are necessary complements to each other in the short and long run. Pursuing all courses of action at once, however, may detract from our ability to pursue others given limited political resources.

Most important, achieving progress on any front in a systemic way forces us to confront many of the same issues discussed in the forthcoming chapters about civic capacity, civic mobilization, systemic agenda building, and performance regimes. In the case of workforce development, it requires a consensus of ideas, substantial resources, credibility based upon values and performance, and deep and growing networks of support. The following case studies and reflections should offer useful guidance for stakeholders and leaders who can urge society to nurture human capital, grow economic assets, and invest in opportunities for the families left behind.

REFERENCES

Annie E. Casey Foundation. 2002. *2002 Kids Count Essay*. Baltimore: Annie E. Casey Foundation.

Bartik, Timothy. 2002. "Poverty, Jobs, and Subsidized Employment." *Challenge* 45(3)(May/June):100–111.

Berg, Peter. 1996. "Training: A Plan for All Workers." In *Reclaiming Prosperity: A Blueprint for Progressive Economic Reform*, edited by Todd Schafer and Jeff Faux, 143–161. Washington, DC: Economic Policy Institute.

Bernhardt, Anetta, and Thomas Bailey. 1998. *Making Careers out of Jobs: Policies to Address the New Employment Relationship*. New York: Columbia University, Institute on Education and the Economy.

Berry, Daniel. 1998. "The Jobs and Workforce Initiative: Building New Roads to Success in Northeast Ohio." *Economic Development Quarterly* 12: 41–53.

Buck, Maria. 2002. *Charting New Territory: Early Implementation of the Workforce Investment Act*. Philadelphia: Public/Private Ventures.

Carnevale, Anthony, and Donna Desrochers. 2002. *Analysis of National Adult Survey, 1992; Current Population Survey, 2001; and Bureau of Labor Statistics Employment Projections, 2000–2010*. Princeton, NJ: Educational Testing Service.

Carnevale, Anthony, and Louis Jacobson. 1997. *The Voucher That Works: The Role of Pell Grants in the Welfare, Employment Policy, and Training System*. Unpublished paper at the 25th Anniversary Pell Grant Conference, November 13–14, the College Board, Washington, DC.

Carnevale, Anthony, and Kathleen Reich. 2000. *A Piece of the Puzzle: States Can Use Education to Make Work Pay for Welfare Recipients*. Princeton, NJ: Educational Testing Service.

Center for Workforce Preparation. 2001. *Keeping Competitive: A Report from a Survey of 1,800 Employers*. Washington, DC: U.S. Chamber of Commerce.

Clarke, Susan E. and Gary L. Gaile. 1998. *The Work of Cities*. Minneapolis: The University of Minneapolis Press.

Clavel, Pierre, and Karen Westmont. 1998. "The Politics of Jobs in Maine." In *Jobs and Economic Development: Strategies and Practices, edited by* Robert Giloth, 195–213. Thousand Oaks, CA: Sage Publications.

Clymer, Carol, Brandon Roberts, and Julie Strawn. 2002. *States of Change: Policies and Programs to Promote Low-Wage Workers' Steady Employment and Advancement*. Philadelphia: Public/Private Ventures.

Draut, Tammy. 2002. *New Opportunities? Public Opinion on Poverty, Income Inequality, and Public Policy, 1996–2001*. New York: Demos.

Dresser, Laura, and Joel Rogers. 1998. "Networks, Sectors, and Workforce Learning." In *Jobs and Economic Development: Strategies and Practices, edited by* Robert Giloth, 64–83. Thousand Oaks, CA: Sage Publications.

Evans, C. and Richard Kazis. 2000. *Improving the Employment Prospects of Low Income Jobseekers: The Role of Labour Market Intermediaries*. New York: Rockefeller Foundation.

Evans, Peter (Ed.). 2002. *Livable Cities*. Berkeley: University of California Press.

Fleischer, Wendy. 2001. *Extending Ladders: Findings from the Annie E. Casey Foundation's Jobs Initiative*. Baltimore: The Annie E. Casey Foundation.

Giloth, Robert. 2000. "Learning from the Field: Economic Growth and Workforce Development in the 1990s." *Economic Development Quarterly* 14(4)(November):340–359.

Giloth, Robert (Ed.). 1998. *Jobs and Economic Development: Strategies and Practices*. Thousand Oaks, CA: Sage Publications.

Giloth, Robert and Dewitt John. 1995. "Mobilizing Civic Infrastructure: Foundation-Supported Job Generation." *National Civic Review* (Summer–Fall): 196–209.

Greater Cleveland Growth Association. 2002. *Jobs and Workforce Initiative Outcomes: A Five Year Retrospective: 1997–2002*. Cleveland: Greater Cleveland Growth Association.

Grubb, W. Norton. 1996. *Learning to Work: The Case for Reintegrating Job Training and Education*. New York: Russell Sage.

Halperin, Samuel. 1998. *The Forgotten Half Revisited: American Youth and Young Families: 1988–2008*. Washington, DC: American Youth Policy Forum.

Harrison, Bennett, and Marcus Weiss. 1998. *Workforce Development Networks: Community-Based Organizations and Regional Alliances*. Thousand Oaks, CA: Sage Publications.

Harvey, Phillip. 1989. *Securing the Right to Employment: Social Welfare Policy and the Unemployed in the United States*. Princeton, NJ: Princeton University Press.

Hughes, Mark Alan. 1996. *The Administrative Geography of Devolving Social Welfare Programs*. Washington, DC: The Brookings Institution.

Iversen, Roberta. 2002. *Moving Up is a Steep Climb*. Baltimore: The Annie E. Casey Foundation.

Jobs for the Future. 1999. *Public Attitudes on Career Advancement for Low Skilled Workers*. Boston: Jobs for the Future.

Jobs for the Future and on Purpose Associates. 1999. *A Framework for Labor Market Systems Reform for Jobs Initiative Sites*. Boston: Jobs for the Future.

Judy, Richard, and Carol D'Amico. 1987. *Workforce 2000*. Indianapolis: Hudson Institute.

Judy, Richard, and Carol D'Amico. 1997. *Workforce 2020: Work and Workers in the 21st Century*. Indianapolis: Hudson Institute.

King, Desmond. 1995. *Actively Seeking Work: The Politics of Unemployment and Welfare Policy in the United States and Great Britain*. Chicago: University of Chicago Press.

Kotkin, Joel. 2002. "A Bit of Chill for Hot Times in the Big City." *Washington Post* (Sunday, March 24):B01.

Lafer, Gordon. 1994. "The Politics of Job Training: Urban Poverty and the False Promise of JTPA." *Politics and Society* 22(3)(September):349–388.

Lafer, Gordon. 2002. *The Job Training Charade*. Ithaca, NY: Cornell University Press.

Lautsch, Brenda, and Paul Osterman. 1998. "Changing the Constraints: A Successful Employment and Training Strategy." In *Jobs and Economic Development: Strategies and Practices,* edited by Robert Giloth, 214–233. Thousand Oaks, CA: Sage Publications.

Lerman, Robert, Signe-Mary McKernan, and Stephanie Riegg. 1999. *Employer-Provided Training and Public Policy*. Washington, DC: The Urban Institute (December 20).

Logan, John, and Harvey Molotch. 1987. *Urban Fortunes*. Berkeley: University of California Press.

Manufacturing Institute. 1998. *The Skills Gap*. Washington, DC: The National Association of Manufacturers.

Martin, Cathie Jo. 2000. *Stuck in Neutral: Business and the Politics of Human Capital Investment Policy*. Princeton, NJ: Princeton University Press.

Melendez, Edwin. 1996. *Working for Jobs: The Center for Employment Training*. Boston: University of Massachusetts, Mauricio Gaston Institute.

Mt. Auburn Associates. 1996. *A Study of Model Development Intermediaries for Annie E. Casey Foundation's Jobs Initiative*. Cambridge, MA: Mt. Auburn Associates.

Mucciaroni, Gary. 1990. *Political Failure of Employment Policy, 1945–1982*. Pittsburgh: University of Pittsburgh Press.

Mueller, Elizabeth, and Alex Schwartz. 2002. *Creating Change: Pushing Workforce Systems to Focus on Family Economic Success*. Cambridge, MA: Abt Associates, Inc.

National Center on Education and the Economy. 1990. *America's Choice: High Skills or Low Wages?* Washington, DC: National Center on Education and the Economy.

National Commission on Excellence in Education. 1983. *A National at Risk*. Washington, DC: GPO.

Northwest Policy Center and Northwest Federation of Community Organizations. 1999. *Northwest Jobs Gap Study: Searching for Work That Pays*. Seattle: Northwest Policy Center.

Okigaki, Alan. 1997. *Developing a Policy Agenda on Jobs*. Washington, DC: The Center for Community Change.

Orfield, Myron. 2002. *American Metropolitics*. Washington, DC: The Brookings Institution.

Orr, L., H. S. Bloom, and S. H. Bell. 1995. *Does Training for the Disadvantaged Work? Evidence from the National JTPA Study*. Washington, DC: Urban Institute Press.

O'Shea, Daniel, and Christopher King. 2001. *The Workforce Investment Act of 1998: Restructuring Workforce Development Initiatives in States and Localities*. Albany, NY: The Nelson A. Rockefeller Institute of Government.

Osterman, Paul. 1999. *Securing Prosperity*. New York: The Century Foundation.

Pearce, Dianne, and Jennifer Brooks. 1999. *The Self Sufficiency Standard for Pennsylvania*. Harrisburg, PA: Women's Association of Women's Alternatives Inc.

Pines, Marion (Ed.). 2000. *The 21st Century Challenge: Moving the Youth Agenda Forward*. Baltimore: Sar Levitan Center for Social Policy Studies, Johns Hopkins University.

Plastrik, Peter, Judith Taylor, and Marlene Seltzer. 2003. *Changing Labor Markets: A Systems Approach to Reform*. Boston: Jobs for the Future.

Regional Workforce Partnership. 2002. *Workforce and Economic Development: An Agenda for Pennsylvania's Next Governor*. Philadelphia: The Reinvestment Fund.

Smith, Whitney, Jenny Wittner, Robin Spence, and Andy Van Kleunen. 2002. *Skills Training Works: Examining the Evidence*. Washington, DC: Workforce Alliance.

Stoker, Gerald. 1996. "Regime Theory and Urban Politics." In *Theories of Urban Politics, edited by* David Judge, Gerry Stoker, and Harold Wolman, 54–71. Thousand Oaks, CA: Sage Publications.

Stone, Clarence N. (Ed.). 1998. *Changing Urban Education*. Lawrence: University Press of Kansas.

Stone, Clarence N., Jeffrey R. Hennig, Bryan D. Jones, and Carol Pierannunzi. 2001. *Building Civic Capacity: The Politics of Reforming Urban Schools*. Lawrence: University Press of Kansas.

Strawn, Julie, and Karin Martinson. 2000. *Steady Work and Better Jobs: How to Help Low-Income Parents Sustain Employment and Advance in the Workforce*. New York: Manpower Demonstration Research Corporation.

Weir, Margaret. 1992. *Politics and Jobs: The Boundaries of Employment Policy in the United States*. Princeton, NJ: Princeton University Press.

Whelan, Robert, David Gladstone, and Trisha Hirth. 2003. *Building a Workforce Development System in New Orleans*. New Orleans: University of New Orleans.

Wilson, William Julius. 1998. *When Work Disappears*. New York: Basic Books.

Susan E. Clarke

2   The Politics of Workforce Development

Constructing a Performance Regime in Denver

Workforce initiatives for bringing about long-term job retention, wage progression, and career advancement for low-income, low-skilled job seekers are significant local policy issues.[1] This chapter draws on the concepts of governance and performance regimes to describe and analyze the trends and conditions shaping the politics of workforce development in Denver, Colorado (Stone, 1998). This casts the analysis of the prospects for less fragmented, more coherent, effective, and equitable local workforce development systems in terms of the political, ideational, and institutional factors characterizing the local policy context. This review of Denver's workforce regime also suggests that the political framework in which such issues are formulated and implemented shapes the effectiveness and sustainability of these efforts. A close look at the Denver scenario allows us to consider some broader issues regarding the design of local workforce development interventions.[2]

WORKFORCE DEVELOPMENT AS A GOVERNANCE ISSUE: DISCOURSE AND COALITIONS

Workforce development issues are intrinsically governance issues. A governance perspective emphasizes the conditions under which workforce decisions must be made—interdependent, complex, loosely-linked actors and institutions with shared purposes but no shared authority—and highlights how problematic cooperation and collaboration among these actors and institutions will be.[3] For systemic change in workforce development practices to occur, stakeholders must generate enough cooperation to make effective decisions under these conditions—that is, craft decision processes that satisfy shared purposes, reduce the costs of making complex decisions, and are seen as legitimate and fair by those involved.

Governance is contingent on the politics of ideas and interests: Discourse and coalitions are central but problematic elements in such collective problem-solving efforts. According to Stone et al. (2001, 26), issue definition is one of the "building blocks"—one of the conditions—of systemic reform: Mobilization and effective reform is contingent on shared understandings of the problem and feasible solutions. They also remind us that the link of mobilization and issue definition is not automatic; competing ideas about workforce problems and contested solutions can hamper reform even in the absence of outright resistance to change.

Regimes are only one type of governance strategy—along with price competition in the market and networks emanating from civil society (Cox, 1997)—for dealing with collective action dilemmas. As a governance strategy, regimes bring together actors with resources and strategic knowledge in relatively stable coalitions to negotiate decisions over shared goals. Selective incentives and "small opportunities" for distributive gains provide the grounds for cooperation and collaboration among disparate actors (Stone, 1989). Although formation of local regimes is a familiar governance strategy for addressing economic development issues in American cities, these regime processes are more tenuous in relation to human capital and livability concerns (Clarke and Gaile, 1998). Stone (1998) contends that rather than "employment regimes" distributing jobs and contracts to selected groups, a "performance regime" capable of systemic changes in workforce policies is needed. A performance regime would push workforce development onto the agenda, giving a strategic direction and priority to these issues (Stone, Chapter 8). There are several challenges in doing so, however: The difficulties in mobilizing participants around workforce issues, sustaining their involvement in the face of competing demands, and creating durable coalitions able to institutionalize new priorities and new resource allocations.

CONSTRUCTING PERFORMANCE REGIMES

Performance regimes are dependent on the shared understandings of problems and potential solutions—discourse—and the active participation of diverse interests in collaborative activities focused on performance outcomes. Creating strategic partnerships and performance regimes for systemic change requires broad mobilization within the public and private sector as well as integration with networks of "brokers," or intermediaries, and civic organizations. As Stone (1998) notes, building support for workforce institutions driven by a performance imperative, rather than distributional benefits, requires establishing a new set of political arrangements with performance as the focal concern. Accomplishing this task will require motivating stakeholders to make the outcomes—good jobs for poor citizens—rather than the processes or the perks their central concern (Giloth and Phillips, 2000). To do so requires more than restructuring control at the top (Stone, 1998, 11). In addition, performance regimes present much more difficult governance tasks than those facing distributional regimes because more than coordination is required. Although many of the players may be the same, the key factor in developing performance regimes is a new set of relationships and motivations.[4]

Building ties around human capital needs is notoriously difficult. The civic infrastructure for human capital agendas is vulnerable to different time horizons, uneven resources, underinvestment, and the lack of "ownership" of an organizational infrastructure capable of supporting and sustaining long-term initiatives. Civic capacity also is vulnerable to decay. Atlanta's biracial coalition, for example, functioned effectively on physical redevelopment and school desegregation issues but faltered in the face of the changing economic and social conditions that demanded different capacities and new forms of collaboration (Stone, 2001a). Similarly, in previous studies (Clarke, Hero, and Sidney, 1997; Stone, 1998), Denver ranked relatively low on civic capacity for systemic school reform although the city obviously mustered sufficient capacity around economic development concerns.

Workforce systems present particularly difficult problems. As Mossberger (2000) points out, incentives to cooperate are "absent, uncertain, or unevenly distributed across industries and firms" in the case of workforce programs. As a result, business participation is often weak and episodic as is the mobilization of strategic public officials and agencies. Partnerships around workforce issues are typically fragile, short-term, and opportunistic rather than strategic; to achieve systemic change and "go to scale" requires broad mobilization within both the public and private sector as well as integration with networks of brokers and civic organizations.

Given the fragile nature of these partnerships, it appears that constructing performance regimes around workforce development issues must engage three challenges: (1) To overcome asymmetrical incentives and enlist diverse stakeholders around a collective goal despite varying perceptions of its immediacy; (2) to persuade participants to sustain their involvement in the face of competing demands; and (3) to overcome collective action problems to create a durable coalition based on performance goals (Stone, 1998, 13). Governance arrangements falling short of these objectives are more likely to be, in Stone's view (1998), "employment regimes" rather than "performance regimes" capable of systemic changes in workforce policies. These performance regimes are more than a matter of coordination. Mobilizing and realigning ties is a question of encouraging active involvement and developing a shared understanding of the problem and potential solutions—what Stone refers to as civic capacity.

To assess the prospects for moving workforce systems in Denver toward performance regimes, this chapter describes the local setting, assesses each challenge to creating a performance regime, and considers the conditions for creating durable reform coalitions capable of the systemic reform of workforce policy. Although the discussion is based on the Denver experience, the factors singled out as influencing the prospects for performance regimes are likely to be evident in other cities as well; these factors suggest a potential framework for examining why performance regimes are more likely in some cities than in others.

THE LOCAL SETTING

In many respects, the political climate for improving workforce development in Denver was auspicious in the late 1990s. The state ranked near the top on many business climate ratings, unemployment rates were at record lows, and there were significant state initiatives for promoting training in high-tech sectors. Denver's mayor is a "strong" mayor; since 1987, a Latino and an African American candidate—Mayor Pena and Mayor Webb, respectively—have won the position of mayor's office in this predominantly white city and governed for over 25 years.

Economic Conditions

Although local officials see the 1990s as "the Denver Decade," a good share of the credit for Denver's success can be attributed to a booming state economy. Colorado shines in nearly every ranking of business performance and economic condition. The Corporation for Enterprise Development (CFED) gave Colorado—one of only three states so ranked—all "As" on its 2001 Development Report Card (CFED, 2002). The Progressive Policy Institute ranks Colorado fourth overall in its 2002 "State New Economy Index," ranking it second in the nation in workforce education in 2002. Numerous other studies rank the state highly in concentration of high-tech workers and creation of high-tech jobs. In 1999, only six states had lower unemployment rates and five states higher job growth rates than Colorado.

The increase in jobs is partially the result of an increase in population. Colorado's population growth has slowed dramatically from the early 1990s when it grew by more than 300,000 people in three years. Census 2000 figures report a state population of 4.3 million, up by nearly one-third in a decade. Most of the 1 million newcomers settled along the Front Range; over 75 percent of the state's population now lives in the ten metropolitan Front Range communities (Olinger, 2001). Colorado's Latino population—17 percent of the state population—is larger than the national average of 13 percent Latino; Latinos are the fastest growing ethnic group in Colorado.

Personal income in Colorado in 1998 had a growth rate of 6.9 percent; that same year the average growth rate for the United States was 4.8 percent.[5] For the eleventh consecutive year, Colorado's per capita income in 1998—at $29,692—rose and continued to outpace the national per capita income ($27,274). By 1999, Colorado's per capita income was $31,546 relative to a national figure of $28,542. The average annual wage in Denver County increased from $30,305 in 1994 to $37,500 in 1998. The increases in wages and incomes, however, failed to keep pace with housing prices; rents increased by 42 percent between 1993 and 1998 and prices for single-family homes increased by 97 percent from 1991–1998.

The Progressive Policy Institute ranked Denver seventh overall in its 2001 "Metropolitan New Economy" Index. Since 1991, 77,000 net new jobs were created in the Denver metropolitan area; the city has the largest job base in the state (459,000 jobs) and 35 percent of all the businesses are in the metropolitan area. The total Denver workforce (295,870+) constitutes 1.46 jobs per worker with a payroll totaling $15.1+ billion (WIA, 2000, 5). Denver's workforce is greater than the combined total of two of its high-growth contiguous counties—Jefferson and Arapahoe Counties. The spatial mismatch problems plaguing other cities are less salient here. Although there is substantial job growth in contiguous counties, the supply of jobs in Denver remains high. Many believe that the current constraints on labor availability (supply) and slower future population growth rates mean that continued stable economic growth in Denver for the next five years will rely heavily on the productivity of a well-trained labor force.

Denver's economic base diversified in the 1990s, bringing in more telecommunication, biomedical, and computer enterprises and making the city more resilient to future economic downturns. Over 41 percent of the jobs in the city are in the service sector. In contrast to many other cities, Denver still offers many entry-level jobs with tracks to livable wages to low-skill workers (Piton, 1999); however, a significant number of these jobs continue to migrate to the suburbs.

Thanks to a generally good economy in the early 1990s, welfare caseloads in Colorado have been declining since 1993. With the introduction of the state Temporary Assistance for Needy Families (TANF) workfare program in 1997, Colorado Works, these declines accelerated and consistently outpace the national rate of caseload decline. Most of the decline in TANF caseloads in Colorado is a result of fewer one-parent TANF cases; therefore, the remaining cases on the rolls are primarily two-parent and child-only cases (Capizzano et al., 2001).

The general economic conditions in Denver remain vibrant although somewhat moderated from the past decade of expansive growth, and challenged by layoffs in the aftermath of September 11th. Colorado's jobless rate was 4.9 percent in May 2002. Although Colorado continued to rank third in the nation in 2001 for venture capital investment as a percentage of gross state product, the economic downturn resulted in over 46,000 layoffs in tech and telecom firms since 2001 (PPI, 2002). By May 2002, Denver's unemployment rate was 5 percent, still below the national average but a staggering increase from the low rate of 2.6 percent in 2000. The overall job growth in the Denver metro area slipped precipitously in the last few years; the state rates also dropped. Denver's employment growth now is projected to be at –2.7 percent, after 2.3 percent growth in 2000 and 3.5 percent in 1998.

The long-term optimism about the local economy stems in part from Denver's distinction in having one of the highest percentages of high school and college graduates in the United States. Further, the strength of the education system has been a major factor in the high level of entrepreneurial growth in the region. There is a general understanding that in order to compete and survive in the global marketplace, there must be continued investment in the training necessary to keep a labor force operating at peak performance. Latinos are now the major public school constituency in Denver; however, the continuing literacy gaps for Latino students in Denver public schools trouble educators and business leaders alike.

Demographic Conditions

Analyses of the 2000 Census classify Colorado as one of nineteen "new growth" states whose foreign-born population is growing at a rate faster than the rest of the nation (Aguilar, 2001). The 80 percent growth rate in the foreign-born population in Colorado over the last ten years—from 142,000 to 255,000—has been driven by Hispanic and Asian immigration to the state (Aguilar, 2001). Not all of this immigration fits the traditional urban pattern, however: With labor shortages in the mountain tourism sectors as well as meatpacking and agricultural sectors, many new immigrants head to rural resort and agribusiness communities in Colorado.

Denver's population rose by 87,026 to 554,836 in 2000. Most significantly, the racial composition of the population changed dramatically; white non-Hispanics are now 52 percent of the population in contrast to 61 percent in 1990. Latinos rose from 23 percent of the city's population in 1990 to 32 percent in 2000; in contrast, African Americans dropped from 13 percent to 11 percent of the population in 2000 (Simpson, 2001).

In addition to this rapid increase in population, Latinos are moving into many historically black neighborhoods. Many city council members now represent districts with electoral demographics significantly different from the constituencies who first elected them into office. Although Latino and African-American populations remain relatively centralized, their growth rates in the suburban counties surrounding Denver increased substantially.

Nearly two-thirds of the Hispanic population in Colorado is Mexican American, but there is a slight decline statewide—from 66.6 percent in 1990 to 61.3 percent in 2000—as the Latino/Hispanic population slowly becomes more diverse, with growth in Central and South American, Puerto Rican, and Cuban groups. Until recently, the Latino population in Colorado has been notable for its low rates of non-citizens. By most estimates, well over 90 percent of Latinos in Colorado are U.S. citizens, and the vast majority are native born with many tracing U.S. citizenship back over several generations. This distinguishes Latinos in Denver from those in other U.S. cities where diverse or very large non-citizen or recent immigrant Latino populations exist.

These demographic shifts hold many implications for workforce development strategies. With the lifting of court orders for school integration, Denver's schools are rapidly resegregating. Latino students, in particular, are characterized by high dropout rates, low graduation rates, and high rates of disciplinary action. Given the autonomy of the Denver Public School system, the establishment of workforce initiatives, such as school-to-work programs, is not under the direct control of city officials. These weak links between a young and growing Latino population and the public schools indicate the need for alternative training sites and nontraditional ties with employers.

Political Context

Since the "regime change" signaled by the election of Federico Pena in the 1980s, local officials in Denver have supported workforce development efforts along with aggressive strategies for public investment in infrastructure. In many ways, workforce development is on the local agenda although it only occasionally rises to strategic status on the system-wide agenda (Stone, Chapter 8). In his inaugural address as President of the United States Conference of Mayors on June 15, 1999, Denver Mayor Wellington Webb emphasized the importance of linking workers with jobs at decent wages. Indeed, he claimed that "it is a fundamental principle of this nation that work will pay" (Gatton, 1999). In recognizing the difficulties of making transitions from welfare to work, he emphasized the importance of child care and transportation as well as job training.

According to Webb, workforce development is some of the city and the region's most important "unfinished business."[6] To make his priorities clear, the mayor established the Mayor's Office of Workforce Development (MOWD), aiming to bring all city and county workforce development services under one agency. MOWD is the lead agency for workforce development and functions as a Special Revenue Fund agency, administering federal and state funds for employment and training.[7]

In Denver, as one stakeholder put it, the strong mayoral system means the mayor and the city council can provide the "ground support" for workforce development initiatives. In his last term in office, Mayor Webb reportedly has stronger name recognition and higher popularity ratings than Governor Owens.[8] The city council is elected by a mix of district and at-large constituencies; it is a relatively professionalized political body with substantial staff resources. In concert with the mayor, the city council now also faces term limits. In the absence of a heavily unionized bureaucracy, the main obstacle to local reform of workforce development is seen as "the need for somebody to remove obstacles" rather than overcoming resistance (Unattributed quotations obtained from confidential sources).

Local leadership opportunities are now challenged by the volatile economy. Facing term limits, Mayor Webb began his last year in office in 2002, facing a significant budget crisis. As the economic downturn caused sales tax collections to slump, the opportunities for new city initiatives faded. By June 2002, the city cut nearly $20 million from its $780 million general fund; plans for cutting the 2003 budget another 4 percent would put spending below 2001 levels (Brovsky, 2002).

Local Workforce Development Initiatives

There are three grand experiments in play in Denver: Welfare-to-work initiatives aimed at moving TANF families into the workforce, Workforce Investment Act (WIA) initiatives focused on disadvantaged groups and dislocated workers, and the Denver Workforce Initiative (DWI) aimed at linking employers and job seekers in sustainable, living wage employment patterns. Few mayors place strategic priorities on workforce development. Denver's atypical claims to political leadership derive, in part, from a historic pattern of devolution of policy responsibilities to counties and local governments in Colorado. Thanks to this historical tradition, significant revenue streams currently channel into the city. As a result of policy devolution, there currently are sixteen different funding streams within the Mayor's Office of Workforce Development.

Clearly one of the most important policy conditions affecting workforce development policy in Denver is welfare reform.[9] Nearly all post-

TANF welfare responsibilities are devolved to the county level. As a consolidated city and county, Denver faces a heavy workfare burden. Many of the concerns about the transition to work for welfare clients paralleled the problems facing the working poor in Denver. The Welfare-to-Work (W2W) formula state grants are passed on to the counties. Colorado receives over $9 million a year in W2W funds. Since its inauguration in 1998, the Welfare-to-Work Tax Credit program, which provides tax credits for employers hiring people who were on welfare for 18 months, has generated 2,140 certifications at the state level (Robert, 1999).

As anticipated by the city and county, during the first year of the WIA—7/1/00 through 6/30/01—the MOWD will have over $8.7 million in youth-specific funds. These funds will target the at-risk youth (i.e., 14–24 year olds) living in high-poverty neighborhoods throughout Denver. During this same time period, $7.8 million will be available through welfare-to-work grants (competitive and formula). The purpose of these funds is to provide post-job entry training and support services to qualified TANF recipients and the noncustodial parents of their children. Additionally, the city of Denver has allocated $6.7 million in supplemental TANF funds to the Mayor's Office of Employment and Training (MOET) to help the TANF recipients secure employment and training options.

These funds can be leveraged to address different target populations: One-Stop partners' funds such as Welfare-to-Work serve TANF groups and specified neighborhoods, whereas WIA funds are aimed at economically disadvantaged groups and dislocated workers, including those outside targeted neighborhoods. This presents opportunities and challenges to governance because the leveraging and coordination of programming is handled by the Denver Workforce Development Board (WDB). The local governance arrangements center on the Denver WDB. The board chairperson must be from the private sector, and a majority of the nineteen members must be private-sector representatives; the rest of the members must include representatives of organized labor, community-based organizations, public assistance, economic development, vocational rehabilitation, educational/school-to-career, and public employment services. Board members serve two-year terms, they receive no compensation, and are mayoral appointments—not subject to city council approval. The board is responsible for program oversight and policy guidance for all federal- and state-funded workforce development programs, including workforce centers.

Although nearly all programs are administratively centered in MOWD, the categorical nature of W2W, having different eligibility criteria and differing institutional bases, leads to charges that it is hard for professional staff and TANF participants to connect with the necessary programs (Robert, 1999). The more client-focused the program, the more necessary it is that different systems work together (Ibid), but the blending and balancing acts often fall to the participants themselves.

The W2W and WIA activities coordinated by MOWD hew to federal guidelines and tend to reflect categorical strategies. In contrast, activities linked to nonprofits and foundations, such as the DWI, which is based at the Piton Foundation, appear more likely to embrace new institutional fixes, linking employers and workers and neighborhood organizations. Often, they also were more engaged in marketplace solutions and long-term employment strategies. DWI's orientation was distinctive for its attention to the internal dynamics of the workplace and for initial efforts to build networks relying on community coaches to link workers and employers. For businesses participating in the DWI sponsored by the Jobs Initiative (JI), DWI for example, specialized training of employees and supervisors was a powerful incentive for larger firms with high employee turnover (AECF, 1999). DWI employers had access to a series of "support products" that emphasized distinctive skills for dealing with workplace dynamics.

In addition, these nongovernmental groups often took on important roles in the larger workforce community. DWI was seen as providing "the intellectual capital" for changing workforce systems by giving direction to system reform initiatives and providing a means of overcoming fragmentation and redundancies built into the system. In many respects, the local discourse on workforce issues was hammered out in DWI sessions. As an institution, DWI was valued primarily as a forum and facilitator— a place where good ideas could be tried out and successes and failures noted—rather than as a program administrator. DWI's vantage point allowed it to leverage resources for the common good and for projects that would not have happened otherwise. More specifically, several stakeholders emphasized the importance of the technical skills and services provided by DWI, including data collection, dissemination of models from other settings, and MIS functions and expertise. As one community-based organization pointed out, these more prosaic services are critical for new service providers and for those moving into new areas.

National reforms in the late 1990s meant that concurrent workforce development initiatives took place in a volatile and fluid local setting. Minimally, this meant that the learning involved in new local initiatives became both accelerated and extended as the composition of both employers and job seekers changed (Giloth and Phillips, 2000). The Center for Women's Employment and Education (CWEE), a TANF contractor, for example, previously "reached out" to those on public assistance who possessed high school diplomas or GEDs and were motivated to enter the job market: Now, "ready or not," participants are required to work or be involved in job readiness programs and CWEE is now providing GED classes, considering serving two-parent families, and extending their case management well into employment (Robert, 1999).

These local conditions presented opportunities as well as constraints for building coalitions and constructing performance regimes around workforce development concerns. To make workforce development a strategic priority for local leaders means addressing the challenges noted by Stone: Enlisting diverse stakeholders, sustaining coalitions in the face of competing demands, and creating a durable coalition around performance goals.[10]

CHALLENGE #1: ENLISTING DIVERSE STAKEHOLDERS

Enlisting diverse stakeholders in workforce issues raises several challenges. The constituencies and strategic resources essential to mobilizing enough cooperation around workforce development policy change are located in both the public and private sectors; the decision processes linking them together vary over time. The interconnections and interdependencies that link these imperfect actors in governance arrangements are critical. Indeed, the patterns of linkages and interactions among these actors are as important as the actors themselves—some patterns will contribute to livelihood concerns, others will constrain such efforts. With a low level of interdependence among stakeholders, the workforce development networks will be unstable and lack the trust necessary to operate effectively.

Several features characterize the mobilization of these diverse stakeholders in Denver. The changing images of the working poor and the lack of information about them—who they are, where they are, and how many of them exist—make reform coalitions more difficult. In addition, the dominance of federal initiatives, the weak state role, overlapping networks, the mismatch of program needs and jurisdictional boundaries, the fragmentation of advocacy groups, episodic business involvement, and the difficult fit with community college agendas shape mobilization.

Images and Discourse about the Working Poor Shift over Time

The visibility of livability issues in Denver is uneven. Searching for the terms *working poor, food kitchen*, and *shelter* in *Denver Post* articles from 1993–2000, 134 articles can be found reporting on livability issues relevant to the situation of the working poor. The incidence of these terms ranged from as few as eight in 1993 and ten in 1996, to as many as twenty-six in 1997 and twenty-six in 2000. The two years representing high points in rhetorical attention appear to be driven by implementation of federal welfare reform and the booming Colorado economy.

The focus of attention shifts as well. In the early 1990s, media attention centered on the homeless population. Working poor, transients, and homeless were often grouped together as problem populations. For all of these groups, the emphasis was on their dependency on social services. By the mid-1990s, the working poor became distinguished as a typically Latino, and often inter-suburban, population. With the advent of welfare reform, the "successes" of workfare programs were considered to be the generation of more working poor. Rather than being grouped with the homeless, the working poor were now linked to welfare clients. The media began to emphasize the barriers to establishing a sustainable livelihood in Denver, focusing on the wages available to less-skilled workers and the disproportionate share of their budgets spent on housing and child care relative to middle-class family budgets.

In the late 1990s, the working poor sometimes were portrayed as competing with former welfare clients for low-wage jobs and affordable housing.[11] The working poor enjoyed a more positive image as beneficiaries of affordable housing. By 2000, they emerged as a distinct target population for politicians and policymakers but remained competitive with other target groups, particularly TANF participants, for policy benefits. This segmentation and competition among working poor and low-income groups has hampered the emergence of a counter-narrative on jobs and the working poor.

Until the late 1990s, some of these shifts in the discourse about the working poor and the definitions of their problems can be attributed to the menu of federal and state programs. The problems of the working poor were often identified in terms of these programmatic niches and were addressed accordingly. During this period, a service orientation dominated the discourse; however, the relatively modest federal attention to workforce development issues meant that local policymakers had few policy windows available and limited resources with which to work.

A change in this discourse began to become apparent in the mid-1990s—ironically, as the state economy blossomed. Despite a low unemployment rate and plentiful jobs, persistent poverty plagued Denver. It also became a distinct issue in the face of the uneven impacts of the fast-growing Colorado economy. Although the robust economy was marked by job growth and low unemployment, it became clear that many of the jobs available paid insufficient wages to cover the housing costs in the Denver market. In addition, many jobs did not pay medical benefits. In the midst of remarkable economic growth, local food banks and homeless shelters reported increased use. This dissonance prompted a more focused attention on working poor populations and distinguished these populations from more traditional users of these facilities.

As one reporter put it, "the Vail syndrome" was emerging in Denver as workers' wages proved insufficient for renting affordable housing in the overheated Denver housing market. Independent of welfare reform and other federal and state initiatives, Denver officials began to recognize the consequences of economic growth for those lacking the skills and education in demand. In addition to uneven economic growth, Denver's redevelopment agenda created new issues for the working poor as gentrification engulfed affordable neighborhoods.

In the late 1990s and early 2000, a critique of current policy approaches to the working poor began to take shape in the media and among local officials. The lack of coherent policy was linked to the tendency to see and treat problems in singular ways—as housing, as food, as jobs. To one advocate, this led to "institutionalizing the street" and an assumption that things were unlikely to improve overall. Job training and workforce development received little direct attention from the media during this period. Indeed, using these terms to search media files yields few articles. Toward the end of his last term in office in 1999, Mayor Wellington Webb spoke out about the working poor, arguing that there was a need to regionalize housing and employment issues. This signaled a different understanding of the issues of the working poor in both the scale of the argument and the linking of housing and employment.

Although the media continued to focus on specific livability issues, the political discourse—in city council meetings and in project reports—began to encompass more systemic concerns. Within Denver's workforce development policy community, there emerged an explicit argument that the changing nature of work and the workforce, in tandem with economic transformations, demanded institutional and policy change.[12] To local advocates, workforce investment systems had to adapt to these new realities (City and County of Denver, 2000).

External Initiatives Dominate the Local Agenda

Federal programs still appear to drive the state and local agendas for the working poor and workforce development in Colorado, although some important local initiatives emerged in the late 1900s. The Welfare-to-Work programs and the WIA programs are the primary workforce development frameworks at the state and local levels. Federal affordable housing tax credits, funds for child health insurance, and other programs also shape policy in this area. The introduction of the Annie E. Casey Foundation's (AECF) JI program in 1995 provided an alternative workforce development perspective. Rather than a critique, this recognition of the importance of federal, state, and nonprofit programs highlights the ways in which these programs structure the local agenda. At a minimum, these programs function as important external stimuli for overcoming collective action problems by encouraging cooperation among diverse stakeholders as a means of accessing federal and foundation funds.

State Roles Are Weak

The state policy agenda in Colorado is dominated by education, growth, criminal justice, transportation, and tax relief issues. Before national welfare reform, the state welfare system emphasized skills development and also featured strong supportive services such as child care and transportation. Nevertheless, the overall strength of the state's social safety net is weak and welfare benefit levels remain unchanged since 1989 (Capizzano et al., 2001).

State welfare reform legislation established Colorado Works, signaling a dramatic shift from the traditional emphasis on education and training to a "work first" model (Capizzano et al., 2001). Both pre-TANF programs and the Colorado Works model reflect the historic reliance on counties for welfare and social service provision in Colorado. With Colorado Works, counties play an even greater role in designing and implementing workfare programs. Although nominally a "state-supervised, county-administered" program, the county discretion in Colorado Works means there is no overall program orientation at the state level (Capizzano et al., 2001). Instead, each county designs its own workfare program in line with state eligibility rules and benefit levels. For a consolidated city–county such as Denver, this became a rare opportunity for local policy innovation.

Although there is a state WDB, workforce development is a relatively minor issue at the state level, thanks, in part, to devolution. The Colorado Department of Labor and Employment has established a Rapid Response Team comprised of individuals from local workforce investment boards, dislocated worker service providers, organized labor, and MOWD to coordinate service and activities on local workforce issues. However, the working poor are addressed primarily in response to federal programs such as child health insurance and workfare reforms.

To many local officials, the state appears remiss even in this reactive mode; the state is perceived as slow to act and lacking commitment to social issues. President Bush's economic stimulus package sent a one-time subsidy of $143 million to Colorado in 2002, earmarked for unemployment offices and job programs, but the funds remain unspent. The state legislature killed a 2001 bill directing some of these funds to workforce centers; the Department of Labor and Employment claims it needs more time to plan the allocations, although the legislature may need to approve some appropriations and does not meet again until 2003 (Pate, 2002). The TANF surplus remains unspent and critics charge that the state misses opportunities to take advantage of waivers for various purposes such as allocating funds for former welfare recipients in the transition stage to work. Similarly, the state had to return child health insurance funds to the federal government because of insufficient enrollments in the state program.

Along with policy devolution, this weak state role leaves the stage wide open for local initiatives. However, the lagging state response to channeling funds, and even weaker response to supporting local initiatives, leaves city officials operating in an impoverished and uncertain intergovernmental context. For Denver officials, this combination of new funds, devolved program authority, and buoyant economic conditions opened the policy window for rethinking local workforce programs.

Local Workforce Development Networks Overlap

The public-sector workforce partners are diverse; the linkages are managed primarily through the MOWD, now in its fifth year of linking individuals in need of employment and employers seeking workers.[13] In August 2000, one of Mayor Webb's senior advisors took over as the director of MOWD after also serving on Denver's Welfare Reform Policy Board. Mayoral office staff are prominent and well-regarded participants in the DWI forums; several staff members also participated in state-level Workforce Development Councils and task forces. The WDB is accountable for oversight of state and federal workforce development programs; several WDB members also serve or have served on other workforce initiatives. Such cross-cutting networks are a distinctive feature of Denver politics. Most workforce stakeholders recognize and accept the initiatives that are under way through the mayor's office. The WDB reports to the mayor and works with MOWD on oversight and policy formulation. Since 1998, several public–private workforce initiatives have been in play.[14]

Some overlap stems from efforts to overcome the fragmentation of a regional labor market into separate jurisdictions. As outlined in their five-year plan (City and County of Denver, 2000), MOWD is currently involved in four regional employment and training activities.[15] In addition, neighborhoods are part of this spatial workforce strategy through WIA's One-Stop Centers. These centers are intended to be the central access for all federal workforce programs, folding in traditional Job Service and Job Training Partnership Act (JTPA) offices. One-Stop services have been established in seven targeted Denver neighborhoods, currently involving 132.5 staff and thirteen different agencies, as well as thirty-nine community-based service providers. These centers are accessible in person and online—"no wrong door" is a trademark of the program, indicating that there are no income requirements to receive services.

Advocacy Groups Are Fragmented

One nonprofit stakeholder characterizes the nonprofit sector in Denver as "weak," with few changes since the 1980s despite capacity-building efforts. Another stakeholder says that community-based organizations (CBOs) are facing a situation in which "the world has shifted on them and they are trying to catch up" because these organizations no longer have welfare cases with which to work and may lack the capacity to participate in new workforce initiatives. Several people consider the different degrees of voluntary and nonprofit organization in African-American and Latino communities as complicating the role of community groups in Denver.

W2W and WIA funds might provide incentives for more cross-organizational cooperation, but these funds tend to be categorical and, thus, are unlikely to encourage a more systemic approach. Funds channeled through nonprofit organizations and foundations as intermediaries may be more effective. In Denver, civil society intermediaries, such as the Piton Foundation, have been significant historically in engaging public and private partners. Their roles as workforce intermediaries proved more challenging and problematic. The Piton Foundation became a key element in the workforce development intermediary network; its JI programs emphasized a holistic workfare policy orientation and blended funds. In its initial phases, the JI-supported DWI chose not to work directly with community-based groups. But in the absence of a city infrastructure capable of delivering workforce development services, DWI eventually decided in late 1998 to rely on community-based groups to implement workforce development reforms. Although DWI contracted with numerous community-based service providers, these providers tended to be small-scale, singular, and often single-issue organizations. Community-based service providers were not particularly well versed in working with employers and job seekers; they may not have had—due to their size and lack of critical mass—the organizational resources and capacities to carry out a sustained engagement with workforce development issues (Plastrik and Taylor, 2001).

The Denver Employment Alliance (DEA) emerged about five years ago, partly in response to concerns about fragmentation, capacity building, and control. Organized by two highly respected, long-time CBO stakeholders and supported by the Enterprise Foundation, the DEA brings together CBO service providers with other stakeholders, explicitly excluding employers. It offers the service providers a coherent voice in workforce deliberations and is considered highly effective. As one DEA member put it, "policymakers are clueless on how difficult it is to implement" reforms, particularly when multiple funding streams are involved. In addition, the DEA provides technical assistance for CBOs and helps standardize the ways in which CBOs do business. Most DEA leaders are also DWI stakeholder members, and many contend that the DEA would not have been established without the aid of the DWI. The DWI shifted the CBO provider focus from the funder to a broader set of partners. In a sense, the DEA is a new collective actor in workforce development emerging from DWI and is a potential example of systems reform.

Business Involvement Is Episodic

Formally, business representation is required in the W2W and WIA programs. Private-sector representatives lead and control Denver's WDB; these representatives also participate in the Chamber of Commerce's WDB. Incentives for W2W participation are relatively indirect. For targeted industries in W2W programs, the benefits include access to a pool of job-ready candidates, training supervisors to handle these new workers, tax credits for employing long-term welfare clients, and some transitional wage subsidies. Given the importance of services and tourism in Denver's economy, and the churning of jobs during periods of high growth, how to design workforce development incentives is not a straightforward question. The minority business community in Denver is relatively experienced with national workforce programs. Several minority business owners are active in current programs and serve on various policy boards. Short of this type of commitment, the incentives available to business do not appear sufficient for continued engagement.

More extensive mobilization occurred in 1998 during the Workforce Summit. Cosponsored by DWI, this summit brought businesses in at the early stages of discussions regarding recruiting, retaining, and retraining entry-level employees. Sector-specific working groups were set up, with some continuing beyond the summit. In a sense, targeting sectors creates organized business capacity among disparate firms.

Task force roles also are typical means of participation for businesses (AECF, 1999). Participation can ebb and flow during the different stages of project activities; therefore, business representation may be episodic. Although this episodic involvement is typical, Stone et al. raise the intriguing possibility that external interventions and resources—whether AECF or federal programs—can take the place of business' typical role in mobilization, especially in cities lacking a strong tradition of business civic engagement.

Community Colleges Face Mixed Incentives

Community colleges frequently are portrayed as critical players in workforce development (Fitzgerald, 2000). However, the integration of community colleges into a more comprehensive workforce development system in Denver is hampered by several factors. Community colleges operate with independent budgets authorized by state government in Colorado; they have long-standing political ties and constituencies that make their cooperation in new initiatives more problematic. However, community colleges also see the workforce development agenda in a distinctive way. In contrast to a programmatic emphasis on marketing "products" to find workers and getting them into programs, community colleges are more likely to see their infrastructural development as a key factor in their capacity to provide the training needed. So the DWI's decision to develop its own "soft skills" training modules, rather than rely on community college training programs, created further barriers to mobilizing reform coalitions capable of moving workforce development to a strategic priority in Denver.

Community colleges see workforce development as a "source of future students," according to one stakeholder. These students, however, present distinctive issues. Students who are already working may be reluctant to take time for extra training, and many educational institutions, including community colleges, are not organized in ways that allow them to accommodate these workers' scheduling and training needs. If community colleges rely on workers who return to school for training as a key growth force in the future, these colleges must find the funds to pay for these more costly programs. In Colorado, where community colleges are funded at a per student rate, the growth of enrollment in high-cost programs associated with workforce initiatives, such as technical skills training and certification programs, creates a funding crisis rather than a growth bonus for community colleges. Because the state formula is based on a per capita formula, the growth in costly training programs drains funds that would typically support basic education classes. As a result, there is a growth in part-time faculty to teach basic education courses as resources shift to the training courses. In addition, community colleges compete for this FTE (full-time equivalent) funding; therefore, cooperation across training programs and service areas is difficult. Similarly, if the Colorado Community College and Occupational Education System are to gain more education and training funds from the TANF funds controlled by Denver, each community college president would have to see low-wage worker programs as a priority and compete for these funds (Fitzgerald, 2000, 35).

From the perspective of the community college, the money spent on JI-like projects—sometimes characterized as marketing to gain partici-pants—might be better spent by investing in training institutions so they can revise schedules, add staff, take classes into plant sites, and institute other changes that make the educational institution accessible to work-ers. Community colleges also recognize that many firms now outsource training and prefer on-site training and distance learning. In the absence of such changes and in the face of a healthy economy, community colleges may find it difficult to find participants for training programs supported by workforce initiatives.

This is the case in Denver. There are several "success stories," partic-ularly the Essential Skills program at the Community College of Denver, where a "whole life" approach to building career ladders in child care and central supply technology features a 78 percent employment rate at com-pletion (Fitzgerald, 2000, 30). This program, however, enjoys unusual autonomy over hiring and resources—thanks to the director's ability to obtain grants. More generally, the ability to bring the community college institutions into workforce development systems and to institutionalize their role, is dependent upon recognizing several points of conflict:

- Addressing the decreased ability of community colleges to cross-subsidize courses as their role in workforce development increases
- Acknowledging the community colleges' concerns regarding fund-ing for trainers and upgraded training rather than the access and recruitment goals currently embedded in local policy designs
- Revisiting the conflicts of territorial and functional interests, which community colleges see as limiting systems reforms

Tallying up these factors, Denver has benefited from DWI's role as a forum for debating workforce issues and taken advantage of the overlap-ping networks in the workforce arena to build coalitions and carve out funding streams for local initiatives. The shifting discourse, the weak state role, spatial mismatches of program needs and jurisdictional boundaries, the continued dominance of external initiatives, and episodic business participation are not insurmountable problems to mobilizing participa-tion as the Denver experience shows. Nor do the mixed incentives facing community colleges preclude their selective participation in workforce development issues. The continued fragmentation of advocacy groups—often along ethnic and racial divides—appears more intractable; how-ever, there are several organizational initiatives suggesting that these tensions can be subordinated to a broader agenda. In Denver, enlisting stakeholders and mobilizing their participation around a workforce development agenda does not appear to be a major stumbling block to

constructing performance regimes. Sustaining that involvement, however, is more difficult.

CHALLENGE #2: SUSTAINING INVOLVEMENT IN THE FACE OF COMPETING DEMANDS

Several factors stymie sustained involvement in efforts to elevate workforce systems reforms to strategic agenda status. These include the persistence of competing ideas about the purpose and nature of "systems
reform" as a shared goal, the tensions between political pressures and performance pressures, the potential erosion of the funding resources sustaining participation, and the alternative agendas for addressing the
working poor issues.

Systems Reform Goals Are Ill-Structured

Until recently, the problem space for workforce issues remained somewhat diffuse and ill-structured—that is, there are differences of opinion
on the relevant attributes of the problem and how they link to the overall goal. As a result, it is difficult to form and sustain coalitions independent of their common or divergent interests (Stone et al., 2001, 102).
Although workforce advocates in Denver shared similar policy goals and
recognized the need for "systems reform," the persistence of workforce
development as an ill-structured problem limited their sustained involvement in common initiatives.

Much of the support for systemic reforms stemmed from a frustration
that "nobody would devise a system" like the current workforce development process—one constrained by multiple and often conflicting regulations associated with different funding streams. What really constituted
systems reform was a continual debate. The most frequent characterizations
put emphasis on "connectedness" between employers and community-
based providers, getting all organizations in the system "to do what they
do best." This means "not just a network, but a system," characterized
by shared credit rather than competition over funds. This would require
shifting the focus from where the funding came to who provides the services. When asked where Denver stood relative to that standard, the most
typical response was "about 4–5" on a 10-point scale.

The varying size of nonprofit organizations that are active in workforce development contributed to this ill-structured problem space. A
performance-based perspective emerged from some smaller nonprofit organizations: As they saw it, there are many workforce systems in place but
few are funded through the "Big Systems"[16] (i.e., DWI, DEA). In this view,
true systems reform would be performance based, where organizations

are judged and funded on the basis of their effectiveness.[17] The increased coordination and integration demanded by the dominant view of systems reform carried a price for such organizations, specifically the transaction costs entailed in meetings and efforts to standardize data collection and procedures. Few were persuaded that more coordination was beneficial. Those dubious of the coordination and integration initiatives of the Big Systems suggested reallocating funds to organizations rather than to "million dollar projects with multiple staff." This reallocation would be structured through various procedures, creating open competitions among groups motivated by common goals such as retention and placement. This would empower the organizations to develop their own strategies, would reward the best practices that met the goals without presuming only one model, and could minimize meetings and maximize rewards for performance.

Performance Often Conflicts with Politics

In many cities, the tension between targeting certain population groups who need a second chance at gaining decent employment and larger questions of restructuring the workforce development process crop up repeatedly. This tension often tends to be resolved by resorting to the program focus rather than the system change initiatives (Stone, 2001). This is not surprising because the stakeholders primarily consist of organizations with ongoing programs, gaining new resources by targeting new populations—such as CWEE's shift to working families from a previous focus on welfare mothers—or enhancing and expanding current programs for second chance populations in response to program incentives.

Efforts at rationalizing existing workforce systems often appear to challenge the community-based groups who are needed to implement new policy changes; thus, these challenges threaten their sustained involvement. In Denver, these tensions were real and complex. Some respondents referred to the debates over the role of CBOs as just another set of "turf wars," whereas others indicated that this particular cycle of turf wars stemmed from Piton's initial reluctance to form partnerships with community-based groups. Some pointed out that the disagreements stemmed from the seeming redundancy of the JI design with what Denver CBOs claimed they were already doing. Much of this dispute centered on measurement and assessment of outcomes. Most groups claimed they already did outcomes assessment as part of their standard evaluation processes. JI's performance-based outcomes funding now required groups to take on measurement and assessment tasks in order to be funded; these tasks were perceived to be of dubious relevance to their own mission. As in Milwaukee, the focus on metrics and a seeming lack of real discretion often jeopardized small groups' ability to participate and provide fresh ideas. Not that most groups resisted assessments and evaluations of their efforts; the issue appeared to be the effort involved in standardization rather than the assessments themselves. With more groups involved in delivering workforce services in Denver, and more funders demanding performance measures, the outcry over performance measures rose, and the ability to effectively measure their performance declined (Fung and Zdrazil, 2001, 32).

The Local Geography of Workforce Development Is Contested

As the Milwaukee study points out (Fung and Zdrazil, 2001), the local geography of workforce development policy is crucial. Those agencies charged with workforce responsibilities are embedded in a locally-based network of CBOs, other government agencies, nonprofit organizations, faith-based organizations, and other groups concerned with the working poor. In Denver, workforce development often appeared to elicit conflicts between functional and territorial interests—a focus on workforce development processes colliding with a territorial focus on poor neighborhoods. This perennial conflict now seemed to reflect contradictions between "old ways of thinking" and new clients to be served. To the extent that federal and foundation workforce development monies seemed to repeat funding patterns to the same territorial interests, these patterns signaled a continuation of the "old ways of thinking" to some business interests.

But to many business leaders and nongovernmental organizations, this signals an inability to break out of old funding patterns and political relations. CBOs are vocal political participants in Denver; to some stakeholders, they appear to tie the mayor's hands because they demand inclusion in workforce development initiatives but often are ill-equipped to meet the performance standards. Because most workforce development funds flow through government structures (with the exception of the JI in Denver), the political sensitivities to CBOs are perceived to undermine the prospects for strategic direction. Indeed, even some public-sector stakeholders in Denver questioned whether these traditional territorially-based structures were the most appropriate vehicles for systems reform of workforce development processes. The "marketing" elements in DWI projects were perceived by some as a means of going around CBOs to directly address workers and employers.

Business Needs Do Not Always Fit Workforce Development Agendas

The employer-driven orientation of the JI strategy, in conjunction with the equity issues embedded in the second chance targeting, proved a challenging mix for most employers in Denver. To one business stakeholder, "the city doesn't really understand where it wants to go. . .and who the customer is." In Denver, as in most of the other JI cities, business involvement in JI programs was episodic and erratic. Those participating actively in the stakeholder meetings and the sectoral programs tended to do so out of personal conviction and pragmatic considerations. As a result, although these participants often shared the understandings of workforce development issues expressed by other stakeholders, they did not indicate that their concerns were common in the business community as a whole. Indeed, most active employers had been involved in previous job training programs and saw some merits in the improved access gained to prospective workers. Low business involvement was attributed to a lack of information about the programs available, the benefits possible, and misunderstandings of the second chance populations. One business leader active in public workforce programs admitted there was "less coordination" than expected because of the problems involved in linking workers and jobs.

Some of the more active Denver employers were minority business owners with long-standing involvement in local programs. Employers working on workforce issues through business associations were more likely to attribute the variable participation to the state of the economy. Because a healthy, growing economy existed, there seemed to be little need for organized workforce development initiatives; as the local economy showed signs of slowing, employers predicted more interest in JI-type initiatives. As one public official put it, the public sector has a hard time "keeping the attention" of employers because employers want a quick response rather than involvement in the processes of systems reform.

The "Glue" for Sustaining Cooperation among Diverse Interests Can Dry Up

The "glue" holding these coalitions together emerges from the "small opportunities" for mutual gain available in the workforce development projects and programs noted above. Clearly, the W2W, WIA, and AECF's JI funds are critical to these efforts. These funds provide not only direct benefits to those participating in the programs, but also planning resources, promoting the early engagement of employers in workforce development initiatives.

This cooperation must be sustained, however, even in the absence of continuing external revenues. Local officials look to two other models for sustaining cooperation over time: TEA-21 (Transportation Equity Act) funds for Metropolitan Planning Organizations (MPOs) and the Denver Regional Council of Governments initiatives. Interjurisdictional cooperation is a precondition for access to TEA-21 funds; utilization of MPOs is necessary for project planning and implementation. To the extent that effective linkages of employers and workers require crossing jurisdictional boundaries, TEA-21 funds may play a role. A five-year effort by the forty-nine county and municipal governments constituting the Denver Regional Council of Governments (DRCOG) led to the adoption of the Metro Vision 2020 Plan for regional cooperation in 1997. Although the agreement was voluntary, local adoption of the Metro Vision 2020 Plan has become a factor in the allocation of regional transportation monies by DRCOG. The spin-off Mile High Compact initiative encourages all local jurisdictions in the metropolitan area to sign an intergovernmental agreement committing to the broad visions of the Metro Vision 2020 Plan, including a provision for jobs/housing balances across the region.

Competing Solutions Divert Coalitional Energies

Although there are many stakeholders putting a high priority on workforce development issues, several note the importance of other "solutions"—solutions that reach beyond the urban workforce system—to the working poor problem. To the extent that stakeholders become frustrated or disillusioned with changing workforce systems directly, these alternative goals may divert the energies and attention of potential workforce reform coalitions.

PUBLIC SCHOOL REFORM

Denver's public school system is charged with failing the children of second chance populations. The literacy and dropout rates for Latino students are radically higher than the rates for whites, African Americans, or other groups. Addressing workforce issues for the future will require public school reforms that target the needs of this growing segment of the local population. Furthermore, these reforms must include not only programs for students from kindergarten through grade 12, but also the community colleges that serve as the access point for workers of color who seek to gain credentials and job skills. But the disconnect of city government and the independent public school system, not to mention the autonomous community college system, makes such reforms even more difficult.

SELF-SUFFICIENT WORKING FAMILIES

Now there is a concerted movement toward focusing workforce development on working families. This movement brings together family and work issues, focusing on the "cellophane ceiling," as one nonprofit leader put it, limiting skills and wages for those already working. This approach defines work problems as issues related to upgrading skills and increasing wages rather than providing access to jobs. For some advocates, this links workforce issues more directly to neighborhood concerns; it also shifts the focus from nonprofits to CBOs and neighborhood groups and asks nonprofits to rethink their neighborhood ties. This approach also ties the agenda more directly to livability concerns. Several statewide organizations are working on developing self-sufficiency standards for Colorado families and identifying a Colorado Family Needs Budget to generate support for working families. Among city officials, there is some support for creating a Mayor's Office for Working Families, using General Fund, CDBG, and TABOR retention funds to avoid creating programs aimed at protecting funding streams.

LOCAL EARNED INCOME TAX CREDIT

The local Earned Income Tax Credit (EITC) project developed by the mayor's office is a nationally recognized public-sector innovation, and is the first city EITC in the United States (Nevel, 2002). As welfare rolls declined, the mayor's staff saw the $22 million TANF surplus as an opportunity to try out new initiatives in support of TANF goals. Mayor Webb allowed MOWD to take part of this surplus to support a local EITC program. Denver's EITC would be linked to state and local EITCs. One estimate purports that, once implemented in January 2002, the city EITC would also benefit the 28,000 families in Denver who are eligible for the federal program.

Although there appear to be few incentives for elected officials to support human capital issues, one stakeholder claims the growing city council interest stemmed from efficiency concerns. There was suddenly a lot of money available for workforce development; however, the money was not being spent appropriately. The city council supported the EITC project unanimously because it was seen, according to one observer, as "finally a way to support the working poor" instead of fighting turf battles. Mayor Webb claimed the EITC was the "first creative thing for the working poor" in the past eight years.

Instead of evidence of resistance to pursuing a workforce development agenda, the Denver record reflects diversions offered by competing solutions to the workforce problem. The ill-structured space for workforce issues, with divergent views on how various attributes of the problem link to larger goals, encourages advocates to turn to other related initiatives, such as public school reform and working family concerns. These issues support workforce development but do not directly address labor supply and demand issues. Sustaining the participation of business as well as local electoral constituencies remains a challenge. This concern seems to be interdependent. The tensions between territorially-based groups and more functionally organized groups are interpreted by the business community as "the old ways of thinking" that compete with more efficient strategies. In the absence of sufficient resources to hold these coalitions together, these symbolic dimensions become more critical. The weaknesses in sustaining coalitions complicate efforts to create durable coalitions and institutionalize new practices.

CHALLENGE #3: CREATING DURABLE COALITIONS AROUND PERFORMANCE GOALS

In general, and in contrast to other economic development institutions, workforce institutions are more fragmented, weaker, and subject to volatile funding cycles. As relatively new local policies, workforce development issues may be seen as the purview of multiple agencies. There is rarely a consensus on ownership of the problem and few accepted routines or procedures for dealing with it. Overcoming this legacy of fragmented and weak entities is critical in establishing durable coalitions around performance goals.

The notion of durable coalitions underscores the need for changing relationships and replacing past dynamics with new patterns and linkages in order to institutionalize these new practices. In characterizing the rare instances of performance regimes, Stone et al. (2001, 18) point out that durable collaborations usually require formally organized and staffed entities that are able to maintain high levels of visible activity, focus on concrete actions, and engage in ongoing consultations between grassroots and elite organizations. External resources often play an important role in such collaborations; the impetus for reform often comes from outside of the normal routines. These factors are evident in Denver. Changing workforce systems requires more stable, coherent funding streams, institutionalizing the local public-sector role in workforce development policy, regularizing relations among potential coalition members, and designing regional workforce policy models.

The Mayor Promotes New Paradigms and New City Roles

As a result of multiple and concurrent federal and foundation programs introduced in a short time period, the default workforce development system in most cities is structured by the competition among groups for a share of the pool of public and private funds available. The fear is that although patterns of interactions may have been altered through new institutional arrangements, such as DWI, local efforts still lack coordination and comprehension (Fung and Zdrazil, 2001). Although this can result in the segmented landscape characteristic of the War on Poverty initiatives, and the consequent limits on systems change, this fragmentation of funding sources in Denver became an opportunity for local elected officials to redefine their roles to include steering and coordinating these multiple initiatives.

The Metro Denver Chamber of Commerce reports workforce availability and quality and transportation as key issues in recent years. And, to CBOs, welfare reform created a "do or die" situation; they had to adjust to working with different populations and new programs or lose their funding and legitimacy. The new city roles in workforce systems, however, were crafted in the public sector. The Colorado preference for county devolution in TANF and WIA actually put workforce issues on the agenda of both the mayor and city council. In Colorado, the workforce funding streams from the state to local governments are not unified. Colorado's decision to devolve TANF programs to the county level, and the WIA orientation to county- and city-level institutions, played to Denver's advantage. As a consolidated city–county entity, Denver suddenly became the receptacle for substantial revenue streams from TANF, WIA, and Youth Opportunity initiatives.

As the "working poor" image became more salient in the TANF context and the high economic growth experienced in the Denver area, the mayor used this policy idea to establish a new paradigm, justifying a new role: Growth is not enough to reduce poverty, work may not be enough unless it is at wages sufficient to ensure livelihood, and current bureaucratic programs are not adapting to these new realities. The workforce constituency became characterized as job seekers, including "incumbent workers, emerging workers, or workers in transition." In response to these changing conditions, the mayor's office created a new city role based on this new paradigm, and gained leverage over some of the funding coming into the city from the federal government and foundations.

Fragmented Funding Becomes a Political Opportunity

To take advantage of this opportunity, MOWD needed to assemble staff and flexible revenues to support signature initiatives marking its role in workforce policy. Although revenue streams were flowing into the city, much of the money was targeted and unavailable for new systemic change initiatives. In contrast to other Colorado cities and counties, Denver had to restructure a large city bureaucracy to move toward systems reform of workforce development. Namely, a large human services bureaucracy was in place, geared to traditional welfare services and seen as locked into patronage with minority communities rather than a broader orientation to workforce development. With the mayor's support, the city began to reallocate personnel from state and county programs that were previously administering Aid to Families with Dependent Children (AFDC) and other social welfare programs to the new structures set up in MOWD. Rather than turn any existing bureaucracy "on its head" with new directives, MOWD selectively appropriated parts of the human services budget and personnel into its workforce staff. In addition, thirty-seven employees in MOWD resulted from the merger of Labor's workforce development section and the employment training parts of TANF. These reallocations only partially resolved the staffing issues. Ninety percent of the available staff were AFDC technicians and "had that mentality" according to one observer. In addition, the Civil Service job classifications for old bureaucratic jobs are still in place for recruitment of new MOWD staff.[18]

The largesse promised by federal programs proved problematic. Although WIA seemed to promise a "different way of doing business," as one stakeholder recalled, there was less change than anticipated because WIA retained the same "stovepipe" funding design as the former JTPA. Despite expectations that WIA would consolidate multiple funding streams, consolidation did not occur. Nevertheless, another local official argues that WIA is governing "how things will be in the future because it gives a structure to the system" and is "better thought out" by emphasizing three types of services to be provided: One-Stop Centers, intensive services, and training by certified providers.

In the short term, however, the transition from AFDC to TANF gave the city more opportunities to serve a greater population and to do things differently. In particular, TANF surpluses and their diversion allowed the city to make things happen, according to one stakeholder, rather than let them "evolve." When Denver's Welfare Reform Board decided to implement federal regulations allowing TANF surpluses to go to non-TANF clients, the increased flexibility essentially capitalized MOWD's workforce development initiatives. By appropriating some of these funds and using the federal and state regulations devolving TANF, WIA, and Youth Opportunity authority to its advantage, local officials began to carve out a new workforce development policy niche. MOWD now directs the WIA One-Stop Centers, TANF diversion funds, various Youth Opportunity programs, and W2W competitive grants. The budget, consisting mostly of federal funds, is now over $14 million. As one indicator of this local political will and new priority, the year 2000 marked the first time the city allocated general funds ($500,000) to workforce development. The city is expected to increase the funding of workforce development in 2001 as the demand for skilled services increases and becomes more articulate.

GETTING PRODUCTS

To some extent, earlier versions of the MOWD office were considered to have the necessary infrastructure but no products. In the past, the mayor's office contracted out most services; however, as the JTPA funding declined over the last six years, the agency began to bring some services in-house. The resulting melange appeared fragmented and directionless. Now MOWD is operating with a more strategic, "business-like" approach to determining whether it is best to buy services or generate the services directly and when to directly manage programmatic grants. Currently, this office manages a diverse range of programs, including recent awards of a competitive Welfare-to-Work grant, a Youth Offender grant, and a Youth Opportunity Demonstration grant. MOWD also has assumed the management role for the Denver Department of Human Services' employment staff.

CHURNING STAFF

The JI borrowed elements of an "innovation ecology" model by devolving financing and operation authority to labor market intermediaries and presuming that these brokers would generate contextually-specific knowledge and innovation (Fung and Zdrazil, 2001, 16). The latter design feature required substantial monitoring to ensure program goals were met. It also presumed talented people would be available at critical junctures within the system. There is no shortage of such people in Denver; however, there exists a tendency to churn these people through the system. Turnover in staff and leadership at DWI became a serious—possibly fatal—problem. At MOWD, movement on the mayor's agenda depended on the retirement of a civil service employee and placement of the Mayor's Special Assistant as MOWD Director. Perhaps to an unusual extent, the linkages within the workforce development system in Denver rely as much on personal relationships as structural incentives for cooperation. As a result, a series of segmented relations in this system rather than routines for coordination and cooperation exist. In the absence of certain key people currently working on Denver's workforce issues, there is no guarantee that these linkages and cooperative initiatives would continue in their current state.

Windows of Opportunity Open Briefly

The mayor's office is now the arena for integrating some of these multiple funding streams and cross-funding some initiatives. By reasserting the public role and voice in workforce issues, capturing significant shares of the available funding, and employing market rhetoric to explain new goals and procedures, this office is creating a public sector with new mechanisms for delivering employment services. If the mayor's office can effectively steer the larger workforce development process, it may become the "guardian" of that process in Denver (Stone, 2001).

The window of opportunity for systems reform through this venue is small, however. Thanks to term limits, Mayor Webb and a high proportion of the city council will be out of office in eighteen months. These term limits will also most likely bring an end to the tenure of the MOWD Director who is also part of the mayor's staff, and who used the federal and state regulations to engineer the reorganization of workforce funding and personnel at the city–county level. In the absence of such a policy entrepreneur, and the absence of the political commitment of local elected officials, the durability of existing arrangements is questionable. Indeed, it is possible that the new linkages, programs, and procedures introduced to date will falter.

In Denver, there is agreement that the window of opportunity for systemic reform of workforce development is open—for about five years now—although there is less agreement on why and how long it will remain open. Those who see workforce development as a matter of upgrading skills and gaining higher wages believe that a healthy economy improves the prospects for initiatives targeting those goals; they believe that the window remains open as long as the economy thrives and certain skills remain in demand. Paradoxically, those viewing workforce development in terms of marginalized workers and underemployment note that workers move through a series of low-wage jobs available in abundance during a strong economic period and may have little interest in training. In their view, the window opens as the economy slows and the supply of low-wage workers increases. In the aftermath of September 11th, this latter scenario becomes more relevant.

Realigning Allies Is Incomplete

For workforce development to achieve systemic agenda status, durable coalitions formed around performance goals are necessary. In Denver, this requires realignment of a number of critical relationships: External funders and local intermediaries, the mayor's office and local intermediaries, and intermediaries and neighborhood groups.

Realigning the relationship of external funders and some local intermediaries proved troublesome. In May 2001, Piton and the AECF ended their relationship on the JI project. Many factors seemed in play.[19] To many stakeholders, the JI project seemed to be a mismatch of what Denver groups wanted and what AECF needed. Divergent views of workforce problems in Denver and the outcomes to be sought through the JI project were two areas of disagreement. Even using Piton as the intermediary elicited some concerns. Piton was often perceived as a foundation that funds themselves to do direct service provision and thus diverts funds from other providers. Some contrasted the JI model with the new AECF-funded project, *Making Connections*, which was also using Piton as an intermediary. In this neighborhood-based project, systems reform is just one piece of the strategy and Piton's role is that of a partner in a circle of stakeholders rather than as the head of the table. AECF funding for the *Making Connections* project at Piton dwarfs previous JI funding. *Making Connections* also is perceived as integrating work and family concerns in ways that the JI project did not. Finally, timing also mattered. With the entry of TANF and WIA funds, and the arrival of Youth Opportunity funding, the JI project seemed to offer fewer resources and more strings.

The decision to end the Piton/AECF relationship reflects certain aspects of governance failure (Jessop, 1998; Stoker, 1998). Early on, the original policy design included oversimplification of the conditions in which networks operate and, possibly, incorrect or insufficient information. The programmatic emphasis on soft skills did not appear to be based on empirical assessments of the workforce conditions in Denver or on consultation with a broad range of groups, particularly those in the Latino community. Furthermore, the needed flexibility and accountability proved elusive. Flexibility entails robustness, sensitivity to motivational complexity, and variability to encourage experimentation (Stoker, 1998). The vaunted flexibility and adaptability of networks, however, can conflict with the need for guidance and use of past experiences.

For some in DWI and other workforce organizations, the guidance and reflexive opportunities built in to the processes by AECF seemed to come at the expense of their ability to develop a flexible, adaptive network. Even though AECF allowed sites to set their own outcomes—given their particular set of strategies, resources, and capacities—DWI and many of the CBOs balked at AECF's accountability demands. Not that they were unconcerned with outcomes or felt no need for accountability; rather it became a question of to whom they were accountable and how their performance would be measured. These tensions between accountability, flexibility, and efficiency can undermine any governance process. Ironically, the DWI stakeholder meetings empowered JI participants to the extent that they decided to head in a direction considered more appropriate to the Denver context.

More explicit partnerships between MOWD in the mayor's office, DWI, and DEA may contribute to durable coalitions by building on and sustaining the institutional strengths developed in these spheres. From the perspective of one stakeholder, DWI was in a position to run informal and formal RFP (request for proposal) processes that would allow them to attempt projects that would not otherwise be possible in the public sector because of bureaucratic procedures and grant constraints. Bringing employers into the initial design process and involving them in training programs is critical. Monitoring and evaluating these projects, particularly work-site evaluations, and "going public" with the results through DWI and DEA fora, seem to mesh the capacities of the different organizations and strengthen the linkages across critical elements of the workforce system.

Finally, durable coalitions may founder if links between local intermediaries and grassroots groups remain ill defined. These tensions surfaced over control of One-Stop Centers. Although WIA promoted these centers, it is unclear how the centers will be coordinated with existing services and the missions of CBOs in those neighborhoods. The centers are seen as institutions that harness many workforce elements at the community level—and thus contribute to systems reform—but they also introduce the possibility of, as one stakeholder put it, providing "narrow services to narrow groups." In Denver, debates over neighborhood representation and voice centered on capacity-building and control issues that were linked to the One-Stops' initiatives. DWI considered establishment of Community Advisory Boards (CAB) for the One-Stop Centers as a means to increase neighborhood support for the One-Stop Centers and increase the centers' responsiveness to communities. Although the neighborhood capacity-building goals and the channels for community involvement were considered important, the proposed CABs raised questions. Even to supporters of a stronger neighborhood voice, these fora "would be a disaster" because of the substantial possibility of friction between CABs and the One-Stop Centers they were meant to advise. CABs potentially could become gatekeepers in the workforce development process, adding another institutional layer to manage. The unintended consequences of this formalization could include obstructionism and nonrepresentative voice.

Regionalizing Workforce Development Strategies: Preferred Solution But Not the Actual Policy Choice

The prospects for a durable coalition also are limited by the difficulties associated with regionalizing workforce development strategies. To the extent that labor markets are regional rather than local, and increasingly "dismantled" through outsourcing and other resource reorganization practices by firms, the role of local intervention alone becomes problematic. In Denver, there is a recognition that labor and housing markets are indeed regional and that policy intervention must be structured to take this into account. In a recent State of the City address, the mayor emphasized this regional context and underscored the fragmentation and redundancy built into the current local intervention strategies. Although this was seen as a primarily rhetorical gesture, one that "never got traction," some local leaders continue to push for regional coordination, believing it is the necessary scale for constructing durable solutions to workforce issues.

Several barriers to regional workforce development strategies are evident. Those working on regional issues contend that workforce issues bring in a labor bureaucracy unfamiliar with working with local officials. In addition, labor agencies are not inclined to support employer-oriented strategies, particularly those originating at the local level. Current rifts between the state Department of Labor and the WDBs in the metro counties over state civil service jobs exemplify the prevalence of a "gotcha" mentality. The legacy of past CETA (Comprehensive Employment and Training Act)/JTPA programs includes institutional structures as well as continuing civil service personnel who, in the views of some, do not see much difference between their past Private Industry Councils (PICs) and current WDBs. There is also a sense that federal workforce programs continue to reward inputs rather than outcomes; WDBs are unlikely to promote regional cooperation until rewarded for doing so. Although business groups rank workforce issues as a top priority, they have yet to demand coherent regional strategies with employer orientations. Groups like the Metropolitan Mayors Forum are not held accountable for regional problems (e.g., affordable housing and workforce development). In short, cooperation on regional workforce issues "lacks a champion" as one advocate sees it.[20]

Although no such champion exists, Denver still enjoys a history of innovation on regional cross-jurisdictional strategies.[21] With the approval of a strong majority of voters in the six contiguous metro counties (i.e., Adams, Arapahoe, Boulder, Broomfield, Denver, Douglas, and Jefferson counties), the Scientific and Cultural Facilities District (SCFD) was established in 1988—and again in 1994 for another ten-year period. The SCFD is intended to support cultural institutions and activities benefiting the metro area through the creation of an earmarked 0.1 percent sales tax. Now Denver's "blueprint" for interjurisdictional cooperation, the regional tax-sharing model pioneered by the SCFD, is contingent on creating regional special districts.

Other local models of regional cooperation include the Metro Denver Network (MDN), which was developed by the Chamber of Commerce. This partnership of fifty-six cities, six counties, and forty-two economic development organizations is aimed at coordinating metro area economic development activities by providing One-Stop services for companies that are considering relocating to the area. MDN responds to inquiries by preparing customized proposals for all matching sites in the Denver area. The city is in the process of centralizing this information at MDN and providing this service to both the local government and inquiring firms. The incentive to share information and cooperate across jurisdictions stems from the desire to improve the intelligence functions demanded of both firms and local governments.

Finally, some stakeholders see the DRCOG as a more seasoned, available mechanism for coordinating workforce policy at the regional level. DRCOG relies on voluntary participation and cooperation; it provides data collection and information on regional labor markets but has not yet been mobilized for policy intervention. To accomplish DRCOGs Metro Vision 2020 Plan goal for a jobs/housing balance, financial incentives for regional cooperation may be needed. Voting for mandatory compliance on these goals and establishing additional DRCOG control over transportation funds may provide the incentives necessary.

Efforts to apply these models of regional cooperation to workforce issues have had mixed results. The MDN model is evident in the Metro Job Team approach. The Denver Regional Workforce Collaborative is a broader policy-oriented initiative aimed at regional cooperation on workforce development. WIA seemed to promise a means of promoting regional workforce development, similar to that promoted by ISTEA mechanisms, according to one nonprofit observer. Governor Romer, however, did not "bite the bullet" and appoint a Metro Denver Workforce Development Board for WIA; instead, there are five separate boards for each county in the metro area. Although the individual boards are interested in more regional strategies, their cooperation to date is informal. Consequently, service providers cannot take on a regional orientation because they are dealing with five boards rather than a regional organization. The inability to transfer these models to human capital policy arenas, such as workforce development, dictates that regional governance may be restricted to projects with only indirect benefits for human capital development.

Although sustaining participation is difficult, the prospects for a durable coalition and institutionalization are more promising. This unexpected view stems from the political leadership and entrepreneurial skills of current members of the Webb administration. Their need to promote the working poor coincided with a period of greater federal funding for a range of labor supply and demand polices. Given Colorado's devolution history, responsibilities and revenue came to the city rather than resting at the state level. Although there is no question that the Webb administration is committed to the issues of the working poor, the confluence of these programs and revenues provided an open window, allowing the mayor to convey a new way of viewing workforce issues that articulated new city roles. Yet, these political skills and opportunities were not sufficient to support a regionalized workforce development strategy, although many understood the problem was regional rather than local. Hence, more positive prospects for workforce development do not occur at the desired scale.

Mobilizing Performance Regimes to Change Workforce Systems

If we conceptualize changes in workforce systems in terms of constructing performance regimes, we ask how well Denver overcomes the mobilization, sustainability, and institutionalization challenges (Stone, 1998, 13). Overall, Denver's record in addressing these challenges is mixed. The argument here is that mobilization does not present an intractable problem, but that sustaining that involvement and institutionalizing these initiatives is more problematic.

Even though Denver enjoyed strong economic growth in the 1990s, workforce issues remained salient in the face of the "Vail syndrome"—the persistence of poverty in the face of growing wealth. Thanks to the confluence of revenue streams coming to the city in support of workforce development, numerous incentives are available to enlist diverse stakeholders around workforce issues. Many of the initiatives rely on the participation of community-based groups and employers for implementation; these groups benefited from joining forces. The DWI forum fostered a common understanding of workforce problems and created new, broader relations among stakeholders. Its role as a workforce intermediary raised more complex issues. The broader question is not the effectiveness of DWI, but the ways in which the choice of such intermediaries shapes the political landscape.

Sustaining this participation is proving to be a more difficult task. The competing demands challenging sustained involvement include the persistence of competing ideas about the purpose and nature of "systems reform" as a shared goal, the tensions between political pressures and performance demands, the potential erosion of the funding resources sustaining participation, and the alternative agendas for addressing the working poor issues. Any one of these is sufficient to encourage groups to "exit" from workforce development activities. In Denver, the requirements for assessing the performance of stakeholders in carrying out workforce initiatives continue to be the most contentious elements challenging continued participation. All government programs require some type of assessment and evaluation, of course. It is not assessment per se but the need to standardize measures and data collection that appeared onerous to smaller organizations in Denver. Dealing with this accountability challenge is likely to be critical to sustaining involvement in workforce initiatives.

It is also integral to create a durable coalition around performance goals. Rather than seeing this as a matter of boosting the capacities of each organization, it is more appropriate to consider this a matter of institutionalization of workforce policy roles, responsibilities, and routines. Workforce development policies unfold in arenas where the rule-setting, hierarchical governance strategies of the public sectors intersect with the more networked strategies found in civil society and the price competition mechanisms of the private sector. These institutional settings encompass features that help or hinder reaching agreements, coordinating preferences, and providing options (Heclo, 1994). Institutions matter; they can change how groups understand their own interests and affect the types of coalitions formed.

The local public-sector role in Denver is notable. Although a performance regime is not yet in place, MOWD appears to be the driving force for systems reform. With the support of the mayor and city council, MOWD carved out a new city role in steering and coordinating workforce activities, appropriated funds and personnel from a moribund human services bureaucracy and a resistant labor bureaucracy, and initiated a number of innovations, such as the local EITC, enabling the mayor to take credit for helping the working poor. Political will and the presence of a policy entrepreneur on the city staff have given the public sector a lead role in systems reform. If the window of opportunity remains open, whether due to business pressure, a compatible agenda from the new mayor, or stable national funding, the prospects for creating a durable performance regime coalition in Denver increase. Overcoming the barriers to workforce regime formation will now require broad mobilization within the private sector as well as better integration with networks of "brokers," or intermediaries, and civic organizations.

In Denver, there is a sense that the conditions for such a mobilization exist. Two key factors are present: The "small opportunities" that provide the "glue" to hold coalitions together and a window of opportunity for change. The glue consists of the multiple federal funding streams coming into the city and the efforts of MOWD to use these funds to promote changes in the workforce development system. Both the resources and the political will are critical; in the absence of either, as in past periods, mobilizing reform coalitions will prove futile.

Timing is also a vital element. The sense that "the time is right," that there is a change in the political climate conducive to certain reforms, and that the local and national political mood favors certain issues, signals an opportunity to introduce reforms to receptive audiences. Now there is a perception, however, that the window may be closed by external changes, including economic recession and possible cuts in WIA and TANF funds.

Also, there is a sense that the mayor's political capital will diminish in the last year of his term. Consequently, some stakeholders believe the issue is whether funding will "dry up before we can do it" (i.e., systems reform).

In any American city, the odds are low that performance regimes will form and persist in pushing workforce issues as strategic agenda items. Structural features, such as privileging growth and framing local economic development in terms of firms' needs rather than labor concerns, limit the salience of workforce issues. Mobilization around workforce agendas marks important historical moments that reveal how the political framework shapes the sustainability and durability of any workforce initiative. Considering Denver's demographics and political history, it is unlikely that a new mayor and city council would reject the significance of workforce issues; however, other priorities may displace the current attention to this issue. The devolution of workforce and welfare responsibilities to the city–county levels in Colorado provides ample incentives and mechanisms for Denver officials to continue to pursue a local role in changing workforce systems. Their effectiveness in doing so is contingent on their ability to contend with the factors influencing the sustainability and durability of workforce coalitions.

NOTES

1. This paper draws on a larger analysis of the politics of workforce development in Denver supported by the Annie E. Casey Foundation (Clarke, 2001). Although the empirical focus is on the AECF JI program, the broader concern is examining the conditions under which performance regimes can be established around workforce development agendas. I gratefully acknowledge the research assistance provided by Nicole Rosmarino, the generous spirit of Denver respondents, insightful comments from other project participants, and Bob Giloth's thoughtful and patient guidance of the overall project.

2. Some of these issues emerged in discussions during the April 2001 Denver Workforce Initiative project meeting; others are garnered from my interviews with Denver stakeholders in 2000–2001.

3. The literature on governance processes provides some consensus on these critical elements of governance processes (Clarke, 2000; see also, Jessop, 1998; Rhodes, 1996; Rosenau, 1992; Stoker, 1998). Many times local officials may be one of many actors with stakes in local decisions; no one actor will be able to produce the desired outcomes because of the nature of interdependent resources and actions. Coordination of networks spanning public and private sectors will be critical to leadership. There is value added in combining resources rather than acting alone. Local officials face shared purposes among multiple actors but in the absence of any hierarchy of control. As a result, decisions are made by negotiations and interactive processes, building on trust and consensus, and although the

outcomes may be similar to those produced in the past by traditional governmental institutions, the processes are distinctive (Clarke 2001, see Figure 1).

4. The concept of civic capacity suggests that policy reforms—systemic changes—depend on intersectoral ties within the community (Stone, 1989, 2001). Mobilizing and realigning these ties is a matter of encouraging active involvement and developing a shared understanding of the problem and potential solutions. These ties provide the trust, iterative experiences, and reciprocity necessary to risk systemic change through cooperative, collaborative efforts. Civic capacity will vary by issue; the patterns of linkages and the decision processes are neither static nor universal.

5. Colorado Economic Perspective, First Quarter Fiscal Year 1998.

6. Nevertheless, in 1996 Mayor Webb opposed Initiative 100, a local ballot ordinance aimed at setting a living wage. Although the measure was defeated by over 75 percent of the voters, the state legislature was sufficiently alarmed that motions to outlaw any such local ordinances were introduced (but not passed).

7. MOWD took over the responsibilities of the former Mayor's Office of Employment and Training (MOET). MOET administered JTPA programs and a wide range of employment and training services. The shift to workfare models and the consolidation of programs and personnel under MOWD created both structural and programmatic upheavals (Capizzano, et al., 2001).

8. It is worth noting that the state political context is changing. For decades, Colorado operated with a divided government: Republicans controlled the state legislature while Democrats won the governor's office. During the 1990s, Democratic Governor Roy Romer championed many programs benefiting children, especially those from working poor families. When he left office (due to term limits), Republicans won the gubernatorial race as well. For a two-year period, Republicans controlled state government. In 2000, the Democrats gained a thin majority in the Senate; however, in a state dominated by rural and suburban voters, state support for urban initiatives is often diffuse and unreliable.

9. In 1992–1993, there were about 42,000 households on welfare in Colorado; by 1999, there were about 13,000. Over one-fourth of these are child-only cases (i.e., a child is living with a family member who receives a small stipend for child care but no benefits themselves). In Denver County, where a disproportionate amount of welfare cases are located, the rolls dropped from 11,431 in 1990 to 4,276 in 1999.

10. The following observations are based on interviews conducted in Spring/Summer 2001.

11. In the case of the redevelopment of Lowry Air Force Base, for example, federal guidelines led the city to put a priority on providing a share of housing for homeless families. When the developer balked, arguing for a greater share of affordable housing for the working poor, the city agreed to support the goal of economic diversity and to locate housing for the homeless in other areas of the city.

12. As city and county policymakers see it (City and County of Denver, 2000), these are the key factors: (1) Technology is redefining work and workplace skills

by demanding lifelong learning; (2) the earnings gap between those with skills and those without is widening; (3) business is reinventing its methodologies and functions, creating high performance organizations, flattening layers of management, and sharing decision-making with front-line employees; (4) problem solving, teamwork, and communication skills are increasingly essential for success in the workplace; (5) youth, incumbent workers, and job seekers must be served by a system of learning that offers them the opportunity to continually enhance their skills; (6) linkages between economic development and the quality of employment and training are more critical in dealing with a work environment so heavily dependent on skills; (7) the job market now and in the near future is one where the most important resources workers have are their workplace skills and their ability to learn new skills; and (8) most people will change jobs five to seven times during their careers and, given the pace of organizational and technological change, be asked to upgrade their job skills on a continuing basis.

13. The public sector partners include: City and county of Denver and Mayor's Office of Workforce Development *Services for Employers*: WIA programs, Resource Center, JobLink System, Welfare-to-Work Program, Employment First Program, TANF Program, Non-Custodial Program, Administration; *Services for Job Seekers*: WIA programs, Youth Opportunity Programs, JobLink Employment System, Welfare-to-Work Program, Employment First Program, TANF Program, TAA Program, WFA Program, Homeless Veterans Reintegration Program, Resource Center, Administration; *Education and Training Resources*: Bridges to Work Job Placement and Transportation Assistance for Employers and Job Seekers, Denver Employment First for Food Stamp Participants, Disadvantaged Worker Program, Refugee Tuition Voucher Program, EDWAA-Dislocated Worker Tuition Voucher Program, Welfare-to-Work, Veteran's Program, various Youth Programs.

Denver Human Service Department *Services for Employers*: Welfare-to-Work Program, Child Support Program.

State of Colorado and Colorado Department of Labor and Employment *Services for Employers*: WIA programs, including W2W Tax Credits.

Colorado Community College and Occupational Education System *Services for Employers*: WIA programs, Youth Opportunity Program.

The Mayor's Office for Economic Development funds part of the manufacturing outreach and training efforts in the DWI coordinated by the Piton Foundation.

14. The *Denver Mayor's Workforce Summit* in October 1998 involved over 500 Denver area businesses who redesigned the city's employment and training resources from the employer's perspective. The summit featured employer-led events focusing on recruitment, retention, retraining, and resources.

The Employer's Desk: Established in October 1998, the MOET now assists employers who need to access workforce resources, prescreening assistance, workplace training, tax credits, and specific labor market information.

The DWI: A partnership of the Denver Chamber of Commerce, the city of Denver, not-for-profit agencies, and the Piton Foundation that emphasizes seven critical employment sectors. Currently, it matches low-income job seekers with good jobs in the health care, teleservices, and manufacturing industries. Its products include: *Community Coaches™*, a program where coaches recruit and aid in job retention by providing a support network for new employees; *Workin' It Out,* a cognitive skills curriculum aimed at new entry-level workers on the job, featuring opportunities for new workers around conflict cycle, understanding the unwritten rules of the workplace, and personal responsibility; *Managing to Work It Out,* a skills curriculum aimed at supervisors of entry-level employees in DWI partner companies; *Learning to Work It Out,* designed for job seekers in pre-employment programs; and *Beginning to Work It Out,* developed particularly for the needs of youth.

Bridges-to-Work: A service that links suburban employers with a ready workforce and offers transportation assistance to and from employment in Denver's surrounding growth areas.

Denver Department of Human Services: Recently relocated into a new $36 million building and now conducts outreach to low-income neighborhoods.

Denver Employment First: Mandatory employment and training program for able bodied food stamp participants located in the Denver One-Stop Career Center Hub. Employment First clients have access to One-Stop employment and training resources.

Denver Housing Authority/HOPE IV: Opened the Quigg Newton Community Center and the Campus of Learners, and is in process of demolishing an old and distressed ten block area of Denver (Curtis Park Housing Development) to make way for a mixed-income housing program for its residents.

Empowerment Zones/Enterprise Communities: Committed to developing programs for services such as child care, health care, and transportation that decrease obstacles for *Enterprise Communities* residents entering the workforce. These efforts are assisting the *Enterprise Communities* residents through community-based organizations and other neighborhood resources on programs that build residents' jobs skills and, in turn, their ability to compete for higher wage positions.

Enterprise Foundation: The *Community Employment Alliance Initiative* (CEA), an initiative of the Enterprise Foundation, has played an active role in the employment and training arena. By focusing on neighborhoods and involving employers in the program design, this initiative has created new programs that address the needs of employers and disadvantaged job seekers. These programs include: *Focus on Neighborhoods–Community Employment Alliance's Initiative strategies* that focuses its efforts on Denver neighborhoods with the highest poverty rates; *Work at It!,* a training program for TANF recipients; *The Home Depot Program,* funded through a national Discretionary Welfare-to-Work grant that will place ninety welfare-to-work eligible individuals at three Home Depot stores.

Offender One-Stop (adult): Spearheaded by the Colorado Department of Corrections, specializes in employment and training resources to offenders in the Metro Denver area.

Out-of-School Youth Grant: A $2.25 million demonstration project aimed at out-of-school youth (ages 16 through 24) in three targeted Denver neighborhoods. The design of the program places out-of-school youth into long-term employment. Program activities include educational and vocational skills training, job placement, and job readiness/assessment. The Out-of-School Youth

Grant targets the Five Points, Cole, and Whittier neighborhoods and is located in the Denver One-Stop Career Center at CCD East Campus on 3532 Franklin Street.

Targeted Assistance Grant (TAG): A special project that provides tuition assistance to eligible refugees for vocational training in order to enhance employment skills.

Youth Offender Grant Program: A demonstration project aimed at youth offenders and at-risk youth in targeted neighborhoods. The program is designed to place youth offenders and at-risk youth into long-term employment. Program activities include educational and vocational training programs, job placement, and job readiness assessment. The Youth Offender Grant targets youth ages 14 through 24 in the Barnum, Highlands, Jefferson Park, Sun Valley, Villa Park, and Westwood neighborhoods. The new Denver Youth One-Stop Career Center is located at the Denver Area Youth Services (DAYS) building.

In line with the emphasis on linking with neighborhood-based providers, the MOWD has active contracts with thirty-nine community-based service providers. MOWD also has a contract with the AFL-CIO to provide vouchers directly to training providers for job readiness preparation specifically targeted for AFL-CIO eligible participants. The AFL-CIO Metro Reemployment Center (MRC) provides the services under MOWD's direction.

15. These spatial strategies include: (a) The Metro Job Team (MJT), a single point of contact for all metro Denver area employers. This regional collaboration is located at the main *Job Service* Center in Denver, and receives all in-coming job orders from metro area employers; thus, eliminating the need for employers to contact the Service Delivery Area (SDA) in their specific regions. The MJT enters the job order information into the statewide JobLink system that, in essence, creates a statewide database that is available to any job seeker. The SDAs in this collaboration each pay a proportionate share of the staff salaries and benefits.

(b) The Center for Regional Neighborhood Action (CRNA), funded by the Partnership for Regional Livability, invited MOWD, the other Service Delivery Areas (SDAs) in the metro area, foundations, community-based organizations, employers, and federal officials housed in the Denver Region to participate in a collaborative called the Denver Regional Workforce Collaborative. The objectives of the collaborative are to connect employers and employees throughout the region and to coordinate regional workforce development efforts. Three major focus areas emerged from the discussions locally and at a partnership meeting in Atlanta: *Policy,* increasing the knowledge base and common understanding among policymakers of the importance of regional cooperation in workforce development, characterized as JOB NET; *Performance,* determining the practical opportunities and challenges of building the capacity to act regionally, seen as JOB SUPPORT; and *Knowledge,* developing a capacity for mapping and analysis of the present and future regional job market, labeled as JOB MAPping. The collaborative is currently structuring itself into committees to brainstorm and identify strategies to accomplish the Job Net, Job Support, and Job Mapping areas.

(c) The Denver Area JobLink is envisioned by CRNA, in concert with the Collaborative; these groups prepared and submitted a proposal to the United States

Department of Labor for a planning demonstration grant for training the Denver region's working poor to become tomorrow's technology workforce. The project will bring together all key stakeholders to design an action plan for a high performance workforce development system for the region's technology and telecommunication industry.

(d) Finally, anticipating some of the potential governance failures from overlapping systems, MOWD periodically invites the Chairs of the WDBs in the metro area and the Directors to a breakfast meeting to discuss the challenges and opportunities of having five workforce development boards in one labor market. Specific concerns entailed the feasibility and success of marketing in this labor market, service to employers in multiple regions, recruitment of qualified workers, certification of training providers, recruitment of board members from the same pool of employers, and the list continues. This regional strategy focuses more on operational issues given the multiple regions in one labor market.

16. This characterization as a "Big System" by other local groups appears to refer to who has access to external funding streams rather than the actual volume of revenues, funds leveraged, or size of organizations.

17. Although it is difficult to evaluate these comparisons in the absence of standardized measures, some of the smaller nonprofit organizations claimed higher job placement rates at one-third the cost of government-supported programs.

18. In fiscal year 2001, the MOWD office had 104 employees and a total budget—of mostly federal dollars—over $14 million.

19. As the research unfolded, a number of tensions stemming from the historical design of the Denver JI became more evident. Although participants appreciated the JI intervention, there were concerns about the impacts of assessment requirements for outcomes funding and, to some, a fear that the JI model could potentially destabilize long-standing institutional arrangements. Also, the pattern of personnel changes plaguing the project from the beginning took their toll. The AECF continually expressed unease with DWI's relatively low performance on placements; these low rates—about 800—persuaded some that DWI's early investment strategies had "failed." On all sides, there was a sense the project faced a crisis of strategy; the competing policy solutions—public school reform, EITC, etc.—contributed to this strategic dilemma. Much of the anxiety and resistance to the performance measures and the accountability issues stemmed from this uncertainty. By the end of May 2001, the local intermediary, the Piton Foundation, announced they planned to continue their workforce development activities but that they would do so without AECF support. In effect, this ended the JI project but not necessarily the prospects for formation of a performance regime in Denver centered on workforce issues.

20. In contrast, Waste (2001) reports six examples of successful workforce regional alliances in California: The Institute for the North Coast (Humboldt County), the Sacramento Regional Action Partnership, the Joint Venture Silicon Valley, the Gateway Cities Partnership (Los Angeles), the Economic Alliance for the San Fernando Valley, and the San Diego Dialogue.

21. And public support: a 1993 poll reported that 60 percent of metro residents surveyed strongly agreed that people through the region should cooperate

on funding for art, museums, and the zoo. Thirty-seven percent also agreed that it is fair for residents to financially help regional organizations and another 41 percent agreed somewhat (Brimberg, 1993).

REFERENCES

Abt Associates Inc. 2000. *AECF Jobs Initiative: Evaluation Report on the Capacity Building Phase (March 1997–March 2000) Cross-Site Report.* New York: New School University (November).

Aguilar, Louis. 2001. "Colorado a Haven for Immigrants Hispanic, Asian Influx Reaches Beyond Cities." CENSUS 2000: A SPECIAL REPORT. *Denver Post* (August 6):A7.

Annie E. Casey Foundation (AECF). 1999. *Private Interests, Shared Concerns: The Relationship between Employers and the AECF Jobs Initiative Final Report.* Baltimore: The Annie E. Casey Foundation.

Brimberg, Judith. 1993. "Poll Shows Culture Favored over Rockies." *Denver Post* (December 14):B3.

Brovsky, Cindy. 2002. "Webb Set for Final Year." *Denver Post* (June 28):A1.

Capizzano, Jeffrey, Robin Koralek, Christopher Botsko, and Roseana Bess. 2001. "Recent Changes in Colorado Welfare and Work, Child Care, and Child Welfare Systems." *Assessing the New Federalism Project: State Update #9.* Washington, DC: Urban Institute.

Corporation for Enterprise Development (CFED). 2002. *2001 Development Report Card.* Available at www.cfed.org.

City and County of Denver. 2000. Workforce Investment Act—Five Year Plan for the City and County of Denver, revised April 14, 2000.

Clarke, Susan E. 2000. "Emerging Forms of Governance in the Context of Globalization." Background paper prepared for the UN Centre for Human Settlements, Third Global Report on Human Settlements (July).

———. 2001. "Interests, Ideas, and Institutions: The Politics of Workforce Development in Denver." Report prepared for the Annie E. Casey Foundation (July).

Clarke, Susan E. and Gary L. Gaile. 1998. *The Work of Cities.* Minneapolis: University of Minnesota Press.

Clarke, Susan E., Rodney Hero, and Mara Sidney. 1997. *Civic Capacity and Urban Education: Denver, 1993–1997.* Report to the National Science Foundation (NSF S#134.331).

Cox, Kevin. 1997. "Governance, Urban Regime Analysis, and the Politics of Local Economic Development." In *Reconstructing Urban Regime Theory: Regulating Urban Politics in a Global Economy,* edited by Mickey Lauria, 99–121. Thousand Oaks, CA: Sage.

Fitzgerald, Joan. 2000. *Community Colleges as Labor Market Intermediaries: Building Career Ladders for Low-Wage Workers.* New York: New School University Community Development Center.

Fung, Archon and Scott Zdrazil. 2001. "Ecologies of Workforce Development:

Patterns of Interaction and Prospects for Reform in Milwaukee, WI." Unpublished paper.

Gatton, Dave. 1999. "Webb Calls for New Partnership with America's Communities." Washington, DC: U.S. Conference of Mayors, June 28.

Giloth, Robert, and William Phillips. 2000. "Getting Results: Outcomes Management and the Annie E. Casey Foundation's Jobs Initiative Research Brief: September." Baltimore: The Annie E. Casey Foundation.

Heclo, Hugh. 1994. "Ideas, Interests, and Institutions." In *The Dynamics of American Politics*, edited by Larry Dodd and Cal Jillson, 366–392. Boulder, CO: Westview Press.

Jessop, Bob. 1998. "The Rise of Governance and the Risks of Failure." *International Social Science Journal* 155:29–45.

Mossberger, Karen. 2000. "School-to-Work Programs and the Challenges of Business-Education Partnerships in Urban Economic Development." Presented at the American Political Science Association Annual Meeting, Washington, DC (August).

Nevel, Shepard. 2002. "The Local Path to Making Work Pay: Denver's Earned Income Credit Experience." *Local Innovations in Welfare and Work Series*. Washington, DC: Brookings Institution.

Olinger, David. 2001. "Front Range Drives Statewide Boom, Report Says." *Denver Post* (March 20).

Pate, Kelly. 2002. "Federal Cash for Unemployment Sitting Idle." *Denver Post* (June 3): D1.

Piton Foundation. 1999. *Neighborhood Facts 1999*. Denver: The Piton Foundation.

———. 1994. *Poverty in Denver: Facing the Facts*. Denver: The Piton Foundation.

Plastrik, Peter with Judith Combes Taylor. 2001. "Responding to a Changing Labor Market: The Challenges for Community-Based Organizations. Research Brief." Baltimore: Annie E. Casey Foundation.

Progressive Policy Institute (PPI). 2002. *State New Economy Index: Benchmarking Economic Transformation in the States*. Washington, DC: Progressive Policy Institute. Available at www.ppionline.org.

Robert, Chaer. 1999. "Welfare to Work." Editorial: Denver Women's Commission, November 12. Denver, CO: City of Denver, Agency for Human Rights-Community Relations, Denver Women's Commission. Available at www.ci.denver.co.us/women.

Rhodes, R.A.W. 1996. "The New Governance: Governing without Government." *Political Studies* 44:652–67.

Rosenau, James. 1992. *Governance without Government*. Cambridge, MA: Cambridge University Press.

Simpson, Kevin. 2001. "Nearly a Third of Denverites Are Hispanic." *Denver Post* (March 20).

Stoker, Gerry. 1998. "Governance as Theory: Five Propositions." *International Social Science Journal* 155:17–28.

Stone, Clarence N. 1989. *Regime Politics*. Lawrence: University Press of Kansas.

————. 1998. "Introduction: Urban Education in Political Context. In *Changing Urban Education,* edited by Clarence Stone. Lawrence: University Press of Kansas.

————. 2001a. "The Atlanta Experience Re-examined: The Link between Agenda and Regime Change." *International Journal of Urban and Regional Research* 25:20–34.

————. 2001b. Comments on papers presented at Annie E. Casey meeting of six cities project, April 5, Greenbelt, MD.

Stone, Clarence N., Jeffrey R. Henig, Bryan D. Jones, and Carol Pierannunzi. 2001. *Building Civic Capacity.* Lawrence: University Press of Kansas.

Waste, Robert J. 2001. "Drawing Lessons from Regional Successes: New Regionalism and the Prospects for Regional Cooperation in California." Unpublished report. Available at www.csus.edu/calst/Government_Affairs/faculty_fellows_program.html.

Workfoce Investment Act (WIA). 2000. Workforce Investment Act—Five Year Plan for the City and County of Denver, revised April 14.

Archon Fung & Scott Zdrazil

3   Ecologies of Workforce Development
    in Milwaukee

Over the past several years, the design and administration of
modern workforce development policy in the United States has suffered
intense and consistent criticisms concerning its fragmentation, mission
creep, and ineffectiveness. The prime recommendations for addressing
these problems are to rationalize, consolidate, and simplify both the public policies of training and employment and the institutional arrangements
for implementing them. In this chapter, we offer an alternative approach
for understanding local training and employment "systems" and how they
might be reformed. Rather than attempting to develop a synthetic analysis and solution that takes a God's eye view (Lindblom, 1959; Scott, 1998),
our approach begins by examining existing organizations and institutions
in order to understand their capacities, incentives, and strategies in the
context of their political and policy environments. We find that institutions' patterns of interaction in implementing workforce development programs resemble a series of "ecologies." We develop this concept by
exploring the actual workforce development arrangements in Milwaukee,
Wisconsin. Understanding the actors and the "ecologies" in which they
operate sheds light on the failures of workforce development arrangements
and helps to explain why many efforts to reform them have, for the most
part, fallen short of expectations. More importantly, this approach suggests that in order to be successful, reformers must understand the complex configurations, capacities, and motives of various agencies and actors
"on the ground" and tailor their strategies accordingly.

This investigation proceeds in four parts. The first provides a brief
overview of the main criticisms of public policy surrounding workforce
development in the United States, the impulsive solutions they inspire,
and the shortcomings of received reform strategies. It also describes an
alternative approach to examining workforce development operations in
local contexts, focusing on labor market intermediaries and the "ecologies" in which they act. The second part explores the context of our analysis by describing general labor market trends and the shape of public
investments in employment and training in Milwaukee. Section three
applies this theoretical lens to four key clusters of workforce activity in

the metropolitan Milwaukee area: Welfare reform, the implementation of the Workforce Investment Act, the state technical college, and one particular intermediary—the Wisconsin Regional Training Partnership. We conclude by suggesting several governance measures that may improve the effectiveness and equity of these workforce development ecologies.

AN ECOLOGICAL PERSPECTIVE ON WORKFORCE SYSTEMS

Diagnosing the Difficulties of Workforce Development

Many critics condemn the uncoordinated nature of the "system" of workforce development in the United States. After over thirty years of evolution, and with origins in multiple social programs—from job training efforts initiated through Aid to Families with Dependent Children (AFDC) in the 1960s to a variety of targeted assistance programs for dislocated workers, disadvantaged populations, etc.—workforce development programs operate in "silos of activity" with no coherent overall vision and weak connections in implementation. Documenting the multiple actors in these systems has been a primary task for many analysts. Across the country, as the federal government, states, and localities have focused increased attention on developing better workforce development systems, report after report has typically described employment and training programs as delivered through X agencies, regulated and guided by Y programs, and funded by a total of Z dollars. These figures are often quite astonishing. The General Accounting Office (GAO) found that 163 federal programs spent $20.4 billion in 1995 (GAO 1995 cited in Grubb et al., 1999). Oregon counted fifty programs administered through thirteen agencies in 1989, North Carolina spent $800 million on forty-nine separate programs administered by at least eight agencies in 1992, and Arizona found twenty-six programs administered by ten state and federal agencies (Grubb et al., 1999).

Exacerbating this administrative dispersion, programs often pursue conflicting objectives. They target different populations and adhere to different philosophies: Some emphasize human capital development, whereas others focus on work first strategies. Furthermore, many of these programs have been ineffective for most participants, yielding minimal results in the short term and unknown, but possibly no, impact in the long term (Grubb, 1996; LaLonde, 1995). Threading through these difficulties, many programs focus exclusively on the supply side —support, training, and placement services for *job seekers*—of the labor market while remaining unconcerned about important factors in the larger context of work, such as the availability of targeted jobs or the skill requirements of employers.

Collectively, these criticisms have generated a consensus among observers that the whole of workforce development policy and practice in the United States comprises a "non-system" more than a system. The impulsive response among policymakers has been to suggest replacing these baroque arrangements with a simple, coherent, and comprehensive *system* (i.e., articulate an overall vision and to rationalize, coordinate, and discipline currently diverse programs and organizations). This push toward coherence has motivated a variety of recent reforms. In the early to mid-1990s, many states created One-Stop Job Centers to spatially consolidate diverse public programs for job seekers. The Workforce Investment Act (WIA) of 1998 advances consolidation around these centers and also encourages unified planning at the state level for workforce development policies, in part by attempting to decategorize the funding of such programs.

Although self-evidently sensible from the commanding heights, the hubris of rationality in this approach—and so its limitations for understanding and action—becomes apparent upon considering the political and institutional context of workforce development arrangements. At the federal level, ambitious proposals are often reduced to preserve existing, often dysfunctional arrangements. These policies, once implemented, are further transformed through local adaptation and practice. Local agencies and community-based organizations often become "armies of resistance"[1] that defeat policy reforms or remold them to suit their own interests or circumstances.

An Alternative Framework: Ecologies of Workforce Development

If efforts to construct coherent and comprehensive systems fail for these reasons, what are the prospects for realizing more effective and equitable arrangements? We suggest another vantage that strives for a more holistic understanding of how current programs operate and interact on the local level. Much of the research on workforce development has focused on the design and outcomes of particular programs and policies, and failed to attend to these organizational and political questions. Answers to these questions, however, illuminate many of the pitfalls that block comprehensive workforce development reform and suggest an alternative approach. That alternative attempts to understand and craft reform beginning with an understanding of the diverse organizations and actors with an interest in workforce development policy.

More than forty years ago, Norton Long (1958) famously characterized local communities as "ecologies" in which actors such as business representatives, journalists, and politicians played by a variety of rules for various prizes, but in which the whole, though exhibiting patterns, was something less than orderly and rule bound. The notorious fragmentation of workforce policies, organizations, and stakeholders makes Long's notion of ecologies appropriate for this policy arena as well. Politicians, policymakers, agency officials, training providers, workers, and employers are all inextricably tied to one another by various ligatures of workforce development, and yet, each also operates with different and sometimes conflicting goals, agendas, ideologies, and incentives.

The most important of these actors in workforce development are agencies that mediate relationships among job seekers and firms: Labor market intermediaries (LMIs). LMIs are diverse and motivated by multiple interests (Dresser et al., 2000; Bernhardt et al., 2000). They range from neighborhood social service providers that help community residents apply for jobs to large technical colleges. As metaphor and lens, we analyze LMIs as operating in connected but segmented ecologies that are created and maintained by public policies, market imperatives, and the actions of LMIs themselves (Long, 1958; Gittell, 1994). Like a "regime," the notion of an ecology stresses the rules, norms, and structure of workforce systems in a locality. However, the notion of regime or system suggests more coherence, harmony, hierarchy, and intentionality than exists in most workforce development arrangements. In contrast, "ecology" emphasizes the slippage and chaos within the rules and structures and places more analytical weight on the complex and conflicting motivations and strategies of organisms such as LMIs, employers, workers, and officials.

Elements of Workforce Ecologies

Focusing on the public side of training and employment policy, we begin to understand the ecology of workforce development by examining the public policies that constitute, constrain, and motivate LMIs, job seekers, and firms.

The first effect of these public policies is to *constitute the main actors* in workforce development. In the case of Milwaukee, welfare reform and workforce investment policies have created a few powerful LMIs—the "Wisconsin Works" agencies ("W-2," Wisconsin's welfare replacement program) and the workforce investment boards of Milwaukee and its surrounding counties—by granting them control over hundreds of millions of dollars and responsibilities managing workforce development services. Public funds administered by the LMIs—supplemented by additional sources not under their control—sustain a diverse array of smaller labor market intermediaries.

Public policies, in conjunction with market forces, also shape the behavior of large and small LMIs by imposing legal *constraints and oblig-*

ations upon them (e.g., rules about work requirements and training limits under welfare reform). Just as important, however, as part and parcel of privatization, these public policies also create systems of *incentives and rewards* to steer the behavior of LMIs within the space created by legal and administrative parameters.

To capture these financial and reputational rewards, LMIs develop *workforce development strategies.* These strategies can be as simple as the conservative tough-love recommendation to shunt as many clients directly into private employment as possible. Alternatively, some LMIs attempt to develop complex packages of community organizing, social service support, guidance and supervision,[2] training, and job search to advance workforce development goals. Others might build, or join, networks of subcontractors who are skilled in particular services such as community recruitment, job development, or training. Some LMIs attempt to alter the behavior of employers.[3] The effectiveness of LMI strategies also determines, in large measure, the *outcomes* of the workforce development system: They determine whether job seekers in need are effectively trained in valued skills, are placed in jobs and advance to better ones, receive good wages, and whether employers can find qualified workers.

Public policies can also impose *governance arrangements* upon these ecologies. The central questions of governance revolve around how LMIs are authorized, the setting up of constraints and incentives and their monitoring and enforcement, and the steering of the system as a whole.

These elements collectively guide how LMIs operate and interact with each other in the "ecologies" they create and, critically, the results they achieve.

Configurations of Workforce Development Ecologies

Configurations of LMI interaction vary. As points of conceptual reference for considering LMIs in Milwaukee and elsewhere, consider five "ideal types" of workforce development ecologies. These types suggest political and administrative configurations that derive stability from the coherence of their internal logic. That is, in each, the elements of constitutive rules, constraints and obligations, incentives and rewards, LMI strategies, and governance all fit together into an institutional order. Some of these types result from embedded assumptions about what kinds of interventions are likely to be effective in labor markets, whereas others emerge without such direct intentionality. Actual workforce development ecologies are often hybrids that combine aspects of these ideal types.

The first type might be called the *minimalist neoliberal* ecology. The main aim of policy in this regime is to minimize public expenditures on workforce development. LMIs receive very little funding to provide services or maintain their organizations. Very little effort is devoted to maintaining the public governance infrastructure on LMIs. In a charitable interpretation, the underlying economic view is that intentional labor market interventions are likely to be ineffective at best, and that the best route to advancing effective training systems is to let unadorned labor markets operate.

The *laissez-faire rent-seeking* ecology is a second ideal type. Substantial public financing is devoted to supporting LMIs, but they are subject to little external oversight, perhaps because of permissive constraints, ineffective public governance, or undemanding incentive structures. This combination will likely result in a proliferation of LMIs. Some of these will no doubt be well motivated and innovative, whereas others will exploit the system's looseness to maximize their own revenues or press particular goals without building fair and effective workforce development arrangements.[4]

Privatized bureaucracy represents yet a third type of workforce development ecology. Here, the public governance constraints and obligations placed on LMIs are so detailed and restrictive that they determine most elements of their strategies, attempt to eliminate operational discretion, and leave very little room for innovation. These arrangements duplicate the rule-driven arrangements and rights-based approaches of service provision bureaucracies, but offload the performance of these functions to private and nonprofit LMIs. The premise grounding this strategy is that policymakers can specify optimal workforce development strategies.

A fourth ecology, *LMI innovation*, devolves both financing and operational authority to LMIs, but subjects them to rigorous performance monitoring to track their achievement of workforce development goals. Administratively, this ecology resembles the laissez-faire type in that LMIs are well funded and enjoy wide grants of discretion to develop individual strategies, but it requires a much more robust monitoring apparatus to develop parameters and incentives on LMI behavior. The major premise of this approach is that optimal solutions to workforce development problems are not, for the most part, well known, but instead must be discovered in the course of experimentation (Dorf and Sabel, 1998). It relies on LMIs, operating in a disciplined and accountable environment, to generate the knowledge and innovation necessary for fair and effective training and employment.

A fifth type might be called a *coordination* ecology. In typical workforce development environments, parts of the ecology operate according to their own logic. The system as a whole would benefit from greater coordination between the pieces, and each piece would benefit from the expertise of the others. Essentially, employers know what skills they require, but seldom communicate these needs to training providers who end up teaching knowledge that has little market value. Training providers lack the capacity to identify and recruit needy job seekers, yet community-based organizations have ready access to these people. To come full circle, community organizations want desperately to place residents into decent employment, but lack social and economic connections to employers and knowledge of the metropolitan labor market. Consequently, policymakers who favor a coordination ecology focus on forging stable linkages and synergies among firms, job seekers, and various types of LMIs such as community organizations, service providers, and training institutions (Dresser and Rogers, 1998; Greater Milwaukee Committee, 1998).

LABOR MARKET TRENDS AND PUBLIC WORKFORCE INVESTMENTS IN MILWAUKEE

Whatever the shape of ecologies affecting workforce development, their capacity to deliver outcomes is determined, in part, by the structure of opportunities within the local labor market, and partially by the level of public investment supporting them. Our analysis is both informed and restricted by the economic context in Milwaukee.

Milwaukee Labor Market Trends

Milwaukee overall enjoys a relatively healthy labor market. Throughout the 1990s, regional unemployment rates were well below 5 percent, consistently lower than the national average. The regional statistics, however, mask other patterns within the local labor market.

The first significant trend is tremendous population growth in the suburbs compared to relative stagnation in the city of Milwaukee. Whereas Milwaukee's population decreased slightly during the 1990s (by roughly 0.02 percent), the suburbs grew by over 13 percent.

Second, job growth has strongly favored the suburbs. Although job growth has occurred throughout the area—including a significant 35 percent increase between 1950 and 1990 in Milwaukee—it has absolutely skyrocketed in the suburbs—451 percent in the northern suburbs, 352 percent in the northwest, and 1,068 percent in the western suburbs during the same period (Center on Wisconsin Strategy, 1996, 2000a).

Third, deindustrialization has changed the composition of employment available in the region. Whereas durable manufacturing—once largely located in the city—accounted for 26.7 percent of employment in 1975 and the service sector accounted for only 17 percent, these proportions reversed by 1995 when services accounted for 28.2 percent and durable manufacturing 15.5 percent of employment (Center on Wisconsin Strategy, 1996).

These labor market trends pose formidable challenges to intermediaries concerned with improving the distribution of regional economic opportunities. Increasingly, available jobs are located further away from those who need them: 43 percent of current job openings are located in the suburbs where unemployment ranges from 1.9–2.5 percent, whereas unemployment remains stubbornly high in the central city. Jobs available increasingly require higher skill levels: Three out of five job openings require post-secondary education. Jobs that are available to those with fewer qualifications are not likely to sustain families; less than one of five low-skill jobs offer living wages and health benefits (Center on Wisconsin Strategy, 1996, 2000a). And, those jobs are increasingly lower-wage, service-sector positions that offer fewer opportunities for advancement.

Flows of Funds in Employment and Training

To address these challenges, over $500 million is spent on workforce development in Greater Milwaukee every year. This money flows from many sources through various channels—the federal government through community development block grants and competitive Welfare-to-Work grants, the state Department of Workforce Development (DWD) distribution of Temporary Assistance for Needy Families (TANF) block grants, local and national foundations' charitable giving, and local property taxes. This money supports short-term, certificate and associate degree programs at local technical colleges, customized training with community-based organizations, a variety of support services for participants in those programs, and related administration. The flow of funds is not hierarchical or unidirectional. A complex network of contracting across various organizations sustains the morass of training and services.

The highest level governing body is the state of Wisconsin's DWD. DWD oversees two of the largest programs affecting workforce development in Milwaukee: W-2 and the WIA. DWD receives and distributes roughly $370 million in federal TANF block grant money to agencies administering W-2 across the state. Of that amount, $171 million is channeled via the Milwaukee County Workforce Investment Board to the five agencies administering W-2 in Milwaukee. In addition, DWD allocates $10 million of a $20 million Workforce Attachment and Advancement fund carved out of surplus TANF dollars in 1998 to Milwaukee. These funds are to be spent collectively by the workforce investment board and the agencies administering W-2. DWD establishes contracts with individual W-2 agencies and is responsible for establishing their program and performance guidelines.

Like the DWD, the Milwaukee Workforce Investment Board (WIB) is limited to funding and oversight roles. It has an annual budget of $26 million, including the administration of welfare-to-work grants received from the state DWD from federal formula grants, welfare-to-work grants received from competitive bidding from the United States Department of Labor, WIA monies received via formula grants from the state DWD, and surplus TANF money in the Workforce Attachment and Advancement fund. These funds are distributed to local community agencies through open proposal processes. The WIB establishes sets of guidelines and incentives, in conjunction with funding requirements, to steer the direction of the funding.

Although often overlooked, local technical colleges are significant actors in local training. The Milwaukee Area Technical College (MATC), for example, has an operating budget of roughly $200 million, Waukesha County Technical College $57 million, and Moraine Park Technical College $27 million. Beyond these large funds, the city of Milwaukee's distribution of federal community development block grants and local foundations' charitable giving further contribute nearly $2 million and a series of performance-based contracts to local community agencies' operations. At least forty neighborhood-based organizations design and deliver services to community residents. These organizations annually spend approximately $1.8 million explicitly on training programs.

MILWAUKEE'S WORKFORCE DEVELOPMENT ECOLOGIES

One cannot draw a straight line through the various agencies involved in administering the multitude of programs and funds supporting workforce development in Milwaukee. To offer a more detailed perspective on workforce development arrangements in Milwaukee, consider the major efforts in Milwaukee.

Wisconsin Works: Agencies and Their Suppliers

The 1994 W-2 welfare replacement legislation created one of the most substantial—and certainly the most distinctive—workforce development ecologies in metropolitan Milwaukee. Foreshadowing national developments on issues such as the imposition of work requirements on beneficiaries and time limits on eligibility for public aid, the W-2 policy package has been lauded and loathed in equal measure.

W-2's first radical step was to end Milwaukee County's administration of public assistance programs and privatize the administration of welfare programs to outside agencies in six distinct administrative regions of the county through a process of competitive bidding. Two for-profit and three nonprofit agencies, now called "W-2 agencies," won the initial two-year contracts, which totaled $320 million and ran from September 1997 through the end of 1999. Some of the agencies, such as United Migrant Opportunity Services (UMOS) and the YWCA, had long histories in social service provision in Milwaukee, whereas W-2 contract awards enabled the introduction of others, such as Maximus, to Milwaukee. In two suburban counties, five county social service divisions administered W-2, whereas a for-profit agency managed a third suburban county's program.[6]

INCENTIVE STRUCTURES AND LMI RESPONSES

The decision to privatize administration of W-2 in Milwaukee and the subsequent competitive bidding process created five well resourced and powerful labor market intermediaries. Dodenhoff (1998) reports that contracts between the state and these agencies were minimal—running only twelve pages—and left much discretion to the agencies themselves. The funding formula dictated that each agency receive a flat fee for implementing the policy in its administrative area. The agency would draw all costs from this amount, including administration, service provision, and cash payments to participants. If an agency managed to run the programs for less then its initial allocation, it could keep the savings for itself up to 7 percent of the contract amount. Of savings beyond the first 7 percent, the agency would retain 10 percent for profit and the remaining 90 percent would be divided evenly between the state and the W-2 agency. The agency would be required to invest its part of the divided 90 percent in services for participants. The initial two-year contracts did not give incentives or place restrictions on factors such as wages of participants placed into employment, benefits, or job retention.

W-2 rules created four categories of participants. In the highest tier of unsubsidized employment, participants are able to find full-time employment at market wages. The agency need pay only the costs of case management. The costs to the agency rise in lower employment tiers. In the third and fourth tiers of "community service" and "transitions" jobs, participants who cannot find private-sector jobs work at organizations such as nonprofits and public agencies and earn monthly stipends of $600–$700.

This simple formula for W-2 agency financing provides obvious incentives for the agencies to move as many participants into unsubsidized employment as quickly as possible—and move them they did. In the four months after the signing of the W-2 contracts in September 1997, Milwaukee County caseloads dropped by 47 percent (Dresang and Sharma-

Jensen, 1998). Agencies reaped unexpectedly high profits over the course of the first two-year contract (see Table 3.1) (AFSCME, 2000).

Though caseloads have dropped, rules and governance provisions of this LMI ecology do not substantially advance the desiderata for fair and effective workforce development. To be sure, some agencies and individual case managers see it as part of their professional responsibilities to endow participants with lasting skills and promising employment, but these aims were not embedded in the original administrative design of W-2.

Remaining W-2 participants have increasingly been characterized as facing multiple barriers to employment (Stephenson, 1999). At the same time, public policies have become more sophisticated and have begun to incorporate measures of employment and training performance such as placement rates, wages, and retention. Furthermore, a number of W-2 agencies have come under investigation for misuse of public funds; others have been investigated for sub-par performance. The increasingly less-qualified population receiving W-2 assistance, coupled with public pressure for improved performance, has created a bottom-up, entrepreneurial style of coordination among some agencies in which networks of subcontracted agencies deliver specialized support services to participants.

For example, Milwaukee's south side W-2 agency UMOS has an extensive network of subcontractors. Before procuring the W-2 contract with the state, UMOS traditionally collaborated with other social service organizations on Milwaukee's predominantly Latino, Asian, and recent immigrant near south side neighborhoods. Resources from W-2 have allowed UMOS to expand its own internal capacity, but the agency also increasingly issues subcontracts for specialized services and has continued to collaborate with its historical partner organizations. For programs aiming to connect noncustodial parents to jobs, UMOS regularly collaborates with

Table 3.1 Profit Categorized by W-2 Agency from 1997 to 1999

W-2 Agency	Profit	Community Reinvestment*
YW-Works	$3,596,820	$3,002,419
United Migrant Opportunity Services, Inc.	$4,598,972	$3,634,358
Opportunities Industrialization Center	$4,851,076	$2,991,665
Employment Solutions of Milwaukee	$9,927,888	$7,587,690
Maximus, Inc.	$4,612,818	$1,547,079
Total	$27,587,574	$18,763,211

SOURCE: American Federation of State, County and Municipal Employees Legislative Council, Wisconsin (2000).
*"Community Reinvestment" profits must be reinvested by W-2 agencies to advance workforce and local development aims.

and funds over ten agencies, including a neighborhood health clinic, a homeless shelter, a regional employer training consortium, and a statewide legal assistance group, to provide specialized services in language, legal aid, health care, housing assistance, and job training.

The ecology created by W-2 in Milwaukee is a complex hybrid of several of the ideal types described earlier. Its ends with respect to participants are distinctly neoliberal; its designers have consistently emphasized their confidence in the workings of unfettered labor markets. Once they enter work, participants are expected to retain jobs and advance on their own. The formal constraints, incentives, and obligations the policy places on its main W-2 agencies are a schizophrenic mix between the laissez-faire and bureaucratic types. W-2 creates detailed categories, benefit provisions, and procedures and requires its implementing agencies to follow these. To this extent, the program extends command-and-control bureaucratic methods to its private-sector partners through legislation and contracts. In terms of real oversight and monitoring mechanisms, however, current governance over W-2 agencies and their contractors is best characterized as a laissez-faire regime that affords LMIs wide discretion and imposes few demanding performance requirements.

IMPROVING W-2 LMI GOVERNANCE

Improvements in three general areas would likely increase the equity and effectiveness of the ecology of W-2 agencies.

The first and most crucial reform would require altering the definition of performance under W-2 away from caseload reduction toward sustainable employment. Minimally, this would require incorporating considerations of participant wages, retention, and advancement into the public goals that the state asks LMIs to pursue. One promising indication of movement in this direction is that the second round of W-2 agency contracts, which were signed at the end of 1999, pays performance bonuses to agencies based upon wage and retention achievements (Associated Press, 1999; Dresang, 1999). The DWD also indicates that agencies will be paid performance bonuses based on the achievement of standards such as success in placing clients in unsubsidized employment, part-time vs. full-time jobs, job retention, and wages and benefits (Legislative Audit Bureau, 2001).

A second step would be to transform the constraints and incentives on W-2 agencies to allow and encourage them to develop innovative workforce strategies. For example, current rules restrict participants to between ten and twelve hours of training per week as part of their work requirement. Such arbitrary limits severely constrain the ability of agencies to provide sufficient training and experiment with various training approaches. This constraint has been widely recognized, and W-2 agencies have banded together to press for liberalizing these rules (Huston, 1998).

A third area of reform involves the governance—the oversight, performance monitoring, sanctioning, and coordination—of agency activities. Consistent with its anti-bureaucratic origins, governance over W-2 agencies appears to have been fairly minimal. Some embarrassing consequences of this minimal governance have been poor audit reports of agency implementation and various scandals involving alleged financial improprieties within the agencies (Schultze, 2000a–f). More important than these episodes, however, is the lack of general capacity to steer the direction of LMI efforts and strategies by, for example, readjusting incentive structures to reach old goals or target new ones, monitoring actual accomplishments of LMIs to implement these incentives, and identifying best or worst LMI practices.

The Milwaukee Workforce Investment Board and the WIA

The financial flows and programs that revolve around the Private Industry Council (PIC) of Milwaukee County constitute a second LMI ecology. The Milwaukee PIC—composed of representatives from business, labor, community, and educational institutions—is the administrative center of public-sector workforce development in Milwaukee. It distributes $26 million annually in various programs that are competitively contracted. In 1999, this included $6.6 million from the WIA, some $7.5 million under the Department of Labor's Welfare-to-Work program, and $2.3 million from the state's Workforce Attachment and Advancement fund (State of Wisconsin, 1999a, 13). The PIC also monitors and coordinates the implementation of W-2 by the five agencies described above. Finally, it is a major partner in a coalition of public and private groups called the Milwaukee Jobs Center Network that operates the seven One-Stop Job Centers in Milwaukee.

Because the workforce development programs administered by the PIC are relatively new, and because the various programs themselves have diverse performance goals, the PIC's strategies and the body itself appear to be still very much in evolution, and its practices far from settled. That said, the PIC sees itself as serving customers on both sides of the labor market—employers and workers—equally. To help firms fill their staffing needs, the PIC operates a statewide computerized listing service that job seekers browse at area job centers, runs various outreach programs and career fairs, and coordinates and funds customized training programs in which new workers learn job- and firm-specific skills required by an employer.

The PIC delivers "core" workforce development services—such as available job listings, career information, counseling, and regional labor market and trend information—to workers through various subcontracts to LMIs. In fulfilling the One-Stop requirements for the provision of core services under WIA, for example, the same five entities that administer W-2 operate seven Job Centers in Milwaukee.[7] WIA creates a second "intensive" tier for those job seekers for whom core services are insufficient. Intensive services include comprehensive employability assessments, development of personalized career plans, and more extended counseling. Many of these services are likely to be provided by job center personnel as well.

Approximately half of WIA funds[8] in Milwaukee and the surrounding counties—$2.5 million in 2000—are devoted to training and education for disadvantaged adult and dislocated workers. Most of this funding is distributed through training vouchers, also known as scholarships or Individual Training Accounts (ITAs). Case managers determine whether clients are eligible for training and distribute ITAs to cover the cost of books, fees, and tuition at a technical college. A client may then redeem this ITA with any state-certified training provider. The hope embedded in this program is that consumers will use their power through vouchers to drive LMIs to develop innovations and strategies. One reason to doubt the power of an invisible hand to work this magic is that ITAs will make up only a tiny fraction of the customer base of many LMIs, such as technical colleges. Furthermore, customers may lack the information needed to make discriminating choices among LMIs.

Most of the training funds not dispersed through ITAs will be used in closer coordination with employers by supporting on-the-job training and customized training programs. In the former, interested employers hire new employees and provide them with training in return for a public subsidy. In the latter, employers with specific hiring needs (e.g., fifteen auto-mechanics) work with administrators, educational institutions, and other LMIs to develop small, short-run classes of job seekers to acquire the necessary skills and fill those positions.

This mix of job service centers, individual vouchers, and employer-coordinated training has the potential to operate either as a laissez-faire ecology in which arrangements function primarily to maintain LMIs themselves or as an innovation ecology that advances the goals of effective and equitable workforce development. Realizing one alternative rather than the other depends in large measure on the will and capacity of the PIC.

Because the PIC does not deliver any services directly, but instead contracts for all of its programs, its ecology depends on the selection of the subcontracted agencies. In this arena, the PIC has developed accessible and largely transparent procedures for proposal evaluation. Proposals to administer training programs under WIA, for example, are submitted to a review committee comprised of PIC staff and representatives from community groups. The review committee scores the proposal based on a public scale, including previous performance with WIA funds, industry needs and growth potential, and the quality of the jobs.[9] The agency submitting the proposal is allowed to attend all review sessions and discuss with staff possibilities to improve the proposal. If recommended by the review committee, the proposal is submitted to the formal selection committee, which is made up of members of the board. Again, the sessions and scoring scale are public. These measures help construct a transparent, seemingly objective process, one which should facilitate an ecology of innovation. Nonetheless, other considerations regularly affect committees' decisions. Inevitably, board members face community pressure to fund certain neighborhood organizations, which on occasion can flood selection committee meetings with representatives to lobby in support of funding the agency. Such pressures, if unabated, encourage the formation of a rent-seeking, laissez-faire ecology. However, this process also creates the latitude for PIC staff and selection committee members to balance the scoring scale's objective appraisal of best performers, desired outcomes, and other considerations to maintain a broad portfolio and channel funding to diverse organizations.

The Milwaukee Area Technical College

The greatest capacity for skill training and education in the Milwaukee area resides in a single LMI, the MATC. MATC is part of the Wisconsin Technical College System, and is one of four technical colleges in the Milwaukee metropolitan area. Although neighboring colleges occasionally enroll Milwaukee residents and serve city employers, MATC continues to be the dominant technical college in the city and the immediately surrounding suburbs. In the 1998–1999 academic year, some 65,500 students attended the college's four campuses, and 85 percent of these students were enrolled part-time. In that year, the institution's operating expenses totaled almost $200 million (MATC, 1999). Although the public data do not offer baseline information, the institution's quality control surveys report that 93 percent of students obtained employment within six months of graduation—75 percent of these in fields for which they trained—and 70 percent obtained employment in the greater Milwaukee area. Almost one-fifth of these students live in Milwaukee's low-income central city, one-third are minorities, and 18 percent were classified as economically disadvantaged.

Although MATC is relatively well insulated from the political and market tides that buffet other agents, it is influenced by workforce development policy reforms. The implementation of W-2 in Milwaukee in 1997 restricted permissible training and educational activities for students receiving public assistance and mandated that such students find immediate employment. Consequently, over 6,000 MATC students de-registered. Additionally, the college has significantly expanded beyond its core programs to deliver on-site customized training upon request from employers and develop short-term training courses for unemployed people through community organizations and W-2 agencies. Although still operating largely by the logic of its internal ecology, MATC is becoming increasingly embedded in local workforce ecologies as it seeks to forge strategic relationships and exploit market opportunities.

PROGRAMS AND SCOPE OF SERVICES

MATC is focused predominantly on delivering general education and training to students in various regular degree and certificate programs. Outside of this primary realm, however, the college offers peripheral yet expanding contract training programs to local businesses and community groups. These programs are run mostly from the college's Continuing Education and Workforce Development Division. During the 1999–2000 contract period, this division delivered customized training programs to 105 individual employers.[10] Employers contact MATC to provide specialized training to current workers in new technology and equipment. Additionally, the college trains company employees in preparation for industry certification examinations. By state statute, the college charges contracted employers for the full cost of these training programs, or what is termed "full-cost recovery."

The Continuing Education and Workforce Development Division also offers customized training for what it terms "economic development programs." These are programs designed and coordinated by community agencies or W-2 agencies in Milwaukee aimed at training, or in the case of dislocated workers, retraining job seekers for specific occupations. A community agency usually contracts directly with MATC to deliver a specified training curriculum based on funding it has already secured (e.g., from state TANF funds or local WIA allocations awarded by the workforce investment board). MATC delivers the instruction and the community agency offers accompanying support services to students and program administration. Unlike contract training with employers, its economic development programs operate on a "partial-cost recovery" basis by state statute because they serve nonprofit customers. Because MATC effectively subsidizes these operations from other funds, the organization has decreased its commitment in this area. Consequently, community and W-2 agencies have assumed primary responsibility for coordinating economic development programs and subcontract for specific training services from MATC. This arrangement insulates MATC from the performance demands that discipline other LMIs in Milwaukee.

GOVERNANCE

MATC's autonomy stems from its legislative authorization and public funding. Its main source of revenue—42 percent of its total revenue in 1999—comes from local property taxes. State and federal government financing, bond proceeds, and student fees make up the balance of its funding (MATC, 1999). Despite the strong base in the local property tax district, the school has faced potential declining revenue and constraints on future growth because of the combination of stable property values in Milwaukee and state restrictions on increasing the college's rate of property taxation.[11]

Some administrators cite this revenue cap as motivation for the college to pursue innovations in the structure of its core education programs. It might, for example, be able to attract more students by offering additional nighttime or weekend courses, more flexible requirements, open enrollments, and short-term certificate programs. Others go further and argue for expanding the lucrative, full-cost recovery contract training for area businesses and a resolute entry into a world of "just-in-time" training to serve local businesses. These internal pressures have fueled a debate between those who favor more short-term, tailored, and responsive educational programs as the future of vocational education and defenders of traditional one- and two-year degree programs. They have also pushed the institution into an arena with which it has little experience and for which it is not designed to efficiently deliver services. Its organizational structures—staffing, scheduling, accounting, instructional, and marketing operations—are biased toward the traditional full-time, degree-program student.

The ecology of the MATC is thus a rent-seeking, laissez-faire ordering that draws regular funding with weak oversight. Extraneous contract training programs delivering targeted training for unemployed or underemployed job seekers remain peripheral to the organization's operations. Although the existence of MATC's continuing education and workforce development initiatives are exemplary models for technical colleges as forays beyond traditional programming, little evidence suggests that these strategies will become institutional priorities in the near term.

The Wisconsin Regional Training Partnership

The Wisconsin Regional Training Partnership (WRTP) is a distinctive, innovative, and ambitious LMI for which the ecological changes described above—especially those surrounding welfare reform and the WIA—have provided opportunities that have transformed both the strategies and objectives of the organization. Unlike many LMIs, the WRTP does not focus merely on serving a narrow agenda of finding and placing a targeted population (i.e., a certain neighborhood, national or ethnic background, or income level). Since its inception, the WRTP has sought to establish more fair and effective workforce development systems by reforming public policies and governance structures. Its trajectory of growth, struggle, and success illuminates the possibilities for "systemic" reform within complex workforce ecologies.

ORIGIN AND AIMS

The WRTP began in 1993 as an effort to help build a "high-road" metropolitan economy in which firms, particularly those in the manufacturing sector, would remain globally competitive. Today, it is a consortium of more than fifty firms and their unions employing more than 50,000 workers. The WRTP is jointly governed by top managers of area firms and labor leaders (Dresser, Rogers, and Zdrazil, 2000). The mission of the WRTP is to contribute to the regional economy by helping to solve the collective problem of training large numbers of highly skilled workers through an array of collaborative efforts between labor and management.

> The thought was that by establishing common expectations on training among a critical mass of large area employers, the consortium would reduce free-rider threats to sustained training, thus assure industry a better-trained and more committed workforce while demarcating career ladders for workers, and thus build the capacity for industry-wide modernization. By bringing multiple employers and unions with shared interests in the industry together in ongoing collaboration, it would also add to the industry's collective intelligence and capacity to advance its interests, while improving labor-management relations. (Dresser, Rogers, and Zdrazil, 2000)

Compared with other programs we have examined, this organization remains administratively modest. It is staffed by a dozen people, and its annual budget of slightly more than $1 million comes largely from national and local foundation grants and federal funds through operating training programs.

Since its founding, the WRTP has attempted to advance its skill-building mission at three levels. Within individual firms, the organization has helped to establish "Workplace Education Centers" in which workers can learn new skills. WRTP staff facilitate the development of labor management structures within firms to develop operating guidelines and training options at the center. Additionally, WRTP has partnered with the Annie E. Casey Foundation's Milwaukee Jobs Initiative to train and place low-income, central-city residents into jobs that are predominantly within member firms. Beyond these training initiatives, the WRTP also has spread the gospel of training and interfirm cooperation among employers in Milwaukee's manufacturing sector, through individually benchmarking and collectively communicating best practices and advocating for public policies that conform to and facilitate the expansion of proven strategies. Although it began in manufacturing, the WRTP has pressed its model into additional sectors, including hospitality, automotive, health care, and telecommunications.

More broadly, the WRTP has tried to transform governance structures, such as the workforce investment board, into coherent groups that use public investments to create a "high-road"—high-skill, high-wage, high-performance—economy (Greater Milwaukee Committee, 1998). Since its inception, the WRTP has been an activist organization dedicated to advancing the "demand side" or industry by representing firms, providing technical assistance to these firms, and organizing public programs toward firms' needs—rather than emphasizing the "supply side."

INTERACTION WITH LOCAL ECOLOGIES

After a decade of extensive programming, the WRTP has enjoyed substantial growth and success. The group's industry knowledge has enabled it to develop—always in concert with employers and unions, training programs that better serve both trainees and their eventual employers. Whereas most LMIs in the Milwaukee area have specialized in serving job seekers and their main clients, the WRTP's close relationships with, and deep understandings of employers have enabled it to better identify and develop job opportunities. The consequent program success for serving unemployed or underemployed populations, including large numbers of job placements in full-time manufacturing jobs paying over $10 per hour and offering full benefits, has given them distinct advantages in the competition with other LMIs for training and employment contracts with public agencies or subcontracts with the large W-2 agencies.

As the WRTP has negotiated numerous hurdles and expanded its operations, the organization has changed its methods and altered its deeper strategy. Two themes are manifest in the WRTP's recent trajectory. The first is a growing tendency not only to advocate for changes in public policies that better accord with industry needs, but also to construct alternative, supply-side strategies that pull training initiatives together. Initially resolute about tapping technical colleges' vast expertise and resources and orienting them toward industry needs, the WRTP regularly encountered delays in program development that was rooted in local technical colleges' internal governance. Thwarted by the intransigence of technical college procedures, the WRTP has increasingly sought to circumvent—

rather than transform—onerous program development requirements. Rather than relying upon the technical college to provide turnkey solutions, the WRTP has developed its own training materials and effectively reserves several college instructors to be permanently available for WRTP training sessions.

Second, the WRTP has expanded supply-side activities such as case management and recruitment to reduce reliance on public-sector programs and institutions. At the outset, there was broad recognition within the organization that the WRTP did not possess adequate resources and expertise to manage the diverse and often demanding needs of the job seekers participating in its programs. With a more systemic perspective, the organization targeted numerous and well-funded W-2 agencies and job centers, as well as smaller, more specialized community organizations to deliver required support services for participants. Because these services were often provided in an unresponsive or uncoordinated way, the WRTP staff has focused on packaging a range of support services for its participants. This new mission has required a much more intense level of individual case management and has broadened the organization's orientation to the supply-side needs of the labor market.

Threading through both responses has been an adaptive attitude in local program funding partners. The WRTP initially focused on building and supporting a regional workforce development system with a coordinated, central governance. In this scheme, the PIC would provide the lion's share of workforce development financing. As was the case with the MATC, forging a coordinated partnership with the PIC proved unstable. The pace and requirements of PIC funding procedures frequently delayed WRTP's program development and compromised the organization's reputation and ability to satisfy employer demands. Moreover, the PIC continues to seek funding proposals from a diverse array of organizations rather than merely focusing on a smaller number of "best performers." To avoid these obstacles, the WRTP has diversified its funding. In particular, WRTP has developed partnerships with the five W-2 agencies, whose resources now dwarf those available to the PIC. This recent arrangement of coordinating myriad contributors for individual training programs—although different from the WRTP's original vision—is more typical of smaller- and medium-sized LMIs in Milwaukee who face the challenge of operating among diverse, unpredictable ecologies of workforce policy.

IMPLICATIONS FOR GOVERNANCE OF ECOLOGIES

The WRTP now views these recent innovations as a central part of its strategy for advancing a "high-road" regional economy. The number of programs it runs has doubled since these strategic adaptations. Its innovations have drawn the attention of state and national audiences. If the success of its strategy continues, it will demonstrate the importance of involving unions and employer-informed skills training and industry relations to other LMIs and to public governance bodies.

The WRTP's lofty goal of reaching a rational, coordinated system had bleak prospects in the face of multiple ecologies and organizations with conflicting logics and agendas. Given this reality, must organizations like the WRTP resign themselves to playing small roles in the larger drama of metropolitan workforce development? WRTP staffers still see themselves as working toward a larger more coordinated system that can provide recruiting, job training, placement, and support services "at scale." Whereas the traditional, comprehensive vision of governance aims to establish coordination and cooperation through top-down, bureaucratic structures, they now envision a decentralized, entrepreneurial path toward coordinated, and increasingly comprehensive, workforce development systems. The enabling institutions, in this view, are governance bodies that demand high standards from providers of workforce services. In such an environment, high-quality service providers will seek one another out to force partnerships with appropriate divisions of labor. Those who are less capable, either at operating in coordinated partnerships or at delivering their specialized services, will eventually fail and their share of resources will be redeployed. However, in its current form, the broader ecology does not encourage innovators like the WRTP or discourage those with less promising or successful strategies.

Toward Innovation and Coordination

The main institutions of workforce development in Milwaukee operate in a highly fragmented fashion. The W-2 agencies, the PIC and its subcontractors, and the technical colleges all function according to their own distinctive logics, a scenario that frequently results in counterproductive behaviors. These core logics are difficult to alter. We conclude now by offering several suggestions for moving these parts toward the innovation and coordination ecologies sketched above.

Toward Civic Agreement and Capacity

Without pretending to be able to forecast its details, transformation toward a more innovative and coordinated ecology is likely to require the formation of a broad and coherent consensus around the goals of fair and effective workforce development arrangements and the development of governance and implementation capacities necessary to realize such arrangements. In other words, this transformation likely requires a kind of civic agreement and capacity that has been, thus far, absent from the politics of workforce development in Milwaukee.

W-2 was formulated and promulgated in the absence of broad civic support. The basic tenets of that reform—time limits, scant support for and restrictions on skills acquisition, a work first philosophy, and inattention to the quality of employment—depart from the objectives of fair and effective workforce policy. With several years' experience, many in Milwaukee have become frustrated with some of the evident failures of this approach. During this period of reflection upon the effects of the first round of welfare reform, it may be possible to forge a more durable and explicit consensus among policymakers, LMIs, community-based organizations, and industry actors around general workforce goals.[12] Such agreement in principle would mark an important step toward constructing the civic capacity necessary to reform the area's workforce development arrangements.

Toward Improved Performance and Innovation

Backed by such agreement, these parties might begin to build the performance ecology suggested above. We have emphasized that the complex internal logics and patterns of interaction of various LMIs will likely defeat any fixed recipe of reform. Civic capacity rooted in agreement on principle, however, may form the basis for a joint and incremental search for both concrete techniques of improving workforce development and for institutions that govern the organizations that develop and implement those techniques. One metaphor for this search would be a civic conversation—sure to heat occasionally to civic argument—about how best to advance fairness and effectiveness. This conversation, occurring at the level of governance, would support and drive LMIs toward two kinds of performance. First, LMIs would be pressured to improve the methods and techniques in their own areas of specialization, such as recruiting and orienting employers, reaching out to residents of socially isolated neighborhoods, or providing various kinds of training. Second, because any particular LMI depends upon many other actors to succeed, each would become more effective at identifying partners and developing collaborative relationships with them. This dynamic was seen at work with UMOS and WRTP.

Presuming agreement on the system's broad aims, one helpful policy change would be the alignment of state (DWD) and metropolitan (PIC) performance metrics to workforce goals such as sustainable employment, service to those most in need, and filling sectoral labor needs. Although performance contracting and measurement have proliferated in the public management of Milwaukee's workforce systems, metrics are not aligned now with these goals. Therefore, the "system" of LMIs and the bodies that govern them often ignore important labor market characteristics such as the quality of employment. Furthermore, significant accomplishments and innovations, such as those of the WRTP, receive insufficient recognition. Furthermore, properly aligned metrics would enable more searching assessments of whether overall workforce arrangements are realizing their promise, and more informed efforts to improve them.

Civic capacity might also generate the political will necessary to impose these performance metrics—and the consensus goals more generally— upon large and influential LMIs such the W-2 agencies and the technical college system. At present, the size, expertise, and political influence of these large LMIs allow them to resist external direction and act more or less autonomously. Workforce development in Milwaukee cannot become more effective or fair without harnessing their innovative capacities toward public goals.

Toward Improved Coordination

Although pressures for innovation would push workforce organizations of all sizes toward greater fairness and effectiveness in their strategies and services, these pressures might do little to address the problems that arise from the geographic and institutional fragmentation in Milwaukee's workforce development arrangements. Elements of the coordination ecology offer more promising solutions to this set of problems.

First and foremost, effective workforce development requires public organizations to recognize and respond to the regional nature of the Milwaukee economy. For employment and training, the most salient aspect of this regionalism is the "spatial mismatch" between concentrations of employers and open employment in the suburbs and job seekers in the central city. Workforce investment boards should cooperate to overcome this mismatch, perhaps by addressing Milwaukee's fears that greater collaboration would lead to a drain of resources to suburban employers, and suburban fears that greater collaboration would drain resources to Milwaukee residents (see Greater Milwaukee Committee, 1998).

A second dimension of coordination involves encouraging employers and unions to act collectively to advance their workforce development interests. The experience of the WRTP shows how deep industry knowledge and engagement are crucial to the success of workforce strategies. Writ large, this experience would mean building the civic capacity of employers and unions—perhaps along sectoral lines or through industry associations. Coordinated action by entire industries would offer technical and informational benefits to other workforce organizations by, for example, providing accurate forecasts of where job growth will be and what skills will be needed to fill those jobs. Such associations would educate their member firms about the economic benefits of effective workforce development, and about how they can utilize the public systems in Milwaukee to fill their employment needs. This active and coherent user base would then exert political pressures back upon the technical colleges, welfare agencies, and the PIC to become less autonomous and laissez faire, and instead become more responsive and effective.

Notes

1. This phrase is borrowed from Grubb et al., 1999.
2. Lawrence Mead's compassionate "new paternalism."
3. The strategies of two widely lauded LMIs, the San Jose Center for Employment and Training and Project QUEST in San Antonio, both involve substantial components of employer organization.
4. This regime type resembles the "employment regime" described by Clarence Stone (1998) in his work on regime theory and educational transformation. He contrasts "employment regimes," in which public sector institutions operate mainly to provide jobs to service providers and administrators, with "performance regimes," in which they more ably advance public ends such as effective schools.
5. Ozaukee and Washington counties.
6. Waukesha County.
7. Opportunities Industrialization Center (OIC) and Employment Solutions manage two job center locations each, and Maximus, Inc., YW Works, and UMOS operate one site each.
8. See Private Industry Council of Milwaukee (1999) and Workforce Development Area #3 (2000).
9. For customized training and on-the-job training programs, the PIC will only entertain proposals for programs that will place participants in jobs paying a minimum of $8 per hour and offering health care benefits.
10. Bernhardt, personal communication.
11. MATC is one of three technical college districts in the state of Wisconsin that draws a maximum amount of revenue from local property taxes.
12. See Greater Milwaukee Committee Regional Cooperation Task Force (1998) for a statement of such goals.

References

American Federation of State, County, and Municipal Employees Legislative Council, Wisconsin (AFSCME). 2000. *Private Profits, Public Needs: The Administration of W-2 in Milwaukee, WI.* Milwaukee: American Federation of State, County, and Municipal Employees Legislative Council, Wisconsin.

Associated Press. 1999. "Standards Set to Make Sure Agencies Help W-2 Clients." *Milwaukee Journal Sentinel* (November 15).

Bernhardt, Annette, Manuel Pastor, Erin Hatton, and Sarah Zimmerman. 2000. "Moving the Demand Side: Intermediaries in a Changing Labor Market." Unpublished manuscript, December 14.

Center on Wisconsin Strategy. 1996. *Milwaukee Area Regional Economic Analysis.* Madison: Center on Wisconsin Strategy.

———. 2000a. *State of Working Wisconsin 2000.* Madison: Center on Wisconsin Strategy.

———. 2000b. *Workforce Development Resource Directory: A Summary of Metro Area Employment and Training Services.* Madison: Center on Wisconsin Strategy.

Dodenhoff, David. 1998 *Privatizing Welfare in Wisconsin: Ending Administrative Entitlements—W-2's Untold Story.* Thiensville: Wisconsin Policy Research Institute.

Dorf, Michael C., and Charles F. Sabel. 1998. A Constitution of Democratic Experimentalism. *Columbia Law Review* 98(2):267–473.

Dresang, Joel. 1999. "Aid, Custom-Made: After Criticism and 'Confusing' Start, Agencies' Approach Evolves." *Milwaukee Journal Sentinel* (December 14).

Dresang, Joel, and Geeta Sharma-Jensen. 1998. "W-2 Work Or Else: A welfare era passes into state history—AFDC recipients must be switched to W-2 today; jobs remain elusive goal." *Milwaukee Journal Sentinel* (March 31).

Dresser, Laura, and Joel Rogers. 1998. "Networks, Sectors, and Workforce Learning." In *Jobs and Economic Development: Strategies and Practice,* edited by Robert P. Giloth. Thousand Oaks, CA: Sage Publications.

Dresser, Laura, Joel Rogers, and Scott Zdrazil. 2000. "Wisconsin Regional Training Partnership." Paper prepared for A. E. Havens Center on the Study of Social Structure, University of Wisconsin, presented at the Madison Conference on Empowered Deliberative Democracy (January 12–16).

Gittell, Marilyn. 1994. "School Reform in New York and Chicago: Revisiting the Ecology of Local Games." *Urban Affairs Quarterly* 30(1)(September):136–151.

Greater Milwaukee Committee Regional Cooperation Task Force. 1998. "Toward a Regional Strategy for Workforce Development." Milwaukee, WI: Greater Milwaukee Committee (November 9).

Grubb, W. Norton. 1996. *Learning to Work: The Case for Reintegrating Job Training and Education.* New York: Russell Sage Foundation.

Grubb, W. Norton, Norena Badway, Denise Bell, Bernadette Chi, Chris King, Julie Herr, Heath Prince, Richard Kazis, Lisa Hicks, and Judith Combes Taylor. 1999. *Toward Order from Chaos: State Efforts to Reform Workforce Development Systems.* Berkeley, CA: National Center for Research in Vocational Education.

Huston, Margo. 1998. "W-2 Work or Else: Agencies Urge Lawmakers to Alter W-2 Education, Cash Assistance Are Needed for People to Get Jobs, Leaders Say." *Milwaukee Journal Sentinel* (September 16):1.

————. 1999. "W-2 Work or Else: Review of W-2 Agencies Seeks Improvements, Midterm Evaluations Come as County Prepares for Second Set of Contracts." *Milwaukee Journal Sentinel* (January 20).

LaLonde, Robert J. 1995. "The Promise of Public Sector-Sponsored Training Programs." *Journal of Economic Perspectives* 9 (2):149–168.

Legislative Audit Bureau, State of Wisconsin. 2001. *An Evaluation: Wisconsin Works (W-2) Program.* April. Available at http://www.legis.state.wi.us/lab/reports/01-7full.pdf.

Lindblom, Charles. 1959. "The Science of Muddling Through." *Public Administration Review* 19(2)(Spring):78–88.

Long, Norton E. 1958. "The Local Community as an Ecology of Games." *American Journal of Sociology* 64(3)(November):251–261.

Mead, Lawrence. 1999. "Statecraft: The Politics of Welfare Reform in Wisconsin." Discussion paper 1184-99, February. Madison, WI: Institute for Research on Poverty.

Milwaukee Area Technical College (MATC). 1999. *Working Knowledge: Report to the Community 1999.* Milwaukee, WI: Milwaukee Area Technical College.

Private Industry Council of Milwaukee. 1999. *Milwaukee County Workforce Development Area WIA Comprehensive Plan. 2000–2005.* Milwaukee: Private Industry Council.

Scott, James C. 1998. *Seeing Like a State: How Certain Schemes to Improve the Human Condition Have Failed.* New Haven: Yale University Press.

Schultze, Steve. 2000a. "Lawmakers Want Maximus Fired." *Milwaukee Journal Sentinel* (October 26).

————. 2000b. "Maximus Has Admitted to Improper Billing." *Milwaukee Journal Sentinel* (May 9).

————. 2000c. "Maximus to Pay Back $500,000: Firm Also Plans Extra Spending for Poor After Audit." *Milwaukee Journal Sentinel* (October 13).

————. 2000d. "Regulators Accused of Being Easy on W-2 Agencies." *Milwaukee Journal Sentinel* (August 31).

————. 2000e. "State Says W-2 Money Bought Political Advice: Maximus Defends Hiring of Former Thompson Aides for More Than $8,500." *Milwaukee Journal Sentinel* (August 14).

————. 2000f. "State Gets Tab for W-2 Firm's Outside Work." *Milwaukee Journal Sentinel* (August 27).

————. 2001. "W-2 Staffers Given Big Bonuses." *Milwaukee Journal Sentinel* (February 27).

State of Wisconsin, Department of Workforce Development. 1999a. *State of Wisconsin Workforce Development Plan 2000–2004.* Madison: Wisconsin Department of Workforce Development.

————. 1999b. *Milwaukee County Regional Workforce Profile.* Madison: Wisconsin Department of Workforce Development (July).

————. 1999c. *Waukesha-Ozaukee-Washington Regional Workforce Profile.* Madison: Wisconsin Department of Workforce Development (July).

Stephenson, Crocker. 1999. "Hardest Cases Define Welfare's Next Challenge." *Milwaukee Journal Sentinel* (December 12).

Stone, Clarence N (Ed.). 1998. *Changing Urban Education.* Lawrence: University Press of Kansas.

U.S. General Accounting Office. 1995. *Multiple Employment Training Programs: Major Overhaul Needed to Create a More Efficient, Customer-Driven System.* Washington, DC: U.S. General Accounting Office.

Workforce Development Area #3. 2000. *Workforce Investment Act, Workforce Development Area #3 Comprehensive WIA Plan for Waukesha, Ozaukee and Washington Counties.* Madison, WI: Department of Workforce Development.

David W. Bartelt

4 Workforce Systems Change in a Politically Fragmented Environment

HOW DOES a city transform its political culture? How does a political machine with limited local public resources, a fragmented and contentious political process, and a recent history of failed efforts to shape a public–private governing regime engage the issue of workforce development? How does a socially and politically divided city grapple with workforce development issues in a regional economy that is virtually an "ideal type" representation of spatial mismatches and a dual economy? And, how does a governing coalition that is based largely on jobs and contracts begin to address the increasing expectations of outcome-based or performance-based accountability that have emerged as prominent themes in the framing of workforce development programs?

These questions, in the Philadelphia context, constitute the central issue of this chapter: Can a municipal regime, more accurately described here as a governing coalition, begin to include performance criteria in their administrative- and agenda-setting activities when driven by the centrality of workforce development for regional vitality? The importance of workforce development to the economic and community revitalization of inner-city neighborhoods is virtually unquestioned. Similarly, local governments nationwide have been forced to address the manifold family, education, and economic development issues attached to the problem of developing human capital. This discussion begins to define the scope of the workforce issues facing one city—Philadelphia—as it undergoes the challenges and systemic transformations that appear to be necessary for an effective approach to addressing these issues. The questions raised above reflect the challenges embedded in the political and social arrangements that constitute the action arena around many issues in this city, of which workforce development, along with the physical revitalization of the city's neighborhoods, are central to the city's future well-being.

Workforce development and the emergence of performance-oriented public policy have emerged in a symbiotic fashion in Philadelphia. The issue of shifting regimes—from an employment-based perspective to one based on performance—is a step toward recognizing the new realities of workforce development, economic revitalization, and local governance.

At the same time, the emergence of performance-oriented themes in urban political economies often occurs against a narrative of change and resistance—of calls for restructuring local governance that resonate against resistance to change. In this process, familiar concepts of adaptation, cooptation, and pragmatic coexistence are likely indicators of change.

To what extent, then, has a focus on workforce development in the late 1990s generated attention to the issues of performance on the one hand, and effective governance on the other? Philadelphia faces a significant set of barriers to economic well-being that, in combination with fragmented local and state political governmental structures, has effectively limited efforts to coordinate human resource policies in the city and metropolitan region. The region as a whole has experienced a dramatic shift in its economic base, from manufacturing to service industries. It has also experienced a spatial shift in the location of employment opportunities from concentrated city locations to de-concentrated regional centers.

The introduction of performance criteria by both federal programs and key independent-sector entities has helped create a group of key actors—organizations and individuals—who have begun to articulate a performance orientation in several policy areas, particularly in the workforce development arena. When counterposed to the routine politics of resource allocation based on a calculus of inertia, obligation, and reward, these efforts have generated a dual arena for local workforce development policy. Thus, while the traditional basis of local government as an "employment regime" continues to dominate in most policy arenas, including many entities involved with workforce development, a politics of performance has also emerged in which outcomes and impact become key factors in program development and operation.

Using Philadelphia as a case in point, this chapter assesses three major issues related to this process: The ways in which the barriers built into economic and policy environments both inhibit and press for change; the ways in which "performance" criteria have begun to enter the political economy of the city and region, including key actors and organizations; and the ways in which the institutionalized structures of employment regimes in both the public and private sectors are evident. It is the interplay between the "lashed up" arrangements[1] of traditional governing structures (Molotch et al., 2000) and more outcome-oriented approaches that has created both inertial and adaptive forces in the workforce development arena.

Given the entrenched nature of long-standing political and cultural changes, and the immediacy of most economic decision-making—including workforce issues—the nature of change is inevitably one of contested terrain, which is a truism in most approaches to system reform (Giloth,

2000). In the case of Philadelphia, the divergence of parties participating in the shaping and operation of workforce policies and programs appears to make the development of a coherent workforce system almost oxymoronic—at least at first blush. This divergence, however, has provided fertile ground for reform efforts, with some indications of a strategy for navigating this terrain.

There is an underlying issue that has emerged within this analysis that will be examined in the final section of this chapter, namely, assumptions underlying the framework of regime theory. Regime models are broader in scope than traditional elite approaches, and certainly subsume traditional "machine politics" analyses of local and regional political economies. Although there is no necessary assumption that regimes need to function in an internally coordinated and rational fashion, there is a tendency to assume more coordination rather than less.

WORKFORCE DEVELOPMENT IN PHILADELPHIA: ECONOMIC AND POLICY CONTEXTS

Workforce development in Philadelphia has emerged against an economic backdrop of deindustrialization and the spatial relocation of the region's jobs to the suburban counties of the region. Its policy responses suggest a deeply fragmented approach to most local initiatives facing the city, from blight to jobs to taxes to schools—and most immediately to workforce development. The secular shift in the geography of economic activity to suburbs, the Sunbelt, and offshore locations, combined with a concomitant erosion of local tax bases, as well as a political culture that might support local initiatives in communities with limited fiscal capacity, exacerbates this fragmentation.

The twin pressures of shrinking tax bases and devolution at the federal level have essentially delimited the capacity of local government to serve its traditional role as a source of local employment—in short, as an employment regime. Yet, the heritage of this past role[2] persists in the execution of elections, promises made by political leaders to constituents, and the use of various types of neighborhood base organizations as extensions of an increasingly moribund ward system. Community development corporations, parishes, interest groups, and property development firms jockey for a slice of the city's expenditures, with elected officials acting as the distributors. The central feature of performance systems (i.e., accountability) is mentioned at times, but in practice, accountability here refers more to political consequences than to programmatic effectiveness.

Both the city's former housing director and the director of a community development financial intermediary have suggested the limitations of this approach—albeit from different directions and with different goals in mind (Kromer, 1999; Hill and Nowak, 2000). Kromer essentially argues that cities like Philadelphia need to be far more pragmatic in their attempts to deliver housing and community development resources, always seeking leverage in a context of dramatically reduced expectations for potential impact and scale of programs. In his description of the past decade of community development in Philadelphia, Kromer contends that the realities of accountability and patronage are evident. He is remarkably open in his description of the ways in which he and the Executive Director of the Redevelopment Authority would play "good cop–bad cop" in negotiating with community groups and city council members to focus on a pragmatic view of what would work.

From a different perspective, the President and CEO of The Reinvestment Fund (TRF), Jeremy Nowak (with Ned Hill) has offered two arguments that challenge the legacy of the traditional city government. First, Hill and Nowak suggest that only city governments facing a severe fiscal crisis will abandon political practices that make them uncompetitive—that is, their inability to incorporate a performance/quality dimension to their activities. The days when cities could redistribute income are gone for all but a very few of the largest American cities—and even their ability to redistribute income is limited. Hill and Nowak argue:

> Not only has the competitive position of America's cities eroded, but the deadweight of the institutional baggage from the past—political cultures and expectations, management practices and union contracts, and the politics of operating in the current federal system—inhibits or prohibits meaningful reform. If changes are not made to both the bundle of services provided and the taxes charged, city governments will continue to be managers of decline, their competitive position will continue to erode, and their regional economies will continue to bypass them. (2000, 22–23)

In essence, the ways in which cities operate are constrained by past practice, and change is inhibited by the ossified relationships of obligation and reward that characterize a city government that is based on a model of providing employment—directly through its employee base or indirectly through its contracting for housing, economic development, infrastructure, and other projects. The recent venture to build two stadiums comes immediately to mind. Only the opportunity to rewrite the expectations and obligations of city governments—an opportunity that emerges in a fiscal crisis—will allow for such a transformation, they argue.[3]

It is their second point that pulls us closer to the problem of inertia and contending paradigms for regimes. The route from fiscal collapse to a role facilitating central city competitiveness in metropolitan regions is not direct. Hill and Nowak (2000, 26) argue that an enormous amount of political will and a radical restructuring of both local government and inter-governmental relationships must be present, echoing the observations made by Rusk (1999) and Orfield (2001) about governance problems facing many older metropolitan areas. The vivid imagery at the conclusion of this article is instructive.

> Fixing the real competitive disadvantages of distressed cities—outdated tax structures, broken political cultures, uncompetitive staffing levels, vacant and abandoned land, and an inappropriate array of public services—requires the radical experimentation and state and federal support described above. Cities cannot address their competitive disadvantages on their own. State and federal governments have to become partners with them in reform. That partnership cannot be based on old entitlement and categorical models of federal and state aid or on new lines of leaky buckets carrying federal funds through the corridors of statehouses to the desks of big-city mayors. These proposals involve some degree of risk and an enormous amount of change in inter- and intra-governmental relationships. But for many cities, there is very little left to lose. (Hill and Nowak, 2000, 26)

The ultimate issue, of course, is that the governing structures—regional, state, and federal—on which such an argument depends are not well suited to mount such an effort, because they incorporate much of the employment regime in how they perform their tasks. The question that arises is how the inertia of past efforts creates a parallel between traditional models of an employment regime even as performance-oriented models begin to emerge, particularly within the workforce development system.

The Regional Economy

Many communities in the Philadelphia area have been forced to deal with a wrenching transition in the region's economic base. As the city has left the era of heavy manufacturing behind in the past several decades, both the nature of work and the locations of jobs have changed. Before the 1960s, the jobs were largely linked to the manufacturing sector, and were located in the older sections of the city which are further from Center City—in North Philadelphia, Kensington, along the Delaware River, and in older cities abutting river and rail transit corridors (e.g., Camden, Chester, Coatesville, and Norristown). As newer groups of people moved to the city—African Americans, Latinos, and others—they often found housing in the neighborhoods that industry had left behind. With the shift in the basic labor market, educational credentials became more important for jobs that were located both in Center City and, increasingly, in suburban counties.

The workplace here is treated as a regional arrangement of jobs, with greatly varying wages, locations, and types of jobs in different kinds of firms. When we examine the location and types of jobs available, we are looking for opportunities and trends, as well as, ultimately, some guidance as to the expectations that employers have for their employees. Workforce development begins with identifying employer expectations where they intersect with the business development and expansion decisions made by employers.

Members of any community organizing to address the challenges of the contemporary labor market begin with a basic set of issues affecting the entire region. The long-term shift of the Philadelphia metropolitan area has been away from its traditional manufacturing base toward a regionally dispersed, diverse labor market that is more strongly oriented to the service and retail sectors of the economy. The changes in that economy have created a clear sense of direction for business development and labor force opportunities in the city and region.

Many observers have chronicled Philadelphia's transition over the last half century from a manufacturing-based economy to one dominated by services (Adams et al., 1991, 34–45). This history is one of economic transition and locational shift. The neighborhoods of the city that were once dominated by manufacturing industries have been replaced by a spatially dispersed, much more complex mix of manufacturing (increasingly suburbanized), services, retail trade (also more suburban than downtown and neighborhood dominated), and medical/pharmaceutical firms.

The manufacturing sector, once the core of the economy of Philadelphia and its surrounding region, was also the traditional source of entry-level jobs for newly arriving migrants to the city. As the comparatively inexpensive housing of the city attracted new residents, these migrants found that a ready supply of entry-level jobs presented itself, often in the very neighborhoods in which they lived. As these jobs disappeared, many neighborhoods were devalued and became less attractive to people who had other residential choices available, either in the suburbs or in other areas of the country.

In short, the city of Philadelphia has experienced a major shift in the basic economic relationships that shaped much of its development through the period of World War II and immediately thereafter. Manufacturing jobs declined in importance and became spatially dispersed across the region. Many service-sector jobs required a level of educational and skills development that was not immediately available in the public education system of the city; many of these jobs were located in the suburbs as well.

A major factor accompanying the pressures on both wages and job availability has been the long-term economic decline of the region, and the protracted economic pressures of the 1980s and early 1990s. In recent years, both the city and the regional economy have rebounded, with greater opportunities still represented in suburban areas. Data from both the United States Department of Labor and the Census Bureau's County Business Patterns data set amplify these findings.

A report issued by the Bureau of Labor Statistics (U.S. Department of Labor, 2000) suggests that the city has benefited from the national economic expansion of the last several years. Both the region and the city suffered large employment declines during the late 1980s and early 1990s, when the regional employment level fell from 1.95 million jobs (fourth quarter, 1989) to 1.81 million (first quarter, 1993).

The most recent decline in city jobs began before the economic slowdown of 1989. This decline continued after the region's recovery had begun. As such, the 620,000 jobs reported in 1989 represent an employment level that has yet to be regained; however, declines stabilized significantly in the mid-1990s, reaching a low of 540,000 in 1996. Significant growth has been evident in the past three to four years; jobs grew to a level of 582,000 by the end of 1999. In the analysis reported below, the city expanded its employment base to 606,000 jobs in 2000 (see Table 4.1). The report also suggests that job growth is concentrated in several employment sectors, the basis of efforts to expand into advanced manufacturing, professional and data-intensive services, and hospitality. These issues are discussed more fully below.

Although growth has occurred in recent years in the city's employment base, suburban jobs growth has been more pronounced. Data from the annual County Business Patterns (from the U.S. Census Bureau) were examined to provide a more detailed analysis of the locational clusters of jobs—the places where job hunting is more likely to be profitable, and where access strategies should be targeted. These data are presented in two formats: Disaggregated county employment by industrial category for the 2000 reporting year and a comparison of the geographic shift in employment opportunities from 1992 to 2000.

The first breakdown of this information is contained in Table 4.1 (presented in a bar graph in Figure 4.1), which breaks down the location of jobs by the type of business activity of employers.[4] Three aspects of these data are immediately evident. First, suburban areas have a higher proportion of their jobs in manufacturing and wholesale/retail sales firms than does the city of Philadelphia, and the suburban areas are virtually

Table 4.1   NAICS Summary of Employment by Business Types in 2000
Categorized by Location

Location	Industry	Jobs (*n*)	Jobs (%)
City	Extractive	0	0.0%
	Utilities & Construction	13,045	2.2%
	Manufacturing	42,362	7.0%
	Wholesale, Retail	75,093	12.4%
	Transport, Warehousing	28,551	4.7%
	FIRE, Information, Prof. Services	186,135	30.8%
	Social Services	174,257	28.9%
	Tourism	48,777	8.1%
	Other Services	29,420	4.9%
	Auxiliaries	6,207	1.0%
	Not Classified	0	0.0%
	Total	603,847	27.5%
Suburban	Extractive	1,534	0.1%
	Utilities & Construction	92,678	5.8%
	Manufacturing	193,579	12.1%
	Wholesale, Retail	316,573	19.9%
	Transport, Warehousing	35,714	2.2%
	FIRE, Information, Prof. Services	491,373	30.8%
	Social Services	247,760	15.5%
	Tourism	118,291	7.4%
	Other Services	76,135	4.8%
	Auxiliaries	19,257	1.2%
	Not Classified	726	0.0%
	Total	1,593,620	72.5%
MSA	Extractive	1,534	0.1%
	Utilities & Construction	105,723	4.8%
	Manufacturing	235,941	10.7%
	Wholesale, Retail	391,666	17.8%
	Transport, Warehousing	64,265	2.9%
	FIRE, Information, Prof. Services	677,508	30.8%
	Social Services	422,017	19.2%
	Tourism	167,068	7.6%
	Other Services	105,555	4.8%
	Auxiliaries	25,464	1.2%
	Not Classified	726	0.0%
	Total	2,197,467	99.9%

SOURCE: U.S. Bureau of the Census (2000).
NOTE: NAICS, North American Industry Classification System.

identical to the city in the proportion of businesses that are in the FIRE (finance, insurance, and real estate), information technology, and professional services group. The heavy suburban presence of these jobs suggests that employment opportunities are regionally distributed, and that Philadelphia is no longer the presumptive center of regional employment opportunities.

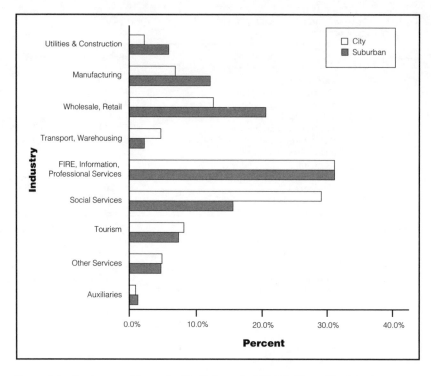

Figure 4.1   Employment Categorized by Industry in Philadelphia and Its Suburbs
SOURCE: Adapted from U.S. Bureau of the Census (2000).

Second, it is not surprising to see that the proportion of all jobs in the region that fall within the manufacturing category is slightly higher than 10 percent, whereas over 70 percent of employment opportunities fall into the sales and services categories. The relative scarcity of manufacturing jobs has been cited elsewhere as a major factor in the disruption of the city's economic opportunity structures for lesser-skilled workers (Adams et al., 1991, 43–48).

A third aspect of these data is also important. The one area in which there is an unmistakable indication of the city's dominance in job types is that of social services, including education and health. Although there is some potential for employment opportunities in the health field, these jobs are most dependent on some form of government funding, and include all the uncertainty that this entails.

When we examine the trajectory of employment opportunities over the recent past, several additional insights can be gained. When County Business Pattern data are compared from 1992 through 1998 (see Table 4.2;

Table 4.2 Regional Employment Data from 1992 to 2000

Location	2000			1992		
	Establishments (*n*)	Employees (*n*)	Share* (%)	Establishments (*n*)	Employees (*n*)	Share* (%)
Pennsylvania						
Bucks	17,798	247,572	11.3%	14,982	194,409	10.2%
Chester	12,177	190,152	8.7%	10,237	153,079	8.1%
Delaware	13,306	217,078	9.9%	13,129	201,228	10.6%
Montgomery	25,800	497,214	22.7%	24,639	422,560	22.2%
Philadelphia	25,782	606,509	27.6%	27,619	575,186	30.3%
Total	94,863	1,758,525	80.2%	90,606	1,546,462	81.3%
New Jersey						
Burlington	10,318	173,890	7.9%	9,176	131,758	6.9%
Camden	12,581	183,883	8.4%	12,174	160,859	8.5%
Gloucester	5,644	77,776	3.5%	4,948	61,983	3.3%
Total	28,543	435,549	19.8%	26,298	354,600	18.7%
Metropolitan Statistical Area	123,406	2,194,074		116,904	1,901,062	

SOURCE: U.S. Bureau of the Census (1992, 2000).
*Share indicates the percentage of employees in Metropolitan Statistical Area for each county.

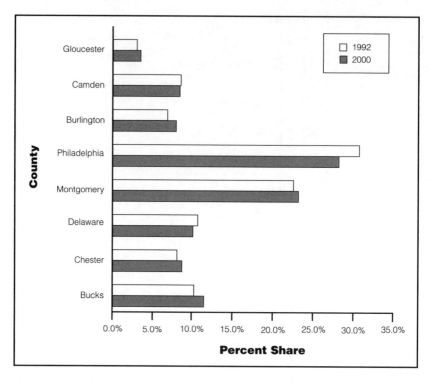

Figure 4.2   Employment Shares from 1992 to 2000 in Philadelphia MSA, Categorized by
County
SOURCE: U.S. Bureau of the Census (1992, 2000).

Figure 4.2), the employment changes over this time period suggest a
growing decentralization of employment opportunities. The number of
employees reported in the County Business Pattern survey grew by over
200,000 over this time period in the region as a whole, and by over
30,000 in Philadelphia itself. However, although the number of establishments also grew, which indicates new business formation across the
entire region, the number of establishments declined in the city of
Philadelphia. Another way of stating this is that fewer establishments
employed more people.[5]
    A ratio of jobs in each county to the total of metropolitan jobs was
developed, creating an indicator of the share of the region's employment
opportunity for each county. The ratio, which points to Philadelphia's
position as the single largest employment center in the region, , also indicates that this share has declined from 1992 to 2000 (from 30.3 percent
in 1992 to 27.6 percent in 2000). Delaware and Camden counties, the

oldest suburban ring counties, also show some evidence of a declining employment share, although less clearly than Philadelphia. Thus, it can be argued that employment opportunities, although more numerous in the suburbs, are also present within the city, recognizing that the largest number of opportunities is present in the suburban counties.

County Business Pattern data are also available categorized by zip code, which sharpens the geographic focus of our inquiry. One of the clearest ways in which the importance of the suburban labor market can be highlighted is by examining locations of employment clusters on a regional map. The map presented below (Figure 4.3) is limited to the Pennsylvania suburbs and indicates the geographic center (centroid) of the zip codes with the greatest concentration of employment in the region. The markers with place names attached indicate these major employment clusters. Data on the areas of greatest office growth, based on data from an office tenant brokering firm (Julian H. Studley, Inc., 2000), are represented by the irregularly shaped, shaded areas.

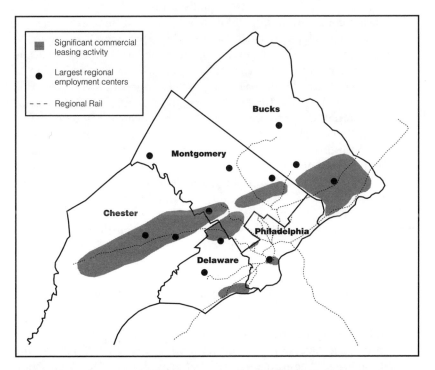

Figure 4.3   Job Centers and Office Expansion in the Philadelphia Area
SOURCE: Redrawn from Julian J. Studley, Inc. (2000); data from U.S. Bureau of the Census (1998).

The suburban employment pattern is clear. Only center city Philadelphia is within easy access of the older manufacturing neighborhoods which are represented by the shaded areas within the city. Areas as distant as Exton, Pottstown, and Doylestown supplement the nearer, but still limitedly accessible, suburbs such as Bryn Mawr, King of Prussia, Horsham, and Langhorne. Although there is some rail access available to these areas, the challenge of the distance between suburban workplace and inner-city residence is significant.

The suburban distribution of jobs is a long-term trend with which most Philadelphians are familiar. The impact on inner-city communities is emphasized when two additional forces are added to the equation. First, the basic distance from the workplace is accentuated by the difficulty of access experienced by many residents of the city. Suburban jobs are accessible most easily to those with automobiles and drivers with easy access to the major routes leading out of the city. Second, with the concentration of the city's population increasingly located on the fringes of the city, older inner-city communities face the frustration of being surrounded by job clusters that are, in many respects, equidistant from them; however, there is significant competition for employment in many of these locations.

Workforce development discussions in Philadelphia have attempted to respond to these patterns by developing strategic initiatives that focus on key employment sectors for the region, emphasizing a combination of growth potential and broad-based employment opportunities across skill levels. A report from the Regional Workforce Partnership (2000) incorporated materials from the regional economic benchmark study prepared by Greater Philadelphia First (GPF) (1999).[6] It should be noted that these two organizations represent key elements of the emerging performance paradigm in the region.

In its benchmark study, GPF used steady employment growth, employment across skill levels, and the improving quality of employment as criteria by which to identify strategic clusters of industries in which the region might invest for further growth. To the extent that this focus on clusters of industries is used as a general basis for economic development, it would appear appropriate to structure workforce development strategies around these efforts.

The key employment clusters identified in this study were:

- *Professional Services:* These are represented by corporate headquarters, higher education institutions, and a range of professional firms (e.g., accounting, engineering, information technology, and legal firms). These are often referred to as "knowledge-based" companies, and often require a high degree of personal interaction.

- *Data-Intensive Services:* These are firms and offices that specialize in so-called "back-office" operations (e.g., banking, financial services, telemarketing, and customer services). GPF notes the growth of a sophisticated workforce and the use of a substantial telecommunications infrastructure as keys to the continuing importance of this sector.

- *Health Care Services and Products:* Long-term investment in medical-related firms and services—hospitals and pharmaceuticals—have given Philadelphia a major competitive advantage in the global health care market. A mix of different skill levels makes this sector a natural for continuing attention for workforce development.

- *Manufacturing:* While recognizing the continuing global pressures that have contributed to the downsizing of the manufacturing sector in the Philadelphia region, this sector is still a major component of the regional economy. The region employs over 200,000 manufacturing workers in increasingly skilled and technically demanding jobs. The continuing health of this sector will call for an ongoing cadre of entry-level employees who will be able to maintain the strength of this sector. As many businesses have reported, difficulties in attracting these employees to entry-level positions exist.

- *Hospitality:* Restaurants, museums, hotels, conventions, and recreational facilities, along with attendant services such as transportation, are the primary types of activities in this increasingly significant sector. The recently concluded political convention, and a major increase in the choice of Philadelphia as both a tourist and business meeting site, are indicators of growth in a wide variety of employment opportunities.

GPF's analysis of regional clusters recognized the interplay of employment opportunities and economic development. This analysis suggested that the continued development of the region's economy would be facilitated by the success of these sectors in attracting employment across skill levels, and by the further expansion of efforts in transportation (for people and goods regionally and beyond), increased entrepreneurship, development of the region's science and technology base, and expansion of a professional workforce—especially a skilled technology workforce.

These strategic factors provided the backdrop for assessing the role of workforce initiatives in addressing contemporary employment issues. The findings of the *Workforce 2000* report (Regional Workforce Partnership, 2000) released in early 2001 cited a series of challenges to the region's economic future, including the following:

- The region faces a combination of slow population growth and a decline in the working-age population (the 16- to 64-year-old age group). Although some suburban counties gained in this critical age group, the losses in Philadelphia, Delaware, Camden, and Salem counties outweighed these gains.
- The clusters suggested by the GPF as areas of economic opportunity are, in fact, sources of employment growth in the region, as well as in the construction industry. Most employment growth, however, is spatially specific, as Chester, Montgomery, and Burlington counties are the sources of greatest growth. Suburban job growth has been accompanied by suburb-to-suburb commuting, as comparatively difficult access from city neighborhoods creates difficulties in using these growth areas as employment opportunities for within-city neighborhoods.
- The report suggests four major workforce challenges for the city and the region:

  1. A technical skills gap, particularly in the areas of information technology and advanced manufacturing areas
  2. A worker readiness gap—from basic skill levels in math and reading—is suggested by many employers as a factor in the inability to fill existing vacancies
  3. Spatial barriers are also an issue, and include transportation issues, child care access, and differential housing costs limiting lower income residents from relocating to areas closer to jobs
  4. Image and attitude issues were also cited, suggesting that employment opportunities need to be accompanied by efforts to address both subjective perceptions of the region and the condition of the region's communities

In short, many city residents seeking to enter the job market will face a combination of difficult access and the shifting skill expectations of employers. Workforce development strategies will, out of necessity, be linked to both the skill sets of job seekers and to an increased knowledge of opportunities across the region. This is not to argue that there are no options available within the city. The persistence of Center City as an area of concentrated employment opportunities must be recognized, although again, competition for this limited employment base will be intense.

These labor market factors form one part of the backdrop for the city's efforts to develop an effective workforce development policy. The other component of policymaking is the public sector as it struggles to adapt to the twin pressures of devolution and a shift to performance-based funding.

The Public Sector

Understanding the public sector's activities in the workforce development arena involves at least three forces: Multiple levels of governance, an expected segmentation of activity derived from the administrative inertia of workforce-related programs that have accreted over time, and the emerging contrast between performance-oriented approaches and traditional forms of resource allocation, reflecting a mix of legislative priorities, employment, entitlements, and administrative survival skills.

MULTIPLE GOVERNANCE LEVELS

One of the major contributing factors in the variable effectiveness of local governments is the fundamental legal constraint that surrounds the very concept of municipal incorporation. Notwithstanding the critical role that cities play as social and political centers of activity, the legal concept of preemption sets real boundaries on city political authority. American cities are the creation of, and derive their powers from, state government (Frug, 1999, 19–20). Even in the case of "home rule," the city is an "instrument of the state" (Frug, 1999, 19).

One might be tempted to treat this as the anomaly of an earlier, small town era—as a matter of legal code rather than a practical constraint—were it not for a reinforcing pattern of income and wealth inequality that, somewhat imperfectly, reinforces this city-suburb boundary. These spatial inequalities are reproduced in local government resources—sales, income, and property tax bases—effectively limiting the capacity of many cities to develop regionally oriented programs. In the practical, day-to-day activities of local governance, then, local government is limited both by law and by the politics of fiscal inequality (Rusk, 1999; Orfield, 2001).

In Philadelphia's case, these limitations have resulted in a stronger role for state activity in a number of areas, including workforce development. Adams (2001, 5–12) has cited education and workforce development as two of the major areas in which state programs and overall involvement have become the most apparent in the Philadelphia policy arena. Because of the long-standing disaffection between state and local political representatives (Adams et al., 1991, 158–161), any potential coordination of workforce development initiatives across the region, or initiatives that involve access to suburban employment opportunities by city residents, routinely suffer against the backdrop of this disaffection.

In the case of workforce development policy, the establishment of Workforce Investment Boards (WIBs) as key elements of federal workforce policy reflects both the statutory and political importance of both federal and state governance in setting the framework for local WIB activity. Furthermore, the funding streams that are combined under the aegis of local WIBs suggest that there will be a mix of public assistance, labor, economic development, and educational funding streams that could be combined in a workforce strategy.

A report issued by the National Governors' Association on the transformation of state workforce systems provides direct insight into how state workforce policies are key to local effectiveness (National Governors' Association, 2001). This report, presented as a series of case studies of the effects of gubernatorial leadership in implementing the Workforce Investment Act (WIA), highlighted Pennsylvania's efforts meeting WIA objectives.

In general, two key factors were linked to success: The development of a more unified workforce development system and the adoption of workforce development as a core economic development strategy (National Governors' Association, 2001, 5). Former Governor Ridge was instrumental in promoting the alignment of workforce development with ten economic development regions (16). Rather than pushing for a formal unification of departments involved with workforce development, coordination at the assistant secretary level was seen as a more effective strategy, especially when developing plans, setting performance criteria, and assessing regional workforce system performance (55).

As noted in several conversations with local workforce development leaders, one of the major changes that separated WIA from prior workforce policy was the separation of oversight from service delivery, as formal "firewalls" were required for local WIBs (National Governors' Association, 2001, 57–58). A key element in the development of local accountability and performance criteria was established from the state level, reflecting federal policies. Pennsylvania is singled out in the report as an example of how best to link workforce development efforts to welfare reform, education/technology investment, and the state's national service corps entity, the Pennsylvania Conservation Corps (60).

Despite these key indicators of systemic change, the report contains several cautions. Not unexpectedly, turf battles were significant, although at the state level, performance expectations contingent on interagency collaboration facilitated a two-year process of greater cooperation. On a more organizational level, the report also noted that significant policy silos exist, in particular those linked to constituency-driven programs and legacy effects (National Governors' Association, 2001, 58–59). These issues are reflected in an examination of the state's workforce enterprises as a whole. This leads to a consideration of the issue of program segmentation.

PROGRAM SEGMENTATION

It is instructive to look at a document prepared by the Philadelphia WIB office to understand the coordination needed to carry out the workforce initiatives for the city provided under the auspices of WIA. A copy of this diagram can be found at the end of this chapter (see Appendix Figure 4.4). A total of eleven funding or administrative sources are identified, including federal (U.S. Department of Housing and Urban Development [HUD], WIA, Department of Education, Department of Labor), state (Education, Labor & Industry), and local (Mayor's Office of Community Services, Commission on Aging) funds. In addition to reinforcing the observations about levels of government, this diagram suggests that a major component of WIB activity is the management of potential "turf" conflicts that have their roots in some distant legislative/political past.

In many ways, this diagram represents a minority—significant, but still a minority—of the public-sector engagement with workforce development issues. During the spring 2002 primary election campaign, the Regional Workforce Partnership—a coalition of public and private-sector organizations engaged in workforce development activities—prepared a summary guide to all state level programs (Regional Workforce Partnership, 2002).[7] The sheer size and complexity of state level programs suggest significant inertia and programmatic fragmentation within the state. The report found a total of forty-nine programs across five cabinet level departments with workforce budgets in excess of $1.2 billion. Only four of these programs were tied, albeit loosely, across two agencies (Labor & Industry and Public Welfare); these include the "One-Stop" offices (jointly administered), career link centers (Labor & Industry), and child care information services (Department of Public Welfare [DPW]). Their total programmatic budget represents the bulk of the state total workforce budget, some $752 million in fiscal year 1999.

What are we to make of this information? First, in addition to the targeted workforce development programs, a sizable amount of public-sector effort is unmeasured; routine expenditures on secondary schools, community colleges, and higher education have an often explicit link to the workforce. The education programs that do appear in this report represent targeted program activity in the areas of vocational education, literacy, and displaced homemakers. Nevertheless, substantial funding does appear to be focused in areas in which there is some evidence of coordination, at least at the state level. This point resonates with the findings of the National Governors' Association report.

This effort at collaboration is far from seamless or coordinated. Classic issues of organizational inertia interfere with top down pronouncements in somewhat unanticipated ways. One example, One-Stop Centers, which are explicitly designed as a shared initiative of two departments, present strikingly different patterns of cooperation in differing locations across the state. In Philadelphia, the fundamental organizational styles of the two departments interfere with effective collaboration.

Pennsylvania's Department of Labor and Industry, charged with administering overall WIA funds through local WIBs, was clearly more ideationally inclined toward an outcomes orientation. Interviews with local representatives indicated a clear understanding of a dual customer approach—employers on the one hand and potential employees on the other. They appeared to be able to interpret the demands of employers for a variety of basic skills, hard or soft, and translate this into a set of performance criteria for job training providers. The DPW, on the other hand, appears to be caught within a conflicting set of expectations. Given that the state's approach to welfare reform defined the issue of workforce development as one of "rapid attachment," performance goals for DPW revolved around getting Temporary Assistance for Needy Families (TANF) recipients placed, regardless of wages or long-term prospects.

Different policy goals, however, are not the only issue at hand. DPW has far more spatially dispersed operations; so much so that there are seventeen DPW offices within the city, each with a tradition of day-to-day operations within precisely defined catchment areas. Until the summer of 2002, there was only one "One-Stop" in Philadelphia; there are now three. The basic concept of a One-Stop Center with linked services and shared responsibilities—linking training, child care, literacy, and related workforce preparation and responding to a dual customer model (employer and job seeker)—is fundamentally at odds with the basic "Weltanschauung" or world view—of DPW.

It is not surprising that an agency that has a history of providing welfare benefits, and that had been pilloried as the major cause of the lack of attachment to the workforce by poor households, would have significant issues changing its organizational culture and its fundamental philosophy. Although this appeared to have slowed the development of the first One-Stop Center, many of the issues may have been the outgrowth of two entities that functioned within their own operational "silo."

COEXISTENCE OF PERFORMANCE AND TRADITIONAL
ALLOCATION CRITERIA

This one example of how performance expectations are differentially understood suggests that the emergence of a performance regime will, for the foreseeable future, occur in a framework of grudging coexistence. Interviews with key workforce development actors in both the public and

private sectors reveal that the intractability of traditional political allocation mechanisms is taken for granted. The entrenched nature of both state
and local decision-makers suggests that those championing a performance orientation have accepted the continuation of these mechanisms,
while creating a set of performance expectations inhering in many of the
recent assessments of the One-Stop Centers and job training contractors.
Standards based training programs have also developed in the customer
service and information technology sectors.

It should not be surprising to find that a significant disjuncture exists
regarding the emerging workforce development governance structures.
Even the basic framework of local WIBs in Pennsylvania reflects this pragmatic compromise. In the original plans for the state administration of
WIA funds, Pennsylvania was to be divided into regions. The combination of suburban antipathy to Philadelphia and pressure from the city's
political apparatus created a dedicated WIB for Philadelphia and regional
WIBs for the remainder of the state.

Considered in isolation from the operational details of both the local
WIB and the Philadelphia Workforce Development Corporation (PWDC),
this set-up could be interpreted as the triumph of the traditional regime
over performance expectations. In fact, both the Executive Director of the
WIB and a Vice-President of the PWDC have discussed how performance
expectations have managed to insert themselves into the highly politicized
atmosphere of Philadelphia's workforce development efforts. Sally Glickman, of the WIB, has focused on transforming the perception that the public system is limited to public welfare issues. Programmatically, this has
meant a focus on raising expectations of service provider performance.
Politically, it has meant trying to engage city government, in particular the
mayor's office, in making workforce development a primary means of
improving the tax base and the economic climate of the city.

PWDC faced significant internal inertia as it made the transition from
the role of providing demonstration and information brokering services
earlier in its history (as the Private Industry Council) to being the primary
conduit for developing performing workforce development projects.
Patrick Clancy, a Vice-President at PWDC, pointed to the often slow and
complex development of the One-Stop Centers in the city as an example
of how performance measures challenge traditional political culture, yet
can be introduced into the workforce development process. Although
many of the issues noted above have slowed the pace of this initiative,
Clancy suggested that the emergence of additional sites over the coming
years would be made easier by the experience gained working through the
combination of organizational differentials and political culture in establishing the first One-Stop Center.[8]

Although responding to state, and indirectly federal, initiatives, most local workforce efforts are mediated by the political culture of divided state and city agendas, with a priority interest in the politics of the local. Although funding might well be from extra-city sources, the hiring, firing and general oversight—including performance criteria—are driven by the exigencies of local politics. In addition, workforce development efforts that are rooted in federal and state oversight often overlap the rhetoric of job creation that has been developed in the economic development entities already found within the city governance structures (e.g., the City's Commerce Department, the Philadelphia Industrial Development Corporation, and the Philadelphia Commercial Development Corporation).

In some respect, the attention to outcomes in job training has its roots in the conditions attached to the funding streams for welfare-to-work.[9] In the five years since welfare reform, PWDC has become much more innovative in developing training approaches that link individual backgrounds to training and vocational placement needs. On a cautionary note, significant issues have arisen over the level of placement and long-term effectiveness of its "One-Stop" Center in Philadelphia—based on performance measures—and poorly integrated functions in the office. For many observers, the way in which parts of the city's former manpower training and other related programs were simply folded into the PWDC has created real impediments for its performance.

In many ways, PWDC can be seen as an exemplar of the ways in which traditional public services are offered against a competing approach based on performance assessment. Still to be explored are the implications of a mixed regime for the future of workforce development. When the "rubber meets the road" as it were, how do traditional political favoritism and a bottom-line approach to "doing the job" coexist? How does a governing coalition mediate contending metrics of performance and political reward?

CIVIC INTERMEDIARIES

Mixed regimes also characterize the efforts of civic intermediaries—organizations that mediate the gap between the public and private sector, and between city governance and specific geographic or interest-based communities. We have already seen how the work of two of these entities, GPF and the Regional Workforce Partnership, has helped shape the sectoral orientation of workforce development efforts in the city. In addition, they have developed several programs that have sought to develop prototypes of sectorally specific labor force development programs—GPF with hospitality and health care, and the Partnership with customer service and information technology training programs.

Other efforts worth mention are: The Latino Workforce Development Taskforce (LWDT) and TRF. LWDT has developed an analysis of the regional economy and its employment potential and barriers for the Latino community in the city and the region, and has developed a strong network of efforts focused on addressing workforce development issues that have arisen. TRF is the principal agent for the Philadelphia Jobs Initiative—one of the six sites selected by the Annie E. Casey Foundation (AECF) in 1995. In both organizations, it has been apparent that the focus on performance is a fundamental aspect of these two very different strategies, and that they have been forced to work within the constraints of the traditional political culture and allocation processes.

In the first case, LWDT combines representatives of community-based organizations, human service providers, staff members from the PWDC, and child care advocates who share an engagement with the specific issues facing Latino residents of the city. LWDT marked its third year of work in June 2002. It had created an analysis of specific workforce needs for the community and used that to develop a network of practitioners to carry out a variety of workforce goals: Literacy and education, accountability of public dollars in terms of Latino community outcomes, and linkage of child care needs to increased engagement with the labor force. As analysis gave way to programmatic development, it became almost second nature for attention to shift from developing "a program" to specifying outcomes—identifying who would participate, with what goals, and with what level of accountability.

TRF offers another example of performance-based decision-making, albeit not without caveats. TRF originated as the Delaware Valley Community Reinvestment Fund, capitalized in the mid-1980s with a foundation seed grant, a loan, and a social investment from a religious organization. The structure of the fund was what is now referred to as a Community Development Financial Intermediary (CDFI)—a financial investment group that attracts "deposits" and invests them in community projects. The distinguishing characteristic of TRF in its early years was its function to combine good investments with the necessary technical assistance to lower the risks of investments in what were widely regarded as risky neighborhoods.

As the Fund began to be more widely recognized for its efforts, it evolved a clearer focus on using a return on investment model that emphasized sound loans and low defaults. Until the Jobs Initiative effort, however, these were largely community revitalization projects that centered on housing and other physical aspects of the community, with some attention on small business development as well. At roughly the same time as AECF developed the Jobs Initiative funding opportunity, TRF had

124 DAVID W. BARTELT

begun to focus on the dilemma of rebuilding communities in the region, which faced stagnant or declining income and employment potential.

As funding efforts began focusing on outcomes, TRF positioned itself to be a reinvestment effort that explicitly valued performance. This did not happen without a sometimes wrenching adjustment by many community-based organizations, especially those who had an undifferentiated view of funding sources. In one key example linked to the Philadelphia Jobs Initiative (PJI), prior relationships with one of TRF's partners in a workforce development project may have contributed to a lack of focus on performance expectations by the community-based organization (CBO). The tradition of being funded on the basis of how many applications were processed drove the fundamental operations of this project, rather than focusing on the number of jobs obtained by community residents. Ultimately, the combination of staff misfeasance and lack of follow through in performance criteria led to the dissolution of the project, creating a significant disappointment in attempts to use a community base for workforce development.[10]

On other fronts, however, TRF has continued to focus on outcomes and impacts both in its Jobs Initiative activities and its other measures. By 2003, it will have an internal assessment process in place that will examine routinely the outcomes and impacts of its investments, incorporating this information in the ways in which it conducts its investments. Additionally, in a relatively nonpublic way, TRF has been instrumental in trying to reshape the housing and community development bureaucracy of the city, the structure of information services in the city government, and the ways in which human service and community revitalization planning might be better integrated.

SUMMARY

Regardless of organization or sector, the inertia of past systems and the emergence of a performance orientation can coexist, even within the same organization. The process of change is just a conceptual construct (i.e., performance vs. employment regimes), but one in which a contested terrain of political reward systems provides, in many instances, an overlay of performance expectations on reward systems. The results are often an amalgam of coexistence, reform, or some combination of the two. Given the entrenched nature of most political reward systems, this is hardly surprising. The issue may well be discovering the contexts within which performance paradigms are most likely to work, and examining the areas in which there are the greatest resistance to change. In the discussion that follows, this pragmatic coexistence has generated a variety of conversations that highlight the issues that are yet to be addressed.

WORKFORCE DEVELOPMENT CONVERSATIONS

To the extent that there is an emergent attempt at developing a performance regime in Philadelphia, it exists at the level of a series of conversations in a sociopolitical space that is both complex and segmented. Two images emerged in discussions about workforce development with several principal actors in the city and region. In one analogy, a leader in the field of welfare-to-work efforts compared the workforce development field to a bowl of spaghetti—many strands, in the same bowl, each entangled with the other but distinct, and with each one leading in a different direction. Another representative of one of the primary private-sector organizations engaging in the economic development of the city and the region made the argument that the assumption of bringing people to the table is problematic when there are "too many tables and too many cooks."

These images reflect some of the tone of interviews with leaders in the city's workforce development efforts. These discussions strongly indicate that there are multiple, simultaneous "conversations" taking place that do not always share common meanings or even terminology. To the extent that there is an identifiable set of performance-oriented political actors in place in Philadelphia, their relationship to existing political arrangements is one that is uneven and episodic. All people interviewed for this project noted, in one way or another, that workforce development often contends with stadium development and neighborhood blight in attempting to gain even a symbolic commitment from public- and private-sector leaders.

One of the inhibiting forces in discussions of workforce development policy is its link in the public's eyes to debates over performance systems in Philadelphia's school system. It highlights the somewhat fragile nature of performance-oriented leadership within the political culture of the city. Although the school system had implemented a measurement and resource allocation system beginning in the mid-1990s, the resignation of the superintendent after the election of Mayor Street in 2000 has raised questions about the longevity of such reforms. "Children Achieving," a mantra for the performance-driven school reforms of the past several years, has been replaced by administrative restructuring as the primary goal, accompanied by chronic budget shortfalls and eventually futile attempts at avoiding a state takeover.[11]

During the spring and summer of 2001, interviews with a series of key informants in the workforce development field were conducted. Additionally, extensive time was spent examining the operations of TRF, the Regional Workforce Partnership, and the LWDT, because of a prior working relationship between the author and these groups.[12] In processing these interviews, it became useful to treat them both as sources of information about various programs in economic development, but also as parts of an ongoing conversation in an ill-defined communication network. Thus, in addition to specific insights about the difficulties involved with generating effective (i.e., outcomes-based) workforce systems, we would submit that there are at least four separate "conversations" or narratives that can be identified as being simultaneously present in this relatively inchoate workforce development "system."

Above all, these conversations were conducted in a political culture that is grounded in a traditional allocation of public-sector "spoils," or less pejoratively, assets. As such, the discussions each came back, at one time or another, to the politics of turf and control. One of the signal aspects of these interviews was the one constant expressed by most of the interviewees—a largely pejorative tone toward other members of the workforce development system. Although the values held about workforce development were fairly diverse among the interviewees, the level of organizational entrepreneurship, for want of a better term, was high.

Consequently, these conversations rarely engaged one another directly. To paraphrase one person interviewed, it's not a problem of getting people around one table, it's the fact that its difficult to even get people engaging in the same limited conversation to get to a smaller table, or to recognize the legitimacy of the other conversations. The following conversations, then, reflect on the realities of how the political culture of specialization and fragmentation militates—at least at present—against a "pure" regime model.

To a striking degree, there are strong parallels between these conversations and some of the issues reported in the wider workforce literature. In a paradoxical fashion, the more that the leaders interviewed stressed the difficulties, if not the impossibility, of focused efforts at workforce systems change, the more they tended to reflect the loosely defined division of labor that is, ultimately, a promising prospect for future efforts at system development. This point is discussed further at the conclusion of this chapter.

Why then are these termed "conversations"? The separation and entrepreneurial assertiveness of these individuals does not obscure the fact that the interviews revealed a sense of potential dialogue—problem areas that have been arising in the development of a practical approach to workforce development that will result in a stronger labor force and better jobs for Philadelphians now at the margin of the labor force. These conversations are extracted from the interviews, and presented as a quasi-dialogue, representing different approaches to the issues that shape these conversations. At the end of these summaries, we will return to the problem of "bridging" these conversations.

A major focus among many employers is the lack of both basic and advanced skills in the manufacturing and information technology (IT) clusters, and to a significant extent in the retail sector. Both basic math and literacy skills are included in this discussion, as well as specific skills sets for the use of computer and computer-related equipment. The conversation that takes place here ranges from advocates for educational reform to the development of standards for training and educational programs to the development of effective adult and mid-work life programs.

A central issue here is the extent to which employer expectations can be identified for trial programs, and subsequently mainstreamed. A substantial element of pessimism concerning system change tends to focus these programs on achievable—and, accordingly, relatively small-scale goals. As a result, the extreme positions in these discussions are represented by those who dismiss small-scale programs as ineffective versus those who dismiss systems reform as ungrounded in experience.

Consider the following scenario. A leading advocate for customer service and IT training standards openly despairs of public-sector entities, such as the PWDC, as offices with no sense of what is needed in the workplace, and with a commitment to immediate placement numbers rather than labor market upgrading. Specifically, he points to the short time frame for training and the absence of support systems for people seeking to re-enter the labor force, or enter it for the first time. Alternatively, a representative of one of the major programs within PWDC is openly dismissive of the attempts of the Customer Service Training Collaborative, and of the efforts of this advocate, as being small scale and unable to generate significant change in workforce development.

On one level, of course, this can be read as a continuation of the "turf" tradition, as both entities are targeting scarce public-sector resources, as well as the needed participation of the private sector. In the back and forth of this discussion, system change—affecting significant changes in educational outcomes, or the development of post-adolescent labor force preparation for the increased skill level demanded by the labor market—can easily be relegated to a rhetorical touchstone rather than a shared component of the conversation.

It should be noted that this depiction of a polar opposition does not represent the entire conversation. The antipathy between these points, however, suggests that much of the discussion "at the table" of skill sets (leaving soft skills to its own discussion) is dominated by how to mesh the impatience of two different needs—the immediate need of the private sector for a skilled labor force and the public sector which is caught in its own dynamic of distributional balance, bureaucratic inertia, and the uncertainty of program development when effective models are not readily available.[13]

EMPLOYER SOFT SKILLS/CUSTOMER SERVICE CONVERSATION

As Holzer (1996) and Moss and Tilly (2001) have noted, the issue of soft skills training has several discussions embedded within it, and has an unavoidably subjective aspect included within it. A mixture of dress, decorum, timely job attendance, and deference to hierarchical work relationships is contained in most programs. The conversation on this topic suggests that two different issues divide participants. The first is one of priority: Does one first address hard skills or soft skills or does one attempt comprehensive skill development? The second issue is one of outcomes—given the significant behavioral shifts that are being advocated in many soft skills training programs, what are the likely outcomes that will reinforce these changes?

It appears to be in the soft skills conversation that the welfare-to-work debate over rapid attachment versus training supports has surfaced and generalized. AECF has emphasized and re-emphasized the need for jobs with sustainable income. Others have emphasized the need to get people into the workforce, considering income advancement as a byproduct of these efforts. In the conversations that we have seen, the issue of soft skills is often a marker for this larger agenda—longer-term training and employee development programs that include social supports for behavioral change versus job placement.

The literature at the national level suggests that the soft skills debate often masks cultural frictions and the contested nature of many "shop floor" relationships, especially when racial differences are involved. Moss and Tilly (2001, 247–248) found that about half of employers criticized black workers' hard or soft skills as well as their work ethic, and that they, in turn, blamed this on single motherhood, welfare dependency, or the inner-city environment—including public schools. Soft skills training discussions begin with this difficult reality: The attitudes at the workplace must often be overcome by the potential employee, and may be very resistant to change. Low-wage employers are reported to have positive views of immigrants and African Americans, salute the willingness of these workers to settle for less, and simultaneously expect the workers to have good soft skills, whereas "managers. . . tend to offer low end jobs that induce poorer work habits" (247). In addition, "customer racial biases appear to dampen the willingness of employers to hire blacks as well" (247). Finally, employers tend to have a view of workers from the inner city that appears to overlay a racialized and stereotypical view of the inner city on the hiring process (Tilly et al., 2001).

In Philadelphia, the conversations we have heard contain each of these elements—a debate over the priority of soft and hard skills that has been "resolved" by citing their interdependency; accepting the problematic nature of the city's labor force as a given among many employers; and looking to the potential employee as the source of change. Among those who would contribute an alternative perspective is the PJI, whose efforts to strengthen human resource components of small- to medium-sized businesses, and to facilitate new firm development within the city that are linked to workforce development to address this issue in a more complex fashion.

Despite the presence of several voices, the issue of the subjectivity and potentially divisive aspects of the soft skills discussion remains largely subterranean. It is not clear that a direct conversation can be had, but it is clear that the voices suggested by Moss and Tilly are present in the workforce system of the city.

WELFARE AND DEPENDENCY

Welfare-to-work contains a serious disconnected conversation between those building opportunity structures and those who are continuing the battle against welfare dependency, essentially a punitive model. To some extent, this discussion overlaps the soft skills conversation, but it is very specifically applied to single women with children. In the aftermath of welfare reform, this conversation has faded, and the concern with long-term employment and child-rearing issues is now a footnote to basic questions of: (1) whether an economic downturn will drive more people back toward welfare; (2) what the end of the original legislation will mean for the current system; and (3) whether effective, flexible supports will be generated from the welfare savings that Pennsylvania has generated (as in the Wisconsin Works model).[14]

These conversations have the effect of shifting the focus of the post-welfare framework from one of workforce development to a more disconnected welfare reform debate. In essence, the programmatic inertia—what several interviewees referred to as the "policy silo" framework—of welfare and associated family service supports is self-consciously embarked on reform. At their best, these agencies recognize the need for a more systematic approach; the Commissioner of Human Services suggests that the One-Stop Centers are more accurately called strip malls—choose the wrong store and you're stuck with what they are selling.

Many within the private sector, however, see these reforms as lacking credibility. One interviewee termed them the "mud" in the system. A disjuncture exists between at least three major themes. Advocates for workforce development constructed around family sustaining income goals, including support services that facilitate such employment, articulate the real possibility that entrenched policy/programmatic inertia will be unable to meet the needs of those seeking to engage the labor market. By contrast, antipathy toward the public sector makes direct conversation about restructuring human and family services very difficult, especially in the politically hostile context between Philadelphia and the Commonwealth of Pennsylvania. Finally, there are those who are primarily wedded to a belief that more resources committed to existing public-sector efforts will be sufficient to supplement the efforts of TANF recipients to link with the labor force.

As the 2002 legislative endpoint to the original TANF legislation nears, and the likelihood that the issue of rapid attachment versus training plus support systems begins to play itself out, there appears little present confidence that a more robust system will be developed in Pennsylvania. Although there have been significant efforts in the past to link employers with service providers to affect legislation,[15] it is unclear whether current conversational rhetoric will allow for a renewal of this coalition.

COMMUNITY DEVELOPMENT

The AECF Jobs Initiative was rooted in a community development discussion that recognized the limits of the traditional Community Development Corporation (CDC) model. In Philadelphia, it is apparent that many CBOs have now become so legitimized by their longevity and success that they were seen by many of those interviewed as being a component of the employment regime model, a part of the "spoils" system—albeit in the face of a declining pot of spoils. The experiences of TRF with the CBO that was the neighborhood intermediary for the Jobs Initiative suggests— staff issues aside—that there is a persistent difficulty of twin conversations within the CBO community, namely, organizational survival tied to a flow of funds and a growing sense that funders are looking for tangible outcomes. This dual mission appears to be a difficult one that inhibits the capacity to effect community economic development through workforce development.

Not surprisingly, many CBOs arose—and continue to develop—out of a concern for distributive justice, either in a global sense of social justice or in a narrow sense of getting one's "fair" share. As has been noted in some of the literature that formed the background of the AECF initiative (Plastrik, with Taylor, 2001; Giloth, 2000; Giloth and Philips, 2000),

CBOs are often fiscally, organizationally, and constituency challenged by the expectations attendant to performance-driven funding.

The experiences of community development entities in Philadelphia (as elsewhere) reflect and resonate with political district concerns, as many CBOs have evolved into political support associations resembling both partisan ward organizations and "consultants" who expect contracts and grants as a normal aspect of their operation. In effect, the CBO movement and those organizations addressing the larger "civic good" form a "call and response" narrative conversation with each other, while each seeks access to or participation in the political regime of the city. As each group bemoans the other's excesses, the conversation shifts focus from potential system reform to seeking influence with an existing regime.

BRIDGING CONVERSATIONS: ROOTS OF A PERFORMANCE REGIME?

Despite the issues that apparently divide workforce development practitioners, it is clear that performance criteria are key elements for each person interviewed, and, to some extent, for their organizations as well. Performance and outcomes are seen as driving forces for effective workforce development. Disagreement existed over what these outcomes should be, and who should assess the outcomes. These issues of cross-organizational legitimacy are at the heart of debates about whether a performance-based public–private coalition will be realized in Philadelphia.

Regimes vary in their ability to coalesce around issues, in the extent of their fragmentation, and in their internal structures. All governing regimes have certain features in common: Local decision-makers share, at least loosely, a set of organizational and interpersonal orbits; provide inputs to policy and affect policy outputs; and typically, link business, political, and cultural leadership. They are, however, also somewhat unique, because they are also subject to the social and organizational dynamics of place, history, and the local economic and political structures within which they operate.

What this examination of workforce development in Philadelphia suggests is yet a further distinction—between regimes that are relatively coherent and unfragmented as they conduct themselves and those that are too loosely configured, too limited in their scope, or too divided in their institutional roots to respond effectively to certain issues. The inability of Philadelphia's governing coalition appears organizationally unable—and we agree with Hill and Nowak that this is not limited to Philadelphia—to address the pressing needs of workforce development and, for that matter, of a broader economic revitalization of the city.

Indeed, what Philadelphia may be experiencing is a formally identified regime that has limited effectiveness. Governance in the city is uneven, even prismatic—with some facets performing adequately while others simply fail. The consensus that exists is "deal oriented"—temporary consensus around limited goals with little in the way of outcomes assessment. Nonregime governance is characterized by its prismatic, multifaceted character, and deal-oriented temporary consensus.

It is apparent that the central missing ingredient cited by a majority of the people interviewed was what might be termed "regime authority." In most discussions of political regimes, one is struck by the ways in which the culture of the deal is subsumed by a somewhat transcendent purpose—a set of political goals that reflect a more generic ideology of a "public interest." Although contending visions of that public interest are inevitable, it is this aspect of a regime that appeared lacking in our discussions with workforce development leaders. Our informants cited an absence of leadership and passion, too many vested interests, inertia, bureaucracy, too many disarticulated subsystems, linking performance objectives to a greater agenda, lack of communication among elected leaders—especially the mayor—and workforce initiatives, and a general sense of the incoherence of workforce development as a whole.

If we consider this local context with performance regimes in mind, we face some basic issues in the Philadelphia case: Are the preconditions for a regime present? Can, or will performance-driven regimes emerge from the disarticulated conversational milieu we have described? On one level, the notion of a private-sector reengagement with public-sector decision-making and independent-sector involvement can be read as the desire for a new entity to emerge that will subsume the best of current efforts. What these conversations also reveal, however, is a large number of people and organizations who are experienced in workforce development, but lacking some form of organized response to the incoherence of the current situation.

CAVEATS, CONCERNS, AND IMPLICATIONS

Several questions have begun to emerge from the analysis about the larger issue of workforce systems change. First, how do we think of the concept of regime and regime change when the evidence suggests that the existing "employment regime" is disjointed and has multiple constituencies that create a powerful sense of inertia? Employment opportunities in minimally accountable public-sector programs are one of the defining aspects of the current regime—in both its governmental and other (private and independent sector) arenas. It is also apparent that the disjuncture between the heavily specialized and isolated departments in city government makes the very concept of a "regime" problematic. Put differently, can we reasonably speak of a regime when a significant paralysis strikes many as the defining nature of city governments, including (especially?) Philadelphia?

A second question is one linked to the concept of performance. It is evident that the private sector is no longer willing to accept simple program completion as a marker for entrance into the labor market. The insistence on performance measures is thus a natural extension of funding allocations based on whether programs actually prepare people for the workplace and deliver them with both hard and soft skills. This natural attraction of performance measures to workforce participation encourages us to look to the way in which a movement to standards has generated new ways of approaching the assessment and restructuring of public education.

One of the persistent issues faced by workforce development organizations, however, is the difficulty in developing a set of standards that will actually impact on employers in ways that will generate stronger outcomes. In this context, the issue of the regime paradigm needs to be addressed from a more pragmatic, or applied, perspective. The roots of this discussion lie in the potential of applying a performance orientation to the issue of municipal regimes in the arena of workforce development—specifically on the likelihood that the performance orientation of workforce system change will be reflected in a new form of urban regime.

When we examine a public-sector entity for which there are demonstrated outcomes that can be referred to for guidance, education is one area that is usually mentioned. Schools are hierarchical organizations that have a tradition of testing and assessment built into the culture. Although using performance as a criterion for differential funding and investments may be a shift in the resource allocation model, educational outcomes themselves have a performance assessment built in. The major task remaining is to use these assessments—or a set of outcomes that are comparable across schools—to guide the resource allocation discussion. Although it is true that one of the most important aspects of the systems reform effort in Philadelphia is the development of similar standards in both the customer service and IT fields, these have been very difficult discussions in which to engage recurring private-sector participation, let alone "buy-in."

Schools also have both the burden and the facilitating force of being place bound. If they are interested in dealing effectively with diminished resources and increased educational challenges, they virtually will be compelled to develop some way to assess effectiveness. In the employment sector, although there is some concern with the nature of the workforce, this is accentuated in firms that are place bound—albeit probably not as much as schools. This is not to discredit the use of the concept, but to begin the discussion of how the two arenas differ, and further, how performance criteria will require a shift in how employers think about their involvement with workforce development issues.

It is also the case that education is an example of a direct service delivery that is highly structured by legislation and oversight, with clear lines of authority that are often attached to control over resources. There is both power and authority deeply embedded in the delivery of educational services, and although performance measures change the decision criteria for resources—and by extension, the way in which education happens—there appears to be no similar model at work within the private-sector world of employers. Regime shifts, if they occur in workforce development, require building new structures in which highly individualized, profit-maximizing firms recognize both short- and long-term benefits by restructuring the governance of workforce development.

Finally, as the process of performance and employment perspectives manage their uneasy coexistence in the contested terrain of Philadelphia politics, I am reminded of Sam Warner's analysis of another model—the private city (Warner, 1968). In many ways, the pattern of workforce development that is taking place is reminiscent of the vision of Philadelphia as city with a public government and a private world, within which the divisions and shifts in emphasis are being worked through. In this world in contemporary Philadelphia, I would suggest that there is indeed an uncertain set of contending forces, one marked by inertial "turf protecting" behavior, whereas another attempts to resolve city issues by insisting on competence and performance.

The issues facing the development of performance regimes in Philadelphia are thus both conceptual and substantive. Does the concept of a performance regime "fit" within the conceptual framework of regimes, particularly limited, less effective regimes from which major players routinely distance themselves? And, at a substantive level, with strong divisions in the conversations surrounding workforce development—and which we take as indicative of similar divisions in other policy arenas—what sociopolitical shift will be needed to alter the current situation?

NOTES

1. This phrase is meant to capture the ways in which communities with different histories "lash together" a range of political, cultural, and social institutional mechanisms for adapting to economic and environmental forces impinging

on them. In their case study of two communities located in close proximity to one another, quite different adaptive responses emerge to an economic/environmental challenge.

2. In Philadelphia, this can be traced back to Mayor Vaux's use of a municipal police force as an employment measure for Irish voters who provided his margin of victory in 1844; later traced through such colorful local characters as Boies Penrose, Barney Samuels, and Frank Rizzo.

3. In a personal interview, Nowak is far more pointed about the prospects for change and establishing a system that is based on achieving significant employment change. His insights are incorporated in the section on "conversations."

4. The classification of these firms is based on the North American Industrial Classification System (NAICS), a replacement of the earlier Standard Industrial Codes (SIC). An Appendix contains the specific NAICS and SIC codes used in the analyses presented in this section.

5. Using these data, it is not possible to determine whether these were full- or part-time employees.

6. Greater Philadelphia First, *Regional Economic Benchmarks*, Philadelphia 1999: Performance indicators were developed based on this report with the intention of highlighting the issues that are important for workforce development by the Regional Workforce Partnership (2000) (with TRF and the Pennsylvania Economy League).

7. Although it cannot be reproduced here, it is available upon request from TRF, or via their website. See "The Workforce Investment System in Pennsylvania: A Summary," included in "Workforce and Economic Development in Pennsylvania," Philadelphia: The Reinvestment Fund, 2002; available online at www.trfund.com/pdf/chart.pdf.

8. This interview was conducted in the summer of 2001; since that time, two additional One-Stop Centers have been opened.

9. This has not been without controversy, as the original outcome measures were simply put—reduce the number of women on welfare and increase the number of women in jobs, regardless of the wage levels or sustainability of such jobs. This was complicated by a fairly traditional approach to welfare trimming by the Pennsylvania legislature, despite financial savings and alternative program proposals (i.e., community college and other educational programs).

10. This is an issue faced in many different cities and with most CBOs whose origins involved fewer performance expectations. See Giloth and Phillips, 2000; Plastrik and Taylor, 2001; Abt Associates, 2000.

11. At the end of 2001, the School District of Philadelphia was removed from oversight by the Board of Education (a mayorally appointed body) and placed under the supervision of an interim board that was appointed jointly by the governor and the mayor. The new governing board, the School Reform Commission, has essentially "triaged" the District's schools, placing poorly performing schools under new management, leaving the bulk of the remainder under the District's supervision, but with far greater standardization of curriculum. The already well-performing schools have been largely left alone. While performance criteria are evident, they remain unlinked, for the most part, to workforce development.

12. All Jobs Initiative sites have a local research liaison, a role that I have played since the outset of the project. The Regional Workforce Partnership is located at TRF; the Latino Workforce Development Taskforce engaged me to prepare a report on the Latino community in Philadelphia, and I have been a participant in their monthly meetings for the past two years. Among other things, these working relationships complemented the formal interviews, which were conducted with the following people: Jeremy Nowak, Executive Director, The Reinvestment Fund; Fred Dedrick, Director, Regional Workforce Partnership; Alba Martinez, head of Philadelphia's Department of Human Services and co-chair of the LWDT; David Lacey, Vice President for Human Resources, Technitrol and former director of the Private Industry Council; Ira Harkavy, Associate Vice President and Director, Center for Community Partnerships, University of Pennsylvania; David Thornburgh, Executive Director of the Pennsylvania Economy League, Eastern Region; Sally Glickman, Executive Director, Philadelphia Workforce Investment Board; Harley Etienne, for Sam Katz, Greater Philadelphia First; Carol Goertzel, Executive Director, Women's Association for Women's Alternatives; Cheryl Weiss, Executive Director, 21st Century League; Gail Zuckerman, Director of Workforce Readiness, JEVS; Patrick Clancy, Vice President, Philadelphia Workforce Development Council; and Mary Jane Clancy, School District of Philadelphia.

13. Two discussions of the limits of the regime model in dealing with different dimensions of these divisions can be found in Bachelor (1994) and Miranda and Tunyavong (1994).

14. The most recent issue of the *Brookings Review*, Summer 2001, contains elaborations of these conversations at the national level.

15. The predecessor organization to the Regional Workforce Partnership, the Philadelphia Jobs Network, led a strong effort to broaden state job training definitions and to effectively broaden the support categories. It was notable for the ways in which employers and human service organizations found common ground.

REFERENCES

Abt Associates. 2000. *AECF Jobs Initiative: Evaluation Report on the Capacity Development Phase* (March 1997–March 2000). Cambridge, MA: Abt Associates.

Adams, Carolyn. 2001. *The City and the State* (draft). Philadelphia: Temple University Department of Geography and Urban Studies.

Adams, Carolyn, David Bartelt, David Elesh, Ira Goldstein, Nancy Kleniewski, and William Yancey. 1991. *Philadelphia: Neighborhoods, Division and Conflict in a Postindustrial City*. Philadelphia: Temple University Press.

Bachelor, Lynn. 1994. "Regime Maintenance, Solution Sets and Urban economic Development." *Urban Affairs Quarterly* 29:596–616.

Frug, Gerald. 1999. *City Making: Building Communities Without Building Walls*. Princeton: Princeton University Press.

Giloth, Robert. 2000. "Learning from the Field: Economic Development and

Workforce Development in the 1990s." *Economic Development Quarterly* 14:340–359.

Giloth, Robert, and William Phillips. 2000. *Getting Results: Outcomes Management and the Annie E. Casey Foundation Jobs Initiative*. Baltimore: Annie E. Casey Foundation.

Greater Philadelphia First. 1999. *Regional Economic Benchmarks*. Philadelphia: Greater Philadelphia First.

Hill, Edward W., and Jeremy Nowak. 2000. "Nothing Left to Lose." *Brookings Review* 18(3):22–26.

Holzer, Harry. 1996. *What Employers Want: Job Prospects for Less-Educated Workers*, 127–129. New York: Russell Sage Foundation.

Julian J. Studley, Inc. 2000. "The Quarterly Studley Report." Philadelphia: Julian Studley, Inc. (2nd Quarter). Available at www.studleyreport.com.

Kromer, John. 2000. *Neighborhood Recovery*. New Brunswick, NJ: Rutgers University Press.

Miranda, Rowan, and Ittipone Tunyavong. 1994. "Patterned Inequality: Reexamining the Role of Distributive Politics in Urban Service Delivery." *Urban Affairs Quarterly* 29:509–534.

Molotch, Harvey, William Freudenberg, and Krista Paulsen. 2000. "History Repeats Itself, But How? City Character, Urban Tradition, and the Accomplishment of Place." *American Sociological Review* 65:791–823.

Moss, Philip, and Chris Tilly. 2001. *Stories Employers Tell: Race, Skill and Hiring in America*, 245–248. New York: Russell Sage Foundation.

National Governors' Association. 2001. *Transforming State Workforce Development Systems: Case Studies of Five Leading States*. Washington, DC: National Governors' Association.

Orfield, Myron. 2001. *American Metropolitics*. Washington, DC: Brookings.

Philadelphia Workforce Investment Board. 1999. Required Contributors to the Workforce Investment System through CareerLink. Updated 2001.

Plastrik, Peter, with Judith Combes Taylor. 2001. *Responding to a Changing Labor Market: The Challenges for Community-Based Organizations*. Boston: Jobs for the Future.

Regional Workforce Partnership, with the Reinvestment Fund and the Pennsylvania Economy League. 2000. *Workforce 2000*. Philadelphia: Regional Workforce Partnership.

Reinvestment Fund. 2002. "The Workforce Investment System in Pennsylvania: A Summary." In *Workforce and Economic Development in Pennsylvania*. Philadelphia: The Reinvestment Fund. Available at www.trfund.com/pdf/chart.pdf.

Rusk, David. 1999. *Inside Game, Outside Game*. Washington, DC: Brookings.

Tilly, Chris, Philip Moss, Joleen Kirschenman, and Ivy Kenelly. 2001. "Space as Signal: How Employers Perceive Neighborhoods in Four Metropolitan Labor Markets." In *Urban Inequality: Evidence from Four Cities*, edited by Alice O'Connor, Chris Tilly, and Lawrence D. Bobo, 304–338. New York: Russell Sage Foundation.

U.S. Bureau of the Census. 1992. *County Business Patterns*. Washington, DC: U.S. Bureau of the Census. CD-ROM.

U.S. Bureau of the Census. 1998. *County Business Patterns Zip Code File.* Washington, DC: U.S. Bureau of the Census. CD-ROM.

U.S. Bureau of the Census. 2000. *County Business Patterns.* Washington, DC: U.S. Bureau of the Census. CD-ROM.

U.S. Department of Labor. 2000. "PLS-3748: Philadelphia Area Added Nearly 39,000 Jobs since Fourth Quarter 1998." (April 10).

Warner, Sam Bass. 1968. *The Private City.* Philadelphia: University of Pennsylvania.

APPENDIX

Figure 4.4   Required Contributors to the Workforce Investment System through CareerLink
Bold text indicates the funding stream name; the first paragraph of text defines the purpose; the second paragraph of text defines the amount of contribution; the third paragraph of text defines the administrative details. "Contributions" to CareerLink are mandated under the Workforce Investment Act. The Act is silent on substantial public and private workforce development investments, including: (1) The private sector, foundations, or other substantial investors in workforce development-related activities; (2) public funding streams that provide important ancillary services for employment retention (such as investments by the Department of Health and Human Services, the Department of Justice, etc.; (3) major investments in primary, secondary, and post-secondary education; (4) discretionary grants from public funding streams; and (5) state and federal economic development resources.
SOURCE: Adapted from Philadelphia Workforce Investment Board (1999).

Philadelphia

WIA TITLE I

Train adults, dislocated workers, and low-income youth for jobs in the local economy; place and retain target populations in jobs; invest in CareerLink infrastructure

Approximately $17 million annually

Administered by the Philadelphia Workforce Development Corporation for the City of Philadelphia

---

VETERANS' EMPLOYMENT AND TRAINING

Provide employment and training services to Veterans

Approximately $630,000, which supports nine professionals to work with Philadelphia-based customers

Resources are state-administered by the Department of Labor and Industry, Bureau of Employer and Career Services.

U.S. DOL WELFARE-TO-WORK

Connect 7,500 "hard-to-serve" long-termTANF recipients to the labor force and provide retention services for one year

Approximately $26 million annually through 2001; $2 million remaining as of 12/2001

Administered by the Philadelphia. Workforce Development Corporation for the City of Philadelphia

---

WAGNER-PEYSER

Train adults, dislocated workers, and low income; provide public labor exchange services to all customers

State resources fund 51 professionals (projected to rise to 80 in 2002) to work with Philadelphia-based customers, as well as the development of technology-based service tools.

Resources are state-administered by the Department of Labor and Industry, Bureau of Employer and Career Services.

TRADE ADJUSTMENT ASSISTANCE

Support retraining for workers who lose their jobs due to the increased import of goods

State resources fund two professionals to work with Philadelphia-based customers.

Resources are state-administered by the Department of Labor and Industry, Bureau of Employer and Career Services.

VOCATIONAL REHABILITATION

Assist individuals with disabilities to obtain and sustain a job.

Approximately $6 million annually

Resources are state-administered by the Department of Labor and Industry, Office of Vocational Rehabilitation.

TITLE V, OLDER AMERICANS ACT

Create jobs for senior citizens in public and community service organizations

Approximately $980,000 annually

Funds are administered locally by the Mayor's Commission on Aging.

COMMUNITY SERVICES BLOCK GRANTS

Provide services, including literacy classes, job training, and community organizing, for low-income residents.

Approximately $3.5 million annually

Funds are administered locally through the Mayor's Office of Community Services

---

HUD EMPLOYMENT AND TRAINING

17 separate funding streams are under the HUD E&T umbrella targeted to youth and adult residents of public, transitional, and Section 8 housing. Most programs complement employment and training activities with other services, such as economic and community development.

Estimated at $100 million annually

Funds are awarded by the Federal Department of Housing and Urban Development directly to local nonprofit providers, public housing authorities, private owners of subsidized housing, and the City of Philadelphia.

ADULT EDUCATION AND LITERACY

Provide services that assist adults to (1) become literate and gain the knowledge and skills necessary to obtain employment and self-sufficiency; (2) become full partners in the education of their children; and (3) complete secondary education

Approximately $3.4 million annually

Funds are granted by the Pennsylvania Department of Education to dozens of local providers. Local efforts to coordinate these programs are spearheaded by the Mayor's Commission on Literacy.

POST-SECONDARY VOCATIONAL EDUCATION

Ensure secondary and post-secondary students who enroll in vocational or technical education programs acquire the skills they need to succeed in their chosen industry.

Approximately $8.5 million annually

Funds are awarded by the Pennsylvania Department of Education to a handful of local providers. The largest local recipients of these funds are the Community College of Philadelphia and the School District of Philadelphia.

STEVEN RATHGEB SMITH & SUSAN DAVIS

5   Workforce Systems Change in Seattle

SINCE THE 1960s, a succession of job training and workforce development initiatives for the disadvantaged has been put in place: Manpower, the Comprehensive Employment and Training Act (CETA), the Job Training and Partnership Act (JTPA), and the Workforce Investment Act (WIA). At the same time, the overall structure of public services for the poor and disadvantaged has been fundamentally restructured. Community-based service agencies have grown dramatically in number and diversity of service orientation over the past thirty years (Smith and Lipsky, 1993). Public agencies at the state and local level were split and reorganized so that by the early 1990s, separate agencies for income maintenance, child welfare, job training, and community and economic development were often the norm in many states. A set of diversified local municipal agencies responsible for helping the disadvantaged further complicated the overall service system.

As this service system was becoming more fragmented and complex, expectations on the performance of job training programs—and services in general—have become much higher. The JTPA of the 1980s implemented a variety of measures to push greater performance among job training programs. But it was widely regarded as a worthwhile attempt that fell substantially short of its goal of improving job training services. Part of the problem was the isolation of the JTPA-funded programs. Service agencies received contract funds and placed workers; however, there was little incentive for service providers to develop ongoing linkages and relationships with other service agencies, private businesses, or other public agencies responsible for the disadvantaged. Indeed, many agencies competed for funds and clients rather than cooperated. Furthermore, JTPA encouraged a very narrow approach to job training that did not fully appreciate the embeddedness of an individual trainee within his or her community. The importance of community ties was also reinforced and underscored by Robert Putnam's (1993) work on social capital. Putnam stressed the linkage between levels of social capital in a community and effective governmental performance. This theme is also echoed in the work of Lisbeth Schorr (1997) on effective social programs.

Compounding these problems in the delivery of services were changes in the labor market including: The increased geographic separation between many disadvantaged workers and potential jobs, the decline of many manufacturing firms, and the growing diversity of the disadvantaged workforce.

These changes in the labor market meant that the fragmented, disjointed service system was even more unsuited for effective performance than in the past. In response, a consensus emerged that effective workforce systems were based on collaborative productive relationships between government, nonprofit service providers, and business, and on a transparent system of services based on outcomes (Jobs for the Future, 1999; Giloth, 2000). Services needed better integration and a much better match was required between the job seeker and potential employers. Helping to provide this match would be third party public and private intermediaries such as community-based service organizations or new coordinating entities. Although a consensus emerged throughout the country among policymakers and scholars on this new approach, significant barriers to its full achievement exist. Yet, indicators of success in the creation of this type of system are developing, offering real prospects for fundamental changes to workforce development systems.

This chapter focuses on the reform of workforce systems in Seattle since the early 1990s, and major public and private efforts to develop more effective, integrated workforce systems. An important player in this change effort is the Seattle Jobs Initiative (SJI); however, many other players exist, including the Seattle King County Workforce Development Council (SKCWD) and state and local agencies, especially those agencies involved with the implementation of welfare reform. An additional player whose role has changed is private business. The importance of involvement from business and industry has been emphasized through the structure of workforce investment boards as well as funding changes that have put the onus on private business to fund services previously provided by public agencies. In the current atmosphere of reformed job training programs, the responsibility for creating innovative programs for low-wage, low-skilled workers has fallen heavily toward the public sector, with not nearly enough deep-seated commitment from private business.

POLICY IMPLEMENTATION AND SOCIAL REFORM

Research on social reform since the 1960s suggests that many well-intentioned social reforms, in particular the federal initiatives of the 1960s, failed to realize their goals because of entrenched political interests and the complexity of changing organizational and individual behavior (Pressman and Wildavsky, 1983; Pressman, 1975; Bardach, 1977; Marris and Rein, 1982; Stone, 1999). Morone (1990) also observed that we as a society tend to have unrealistic expectations about community, leading us to underestimate the differences and political factions at the local level.

The theme of this implementation literature, especially the work focusing on the social reform programs of the 1960s, is one of an enduring pessimism that meaningful change can occur. This generally gloomy assessment tends to be contradicted, however, by the tremendous dynamism in the service system and the accumulating list of effective program examples (Schorr, 1997). Services have changed, sometimes quite dramatically, in recent years and there is a growing recognition that the reasons for the failures of earlier reforms were related in part to the "silo" mentality of many programs so that the needed linkages between job training and economic development programs did not exist. Moreover, successful change was possible if the necessary "buy-in" was obtained from the key local public and private elites who controlled the workforce development service system. Workforce intermediaries could help achieve both goals by facilitating the integration of services and promoting local political support for improved services.

Another key lesson from the reforms of the 1960s and thereafter was that many reforms failed to achieve their goals because they were essentially "parachuted" into a community. The federal government would issue a Request for Proposal, and local governments or community agencies would respond because of the attraction of new monies. The grant would be awarded even though substantial, broad-based community support for the new program might have been lacking. The grant monies would be expended, and the program would end with nothing substantially changed in the community—the pre-existing competitive relationships among providers continued and other potential stakeholders such as private business remained uninvolved. Many communities were jaded by the succession of initiatives that failed to alter fundamentally the way services were provided or to achieve program goals.

Two conclusions have flowed from this reaction against the "top-down" programmatic approach. Pressman (1975) argued policy implementation needed to be approached like political development, with a keen appreciation for the local political context; if successful reform was to occur, then policymakers need to proactively create new political relationships and centers of influence. In short, successful social reform depended upon the institutional and political context.

Second, effective reform was also more likely to be a product of good leaders at the local level who engaged various public and private entities in creative problem solving. Solving the problem of workforce systems will be different in Seattle than it will be in Milwaukee. This emphasis on local problem solving and collaborative engagement also fits with the latest thinking in public and private management that emphasizes teamwork, continuous learning, and collaboration as strategies to effective organizational performance (Katzenbach and Smith, 1999; Cohen and Eimicke, 1998; Kotter, 1996; Senge, 1990).

The implication of this perspective is that reform is more contingent and unpredictable. The top-down, programmatic approach was undergirded by a presumption that policymakers could design programs in a way that ensured their successful implementation. It was also a view that regarded program design as important in capturing the "will of the people" as indicated through their representatives and administrators (see Mazmanian and Sabatier, 1983). But the implication of a more locally-based initiative is that the specific design of the program or reform will be decided at the community level.

This community-based approach tends to conceptualize the purposes of social reform in quite different terms. The problem with many government-funded social programs, including many workforce training programs, was that they tended to create new programs without really changing the structure of services or the overall system of workforce training programs in a local community. A major assumption of this alternative approach to reform is that effective programs require a fundamental reform of the local service system. This means changing relationships among public, nonprofit, and for-profit organizations, and revamping the power and influence of key stakeholders. It also requires changing existing funding streams to allow improved coordination and integration of services (see Giloth, 2000; Stone, 1999).

But simply creating more cooperation or forging new relationships is not enough either. Locally-developed performance measures designed to guide these new relationships and the systems change, in general, are essential if the reform initiative is to stay on track. Thus, systems change approaches the community comprehensively. Building social capital is complemented with a results orientation.

This overall conceptual framework, then, informed our study. Jettisoning the old programmatic, top-down model seems like a good idea, given the implementation problems of the past; however, what are the possibilities and impediments to this new community-based approach whose stated purpose is systems change? Can new entities, including third-party intermediaries successfully achieve social reform?

The focus of our study is the transformation of workforce systems in the Seattle, Washington region during the past several years, with a particular focus on King County, the county that includes Seattle. This city and region are an interesting and very useful site within which to study workforce systems change. In recent years, the area has grown rapidly in terms of population and jobs. In particular, the population of King County grew from 1,507,305 in 1990 to 1,737,034 in 2000—a 15.2 percent increase. During the same time period, the civilian labor force in King County as a whole grew from 869,700 to 1,023,200—almost 18 percent; the civilian labor force was only 683,000 in 1980. In general, the city of Seattle comprises about one-third of King County in terms of population and civilian labor force—approximately 525,000 and 316,000 in 2000, respectively) (Washington State Department of Employment Security Department, 2002a; U.S. Bureau of the Census, 2002a, 2002b).

In the 1990s, considerable change also occurred in the location of people in poverty in the Seattle–King County area. During this time, the fastest poverty growth rate was in King County, outside of Seattle. The number of people below the poverty line in Seattle stayed relatively the same from 1990 to 2000—approximately, 60,000—but increased by 40 percent in the rest of King County to over 78,500. This increase marked the first time that the Census had found more poor people outside of Seattle. Poverty rates increased most dramatically in South King County where housing is much cheaper than in Seattle (Eskenazi and Mayo, 2002a). South King County is also home to a large and rapidly growing immigrant population (Eskenazi, 2001). For example, in the town of Tukwila in 1990, one in fourteen residents were foreign born. By 2000, the number of foreign-born residents had jumped to one in four (Eskenazi and Mayo, 2002b). The number of foreign born in Seattle was substantially less. More generally, Seattle, with about one-third of its population from a minority group, ranks last among the top twenty-five largest U.S. cities in the percentage of minorities. Reflecting the high cost of housing and other social and demographic trends, Seattle has the fewest residents under of the age of eighteen of any other top-25 city except San Francisco (Eskenazi, Mayo, and Boyer, 2001).

Until recently, job growth was increasing sharply in the service sector, reflecting the boom in tourism and the retail industry in the Seattle–King County area. For example, employment in the service sector grew from 242,000 in 1990 to 360,600 in 2000 in King County. By contrast, the role of manufacturing declined from 170,500 in 1990 to 152,800 in 2000 (WA State Department of Employment Security, 2002c). A disproportionate amount of this decline was due to the exodus of manufacturing jobs from the city of Seattle. The U.S. Bureau of the Census (2002b) estimated that only about 25,000 manufacturing jobs existed in Seattle in 2000. With the dot-com bust, the rapid rise in job growth has slowed significantly, especially in high-tech fields. However, the Washington State Department of Employment Security still estimates that there will be continued healthy demand for people in high-tech occupations such as engineers and computer programmers and technicians. Demand in the service sector should also continue at a fairly robust rate (Washington State Department of Employment Security Department, 2002a, 2002b).

In short, Seattle is a large city in the midst of a large county, but it is also not so diverse nor impoverished that systems change through new community-based initiatives would be impossible to achieve within a reasonable period of time. The political leadership was and continues generally to be united in supporting the need for reform. If workforce systems change can happen through a community-based approach, one would hypothesize that Seattle had the political and economic ingredients to succeed. What follows is our preliminary assessment of this hypothesis.

SEATTLE'S URBAN REGIME

Understanding Seattle's urban regime history and political climate is important to understanding the environment that influenced policymakers and unified service providers, agency heads, the mayor, and the city council in their response to welfare reform. These actors lobbied the state of Washington to gain concessions on discretionary program cutbacks, and to spearhead community support for programs such as SJI. In addition to concern for poor peoples' welfare, an important consideration for all was the need to insulate local human service agencies from the potentially huge unmet service needs of former welfare recipients. A key action taken in 1997 by Mayor Norman Rice, the city's first African-American mayor, was the allocation of $3,000,000 of the city's general fund to this workforce development project. The total general fund at that time stood at approximately $500,000,000.

A brief description of the city's history of political leadership and urban regime form is needed to place this community momentum into context.

Mayor Rice's 1997 budget allocation to SJI required approval—just as the rest of his budget did. It was not until the late 1960s that the Washington State legislature, by altering the city's charter, enabled the mayor to create budgets. Until that time, the mayor's influence on the budget was limited to his veto power. Under this constraint, the mayor's citywide vision was not reflected in what is currently an extremely powerful tool: The budget. Agency heads did not feel as reliant on the mayor's good will before that alteration and this decreased his leadership in the city administration (Vega, 1997).

Prior to the charter alteration, empowered city council members made and enacted policy. They did so through powerful committees on which it was incumbent only to get the approval of the council president and the so-called Big Ten. "'If you want to get anything done in Seattle,' says Ross Cunningham, political editor *The Times*, 'you get about six members of the Big Ten together and tell them it's a good project. If you convince them, you're in'" (Banfield, 1965). The Big Ten is regularly referred to in articles treating the Seattle political scene before the 1960s. They were an informal group of "downtown financiers, real estate men, and industrialists," who met regularly to discuss city affairs and attend to their interests, especially downtown business district development (Banfield, 1965). Strong alliances between this business-focused group and the powerful city council formed an important component of that era's regime. Although this does not give a broad picture of the political landscape of the time, it does serve as a valuable contrast to the urban regime form we see in the period beginning in the 1970s and continuing today.

URBAN REGIMES

An urban regime is broadly defined as an informal set of understandings between government and private interests and citizens that can, though does not always, serve to make a fragmented system of resources and authorities into a functional governing coalition.

Seattle's progressive regime has no similar seat of informal power such as the Big Ten and the council president. "There are no kingmakers anymore. There is no one place to go or one person to see for a council wannabe who wants to don the mantle of political legitimacy. Nowadays, a candidate must trek all over town—meeting with small groups from Maple Leaf to West Seattle, graciously waving his or her way through neighborhood Seafair parades, sipping Starbucks in corporate board rooms" (Wilson, 1991). Although "process" was extraneous to the Big Ten et al., Seattle's current political environment often is characterized as being so committed to process as to mire decision making and jeopardize time-sensitive opportunities. If the Big Ten's influence kept business interests in the fore, it is fair to say that their influence has been replaced by a more scatter-shot citizen-empowerment approach that makes it much more difficult to control the political process.

PROGRESSIVE REGIMES

The complicated urban environment is always evolving, making it difficult to conclusively put Seattle or any city into a static regime type. A city always seems to present some evidence of contradiction once a type is established. However, beginning with the election of Mayor Wes Uhlman in 1969 and continuing today, Seattle has had a progressive urban regime. It also has some features of the ideal regime David L. Imbroscio describes in *Reconstructing City Politics,* which would put "the goal of expanding opportunities for the lower class in cities" as the regime's top priority (Imbroscio, 1997).

A key characteristic of a "progressive regime" is an environment where business interests are somewhat marginalized, or an actual anti-business set of principles governs important city decision making. Although policy initiatives vary widely across different mayoral administrations, in general Seattle's urban regime is at least suspicious of the influence of business and market-driven development undertakings.

A good example of this suspicion is the Housing Preservation Ordinance (HPO) passed in 1979 in response to a wave of development projects that diminished the supply of affordable housing downtown. The HPO required developers either to replace any low-income housing displaced by their development, or pay a fee to the city's housing fund. Developers converting residential properties to commercial use were also taxed to help offset the impact to the urban poor. Developers objected that the city was extracting resources from the very people creating public benefit through development. Though state courts eventually overturned the ordinance, the will to impose restrictions on the mobile capital behind downtown development was evident.

It is difficult to capture all the reasons Seattle's regime transitioned from a corporate-centered regime to its current progressive regime. City authorities now answer to multiple constituencies, many of whom see neighborhood preservation, environmental, and other quality of life issues—post-materialist values—as having a higher priority than attracting the mobile capital of downtown developers. Neighborhood and community advocates are now influencing the policy process and are regularly, if not consistently, tipping the scales toward neighborhood priorities. A primary vehicle for neighbor empowerment is Seattle's Department of Neighborhoods, established by ordinance in 1987 to "recognize that neighborhoods are more than places with needs, but communities with tremendous passion, knowledge, and other assets" (City of Seattle, Department of Neighborhoods, 2003).

BUSINESS'S ONGOING ROLE

Although Seattle's progressive regime may be somewhat anti-business, policymakers have nonetheless had to be responsive to an extent. Indeed, mayors Uhlman, Rice, and Schell have all found themselves under scrutiny for advocating on behalf of issues popularly construed as "business interests."

A reference to Clarence Stone's account of how business impacts politics helps illuminate why mayors are beholden, or at least appear to be beholden, to business interests. The business elite "controls resources of the kind and in the amount able to enhance the regime's capacity to govern" (Stone 1989). He describes that a "civic vacuum" in the city of Atlanta necessitates the very active role that business plays in public policymaking. Clearly, there is no such vacuum in Seattle, and community groups compete with corporate interests to take the lead on important city decisions.

Although citizen activists and community groups are more than willing to engage in the process of public decision making and priority setting, business still has influence. Certain development initiatives have polarized citizens against otherwise popular mayors who advocate on business' behalf. Mayor Wes Uhlman, a candidate who was elected in 1969 by "middle class voters, African Americans and the elderly"—all of whom saw the business elite as having ignored their interests (Vega, 1997)—supported business in its wildly unpopular effort to redevelop Pike Place Market. A ballot measure ultimately defeated the redevelopment plan, but this example is characteristic of the lingering influence that business continues to have on public policy, even with a mayor elected, in part, because of his distance from business interests.

In fact, Seattle's business leaders are regarded as socially quite liberal. Unlike many urban centers, this business community supports social welfare programs and takes a measure of responsibility for spinning benefits off to lower socioeconomic status populations (Vega, 1997). Citizens and business alike expect the city to actively support people in poverty by providing homeless services, low-income housing, economic development, and a host of self-sufficiency programs.

Such was the political landscape on the eve of welfare reform as the workforce development system braced itself for a structural overhaul. The city's mayor had a detailed economic development plan and a demonstrated commitment to improving the lives of low-income populations. He was leading a liberal city council that was "deeply engaged" in the impact of welfare reform (Donaldson, 2001). Human and self-sufficiency service providers felt their own and their clients' interests being threatened. The community, including business leaders, expected action and, in a sense, enabled it.

SETTING THE STAGE

In the early to mid-1990s, workforce training programs in Seattle were structurally quite similar to many other programs in other large cities. With funding from the federal Department of Labor, Private Industry

Councils (PICs) directly provided many job training services and con-tracted out other services to local community-based organizations (CBOs). The Seattle PIC had a twenty-member advisory board with the public and private sectors nearly evenly represented. The PIC also had a Joint Executive Board comprised, with one exception, of local elected offi-cials, including the mayor of Seattle.

The PIC, however, suffered from poor linkages to local CBOs, in part because as a direct service provider, the PIC competed with CBOs to serve clients. The ongoing relationship with local businesses was also inade-quate, despite the participation of business representatives on the advisory board. The PIC provided services targeted so closely to the job seekers' needs that attention to employers' needs was noticeably missing. Also, the primary focus of the PIC was on training, especially pre-employment skills, with little focus on job retention and working with individuals and their families over a period of time. PICs were seen as grants administra-tors with little relevance to the business community and few of the resources necessary to provide the wrap-around services needed by low-income, low-skilled workers. Because of Department of Labor (DOL) reg-ulations, eligibility for services funded through the PIC was also very restricted. Other major players in employment training—community col-leges and vocational institutes and local service agencies involved with disadvantaged workers—largely operated their own separate programs with only minimal cooperation with the PICs or other public and private agencies. In sum, workforce services in Seattle were driven programmat-ically by federal and state grant opportunities with little integration among the key players in workforce development.

It was in this context that the SJI was conceived. It would be an inter-mediary organization that would achieve meaningful systems reform and change the way in which workforce training services were delivered. It would also build new, more productive relationships among the key stakeholders in workforce training, including businesses, CBOs, commu-nity colleges, and municipal and county agencies. Where other top-down initiatives had failed, SJI would be a catalyst for fundamental social reform.

SJI was organized as a part of the city of Seattle's Office of Economic Development (OED). It has an advisory board comprised of community leaders and representatives of key stakeholder groups, and a professional staff directing SJI programs. From the beginning, SJI was envisioned as an intermediary entity that would avoid some of the pitfalls and problems of earlier reform initiatives. First, it would not be a direct service provider like the PICs or other initiatives. Thus, SJI could concentrate on building new relationships and networks rather than worrying about the next funding opportunity. Second, it would work closely with CBOs which had not played a central part of earlier training initiatives; these CBOs would provide assessments and case management and could refer clients to appropriate training programs. Moreover, the CBOs contracting with SJI were intentionally diverse, representing the cultural and ethnic diversity of Seattle. Some of the key CBOs include: TRAC Associates, the YWCA, the Asian Counseling and Referral Service, Central Area Motivation Program, the Refugee Federation Service Center, the Seattle Indian Center, and the Washington Coalition of Citizens with Disabilities. Third, job training by the CBOs supported through SJI would be sector specific. For instance, initial training programs targeted the following industries: General manufacturing, health care, office occupations, electronics, aerospace, construction, and automotive services (SJI, 2000). Through sector-specific strategies supported by regularly updated data on local economic trends, it was hoped that greater cooperation among businesses and training programs could be created. The result would be improved outcomes for job seekers. Finally, training services would be available to a broader range of people than was characteristic of the PIC, and the services would be more integrated and longer term, increasing the chances of positive results for job seekers interested in good-paying jobs.

From the beginning, SJI enjoyed strong political support from state and local political leaders. When SJI was first proposed in 1995, Governor Michael Lowry, a liberal Democrat, was in office. SJI also received strong support from then mayor of Seattle, Norm Rice and his director of the OED, Mary Jean Ryan. Based in part on the impressive political support enjoyed by SJI, the Annie E. Casey Foundation provided a matching grant of $700,000; through the OED, the city of Seattle provided matching funds of $350,000. At the time, this sum was all the city had to give, having essentially robbed it from their own Human Services Department (HSD). The mayor and the director of OED successfully argued that HSD's employment dollars ought to more directly link low-income workers to the thriving regional economy. SJI's goals dovetailed well with the concerns of the mayor, Ryan, and their staffs, especially the idea of deploying already-established CBOs in a sectorally-based strategy to connect low-income job seekers with local employers. Indeed, the city leaders were very supportive of the basic philosophy of SJI—and the Jobs Initiative more generally—due to its focus on "job-centered economic development." The idea of a new set of relationships between local employers, labor, the city, CBOs, and foundations was very attractive and fit well with the overall thrust of the state's approach to workforce development. SJI would also spur the creation of more integrated labor market policies, leading to better outcomes for job seekers. The Seattle City Council also liked the idea of "seed-ing" social program innovation that could then be replicated and modeled by other local agencies and even elsewhere in the country.

THE ARRIVAL OF WELFARE REFORM

SJI was officially launched in 1997 after a year of planning. In August 1996, as teams of local community advocates, service providers, public officials, and grassroots organizers were engaged in SJI's planning process, welfare reform was passed into law. This legislation, officially called the Personal Responsibility and Work Opportunity Reconciliation Act (PRWORA) of 1996, has had profound effects on workforce development services in Seattle, including SJI. Broadly, the legislation redirected the focus of public agencies from income assistance coupled with vocational training or education, toward job search and placement activities. In fact, it mandated that grants not be used for "stand-alone" training or education. The old welfare reform program, Aid to Families with Dependent Children (AFDC) was restructured and renamed Temporary Assistance for Needy Families (TANF).

The new law was a great shock to the system of service providers and agencies. Some community activists, service providers, and public officials believed welfare reform would do a great disservice to the many people whose potential for self-sufficiency depended on the training that qualified them for living wage jobs.

SJI was originally planned on a $1.5 million budget; however, Mayor Rice was alarmed at the potential effect of the new welfare law on Seattle. Rice feared the city's human services infrastructure would be overwhelmed when thousands of people dropped from the welfare rolls lost their income safety net. As a result, Mayor Rice in concert with Mary Jean Ryan successfully won approval from the Seattle City Council for an additional $3 million a year for SJI, bringing the total budget to well over $4 million. The rationale was that the additional money was essential if the city of Seattle human service infrastructure was to cope successfully with the aftermath of welfare reform. Thus, SJI is far bigger than it would have been without welfare reform.

The other effects of welfare reform, however, have greatly complicated workforce training for the poor and disadvantaged. Clients remaining on TANF face the looming deadline of the five-year lifetime limit as they cycle through the increasingly intensive programs designed to address their obstacles to employment and place them in jobs. Washington's welfare-related training program is called WorkFirst. It is administered through four public agencies: The Department of Social and Health Services (DSHS), the Employment Security Department (ESD), the State

Board of Community and Technical Colleges (SBCTC), and the Department of Community, Trade, and Economic Development (CTED).

The goal of WorkFirst—not surprisingly given the name—is to move welfare recipients into the workforce as quickly as possible (Klawitter, 2000). Its many detractors refer to it as "first job, any job" to illustrate how the program focuses nearly exclusively on a single measure of success: Reduction of the state's welfare rolls by placing participants in the workforce. By contrast, CBOs involved in workforce development tend to approach the provision of services from the perspective of training clients for careers that pay livable wages, and have clearly defined wage scales and potential opportunities for on-the-job training and advancement. In addition, a client's mental health, domestic violence, substance abuse, soft skills, child care, transportation, and other human service needs are seen as critical pieces in the employment services package. Although immediate employment appears desirable because it lowers welfare rolls instantly, CBOs argue that long-term self-sufficiency can only be achieved through appropriate preparation for careers that pay living wages.

CBOs also worry that the almost exclusive focus on job placement means that the gap between employment and self-sufficiency will grow over time, placing a greater burden on CBOs and other service agencies to offer increased case management, counseling, and training opportunities. Their ability to provide these services is quite restricted through many existing welfare-related programs. Consequently, CBOs worry that they will have inadequate funding to meet increased service demand.

The new burden on CBOs is particularly ironic given the fact that many CBOs were very opposed to the sweeping changes embodied in welfare reform. The changes also represent an interruption in previously established funding and client referral streams. The new emphasis on employment resulted in fewer referrals to training programs, decreased state funding for at least some human services, and a culture change for CBOs: Competition for clients.

Overall, then, welfare reform presented both opportunities and challenges for fundamental systems change in workforce training programs. In particular, it has complicated the task of network building and developing new connections between CBOs, businesses, SJI, and local foundations. It has also made it more difficult to create a unified, integrated workforce development strategy.

AN EVOLVING WORKFORCE SYSTEM

Although welfare reform dramatically changed the funding streams, training programs, and incentives facing service providers and welfare recipients, the federal Workforce Investment Act (WIA) introduced another prominent new player into the local workforce training scene: The Seattle King County Workforce Development Council (SKCWDC). Essentially, WIA was passed by Congress to reform the perceived deficiencies in JTPA and the PICs. WIA required the states to establish local workforce investment boards (WIBs) to replace the PICS as the coordinating body for local workforce training for the poor and disadvantaged. In this spirit, the state of Washington authorized the SKCWDC to act as the local WIB. The King County executive and the mayor of Seattle serve as co-chairs of the organization's board and appoint the board's members. The one most notable functional difference between the SKCWDC and the PIC: The SKCWDC is not a direct service provider, whereas the PIC offered an extensive array of services.

The SKCWDC's responsibilities are wide ranging:

- Research and analysis on the regional economy and labor market, the current and future workforce, and the workforce development system
- The formation of SKCWDC committees on skills gap, wage progression, workforce/one-stop systems development, and youth, to develop strategies for addressing the region's workforce challenges
- Two day-long planning charettes, at which SKCWDC members and others worked to design key aspects of the workforce development system such as employers and job seeker/worker services
- An extensive outreach campaign (SKCWDC, 2000)

SKCWDC administers performance-based contracts with local service providers—both nonprofit and for-profit—for direct service provision to clients. Significantly, they administer and certify the One-Stop Centers in King County, which lie short distances north, east, and south of the city of Seattle. This program, called WorkSource, has three key components: Core services, including outreach, eligibility determination, information and referral; intensive services, including the development of individual employment plans; and training (SKCWDC, 2000, 34).

Locally, SKCWDC concentrates on improving connections between employers and training programs. As noted, the PICs did not place much emphasis on serving employers. The new emphasis on working with employers that was mandated by WIA also required representatives of private industry to make up the majority of the boards of local WIBs. By giving business a formal role in the governance of the local WIBs, it was hoped that business would be more engaged in workforce development.

Thus, SKCWDC and, more specifically, the One-Stop Centers are based on the assumption that employers will not use the workforce development system if it is not easy. Employers need a single point of access where they can find the qualified employees they are seeking. There are many, many public and private programs serving job seekers. What employers do not want is to wander through a confusing maze of programs in order to find employees who have the desired skills. This is especially true in Seattle and King County because many employers historically have had difficulty using the local training system. SJI and SKCWDC are intended to directly remedy this long-standing problem.

SKCWDC has a contract with a for-profit provider called Pacific Associates whose express goal is to insulate employers from the complexities of the workforce system, and give employers the opportunity to deal directly with a professional placement service. The referral stream is relatively straightforward. Ideally, all bureaucratic processes preceding a candidate's readiness for employment are supposed to be obscured from the vision of the employer. This objective, however, requires coordination between service providers, and can be a challenge for SKCWDC and the other players in the workforce system.

For example, if an employer needs fifty employees with three different skills sets and certifications, a single service provider will be unlikely be able to meet the full need. But if information is shared across service agencies, training programs, and community colleges, it is quite likely that the full need can be met. However, the employer is very averse to engaging each agency separately, they need to function as one system.

In general, WDCs are barred from doing any direct service provision, except in cases where appropriate service providers are lacking (e.g., rural areas). This rule is designed to avoid the conflict of interest problems characteristic of the old PIC system. Under JTPA, the PICs provided services directly to clients *and* were in charge of setting the priorities for client needs. Inevitably, this dual role created tension between the service delivery and planning arms of the PICs. Now the WDC can concentrate on a single purpose goal of planning, coordinating, and obtaining performance from its affiliate agencies.

SKCWDC has performance-based contracts with CBOs and other training and service providers. Interestingly, they do not have a contract with SJI even though their missions are quite similar, and SJI applied for affiliate status. This lack of affiliate status may reflect, in part, the history of SJI and the old PIC system in Seattle. Historically, substantial competition between the local PIC and SJI existed. When the city of Seattle made SJI its major workforce development agent, it put SJI in a competitive relationship with the PIC, who viewed its geographic target area as including the entire Seattle–King County region. Also, because the PIC was in the business of providing services, substantial competition for client referrals existed between the PIC and the SJI affiliate, CBO agencies. Although the

WDCs are quite different from the PICs, the SKCWDC has some PIC staff, and has continued some of its policies. Consequently, the relationship between SKCWDC and SJI is quite tentative and yet to be fully clarified.

Another key evolving aspect of the workforce system in the Seattle region is the role of the CBOs. In recent years, state and local governments have restructured their funding and contractual arrangements with non-profit service providers. Initially, many contracts for service were cost reimbursement, with contract funds given to service providers in regular increments (e.g., monthly). This was an imperfect system, but it did offer some measure of predictability in agency funding. The emphasis on performance and outcome measurement, however, has spurred federal, state, and local government to restructure these contracts as fee-for-service contracts. JTPA, for example, only paid service providers once a client was successfully placed. The result is less predictability and greater financial vulnerability, especially for smaller nonprofit service providers lacking substantial capitalization.

The financial vulnerability of CBOs means that, more than ever, they need a regular supply of referrals if they are to remain financially healthy and viable. Consequently, one unexpected effect of welfare reform—substantially lower clients in the welfare system—has presented CBOs involved in workforce training with significant and ongoing challenges. Because of welfare reform, clients who would otherwise be referred to CBOs are now working. Consequently, CBOs are forced to compete for a shrinking pool of potential clients.

This problem of CBO client referrals is further exacerbated by other characteristics of the local workforce system. First, the state of Washington DSHS employs case managers who are responsible for individuals on welfare or recently off the welfare rolls. DSHS case managers often refer their clients to job search programs administered by the state ESD rather than CBOs. Part of this referral pattern may simply be a result of a skepticism of CBOs by the state, but it also reflects the state's concern that referring clients to training programs administered by CBOs—or other service providers—might dilute the "work first" message. Clients might be tempted to go into training rather than seek employment as their top priority.

Even worse from the perspective of the CBOs, clients legitimately eligible for training programs are often not referred to CBOs despite the availability of training slots. One reason is that state DSHS case managers are not well acquainted with the scope and breadth of opportunities for training at CBOs. Until welfare reform, these case managers were basically financial service technicians engaged in determining welfare eligibility, not in helping clients get to work. The new case managers were given two weeks of training, and then given a host of new responsibilities relative to their clients; the Federation of State Employees negotiated this deal in order to prevent layoffs. Learning about the complex training system at the community level has often been very difficult. To remedy this problem, some CBOs have even sent recruiters to welfare offices to make direct contact with clients.

Somewhat surprisingly, the city of Seattle sometimes contributes to the referral problem as well. For instance, the city funds myriad social service programs, including an array of services for the homeless, domestic violence victims, and the disabled. At least some of these individuals are eligible for CBO training programs but the city has been slow to encourage these referrals even when a client is eligible. SJI has worked with the appropriate municipal departments to improve this referral situation with limited success.

Although the CBOs are important as a source of direct services, it is also important to keep their efforts in perspective given the sizable presence of vocational and technical education within the workforce system. The budget of SJI was about $5 million in 2000. The budget of the SKCWDC is difficult to accurately measure because several sources fund the SKCWDC and its programs; however, it is certainly several million dollars. A substantial portion of the direct service dollars of SJI and SKCWDC is channeled to CBOs. Thus, one could surmise that CBOs are spending at least several million dollars for workforce training programs. Although the amount spent by CBOs is significant, vocational and technical education through public secondary schools, community colleges, and public vocational institutes amounted to almost $150 million in 2000 as indicated in Table 5.1 (SKCWDC, 2000, 29).

Despite this large role within the local service system, the commitment of community colleges and vocational institutes to workforce training is quite variable. For instance, some campuses of the Seattle Community College District tend to favor the college preparatory side of their mission rather than vocational and adult basic education. This tendency is probably expected, given the higher prestige attached to college preparation over that of workforce training. Moreover, college-bound students tend to be an easier population to serve due to higher motivation.

The Seattle Community College District has not accessed the WorkFirst Pre-Employment Training (PET) dollars for which it is eligible. Why? The funding is earmarked for a discreet population—low-income custodial parents—in short-term training. This is precisely the kind of student that requires more college resources to serve than the Full-Time Equivalency (FTE) budgeting system provides. Business needs quick turnaround on short-term, modular, competency-based training. Low-income

Table 5.1   Preliminary Resource Map of the Seattle–King County Workforce
Development System

Program	Funding	Percent of Total Budget
Secondary vocational-technical education		
State	$44,900,000	23.5%
Federal	$1,660,000	0.9%
School to work transition	$205,000	
Technical preparation	$400,000	
Postsecondary vocational-technical education		
State	$75,340,000*	39.4%
Federal	$4,120,000*	2.2%
State-approved, joint apprenticeships		
Private career schools		
Wagner-Peyser	$3,125,000	1.6%
Disadvantaged youth training programs (JTPA Title II-B and II-C)	$3,900,000	2.0%
Disadvantaged adult training programs (JTPA Title II-A)	$2,280,000	1.2%
Dislocated workers program (JTPA Title III)	$2,860,000	1.5%
Worker retraining program	$8,345,000	4.4%
Job skills program		
Adult education and basic skills	$34,850,000*	18.2%
WorkFirst (pre-employment training, work-based learning)	$2,950,000	1.5%
Division of vocational rehabilitation		
Services for the blind		
Other state, local, and federal	$6,100,000	3.2%
Seattle Jobs Initiative	$5,100,000	
King County Jobs Initiative	$1,000,000	
Total	$191,035,000	

SOURCE: SKCWDC (2000).
*Amounts calculated by applying Seattle–King County-to-state FTE ratios to state funding.

working students need to access this kind of training at night and on weekends in order to advance in their jobs. Providing that kind of flexibility, considering the budgeting and administrative constraints encountered by the community colleges, is extremely difficult.

In addition, the low-income, low-skilled population is resource intensive to serve. Community colleges do not have resources to follow up on students who stop showing up for class. In the low-income population, not showing up for class could indicate a problem with child care, housing, transportation, domestic violence, or drug abuse. This is a disconnect between what a client gets at a CBO like SJI (i.e., wraparound support services and case management), and how a client is handled in a large institution.

Furthermore, urban community college districts are less entrepreneurial than rural districts in meeting the technical and vocational training needs of their communities. Rural districts tend to be smaller, and there-fore, more nimble. The urban environment, especially in Seattle, is also more likely to value professional work more highly than trades; therefore, urban community colleges tend to focus primarily on preparation for col-lege education rather than for trade jobs (Jobs for the Future, 1999).

Because of this orientation, a substantial portion of the total money spent by the community colleges and technical schools does not go directly to training programs for the disadvantaged and the poor. Among the com-munity and technical colleges, the Seattle Vocational Institute (SVI) is the only major institution that focuses on workforce training for low-income and low-skilled individuals. SVI's mission is to provide education in basic skills and vocational and workforce training opportunities through competency-based, open-entry, short-term programs. SVI strives to focus on jobs with a future and personal educational advancement. It also has close linkages with many local businesses, labor, government, and com-munity groups. For example, SVI's Bright Future Program bridges the gap between high school and vocational training by cross-enrolling high school students in vocational training courses. Participants concurrently earn a high school diploma and certification in a trade. The program also assists with career counseling, job placement, child care, housing, scholarships, and the pursuit of additional higher education. In addition, SVI holds a training contract for SJI's Office Occupations sectoral training.

SVI strives to make its programs financially accessible even to people with very low incomes. Nonetheless, until the state extended the allow-able training period in 2001 from twelve to twenty-two weeks, SVI's offer of training for trades in "as little as six months" was inaccessible to any-one getting a TANF grant. However, community activists pushed Gover-nor Gary Locke to change state policy to allow TANF recipients to enroll in up to twenty-two weeks of career training. This takes the pressure off of community colleges to condense their training programs for TANF recipients. However, a need still exists for shorter training so SJI currently contracts with community colleges to provide it.

EVALUATING WORKFORCE TRAINING SYSTEMS CHANGE IN SEATTLE

On one level, the workforce training system looks vastly different in 2001 than it did in 1994; there are many more players (see Figure 5.1). The old PIC has been evolved into the SKCWDC (although the extent to which the new organization is different than the old PIC is a matter of dispute). SJI is providing a $5 million program working with CBOs, businesses, foun-dations, and state government agencies. Many CBOs are now involved in

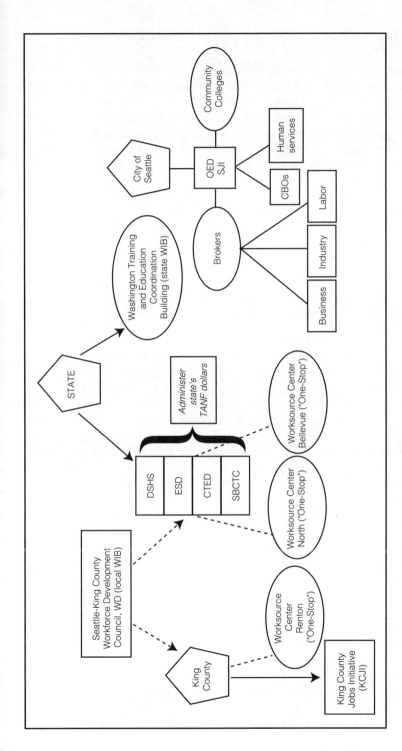

Figure 5.1 Seattle-King County Workforce Development System

workforce training that were previously on the sidelines. Welfare reform and WIA have prompted a host of new initiatives, including the One-Stop Centers with new connections to CBOs, business, and public agencies. King County has even created its own Jobs Initiative, which focuses its efforts on the cities and towns in South King County. This area tends to be poorer than other areas of King County and is the home of many recently arrived immigrants who have no substantial education, English language fluency, or job skills (KCJI, 2000).

But of course, the addition of new players does not mean that fundamental change has occurred. The challenge for workforce systems change is to create new relationships and connections among key stakeholders in order to improve outcomes for job seekers, especially disadvantaged job seekers who are the target constituency for many of the publicly supported training programs.

CHANGING RELATIONSHIPS

One measure of workforce systems change is a relational: To what extent have the relationships between key players changed in a way that produces a more integrated, cooperative service system? On this front, some successful examples of system change are evident. First, SJI, whose mission was primarily system change as opposed to direct service, has forged new relationships and increased the training sector's overall infrastructure. Perhaps their greatest impact has been with the CBOs. SJI has placed great emphasis on building the capacity of CBOs to provide integrated sectoral training. As a result of the efforts of SJI, CBOs are stronger and more central players in providing integrated sectoral training.

One example of this increased capacity to serve is the product of SJI's best practices training for CBOs. Because of SJI training, CBOs screen clients more effectively and completely before making a referral, especially for language or cultural problems that might present an obstacle to successful training. For example, a thorough screening evaluation might reveal language problems that need to be addressed using ESL instruction. Other potential problems—such as religious beliefs—might make some training programs impracticable. These barriers to effective training are now more likely to be revealed before enrollment in a training program, rather than during the training, as had occurred in the past. CBOs' closer screening also increases the community college's efficiency (e.g., fewer dropouts), and puts the community college trainees in a better position for the labor market.

Arguably, SJI has been less successful in enlisting other major players in workforce training in new relationships. As noted, an ongoing agreement between SJI and SKCWDC is still evolving. Although part of the problem appears related to the lingering difficulties in the transition from the PIC to the SKCWDC, different funding streams and the resistance of SKCWDC to close ties to a city department are also complicating factors. In a sense, the integration of SJI with the city of Seattle, Office of Economic Development, is a mixed blessing: It has provided a lot of financial support, legitimacy, and influence; yet, the identification with the city complicates the relations of SJI with other stakeholders. The ties to the city may also be one reason why the advisory board for SJI has not been very active in SJI governance since the initial planning and implementation phase. In particular, businesses and foundations have not been very active in supporting SJI or trying to forge new ongoing relationships supportive of more integrated workforce systems.

Overall, though, it would appear that SJI's integration with the city's OED has been quite positive in terms of helping SJI achieve its systems change goals. The link to the city allowed SJI to obtain far more resources than would otherwise have been possible, and provided immediate legitimacy which attracted local nonprofit and corporate partners. Furthermore, the city has provided a very stable and supportive home for SJI since its inception. Consequently, it has not had to scramble for funding or deal with complicated issues of board development that are typical of many new nonprofit organizations. The challenge for SJI at the moment is that funding from the city is declining so that for the first time, SJI has to devise a sustainability plan that hinges upon finding new sources of revenue. In the current competitive environment for public and private funds, the attainment of this goal will not be easy.

The King County Jobs Initiative (KCJI) is an example of how SJI indirectly prompted the creation of new relationships among key players in the region. KCJI was founded in 1998 soon after SJI began its operations and is set up to function much the way SJI does but instead of focusing on the urban low-income residents as SJI does, KCJI targeted poor residents of South King County. Like SJI, KCJI relies upon existing CBOs and deploys them to help provide case management, direct training, and referral for disadvantaged job seekers.

King County's tax base is significantly lower than Seattle's, and advocates point to the relatively higher proportion of low-income residents in South King County as evidence of the need for more intensive services there. To support KCJI, the county allocated general funds and partnered with the SKCWDC to create a one-stop affiliate site in a KCJI location. KCJI has also benefited from consistently strong support from King County Executive Ron Sims.

Evaluating KCJI from a relational perspective reflects the differences in approach to system change evaluation. On one hand, KCJI—as a conscious imitation of the SJI program model—can be viewed positively as an example of a new funding commitment to workforce training, and a transformed network of relationships among key service providers and planning entities. On the other hand, KCJI is an example of the service fragmentation that has bedeviled the service system for many years—in Seattle and elsewhere. Arguably, a unified KCJI–SJI entity would be in a position to offer a more comprehensive and integrated approach to workforce training. But this unified entity might not have enjoyed the same level of political support as the two separate entities; thus, a unified entity might lack the funding and influence to be very effective.

OUTCOME-BASED PROGRAMS

Another aspect of systems change—outcome-based programs—remains somewhat elusive, although many organizations involved in workforce training in Seattle, including SJI and SKCWDC, are very committed to performance measurement. For example, some SJI training programs operated through CBOs have had low retention rates. In response, SJI worked with the CBO-contract agencies to identify the reasons for the low retention rates. The outcomes of these joint efforts were not only the identification of some key reasons for low retention—e.g., domestic violence and homelessness—but research on "best practices in case management to inform the development of the standards" to improve the way in which the CBOs offered job training and supported their job seekers on a long-term basis (SJI, 2000).

A planning group of SJI and CBO staff now exists to implement these new standards; however, implementation will be a challenge. The CBOs have very different levels of commitment to this initiative, and, as noted, face their own financial pressures related to inadequate referrals. Many CBOs also lack the resources or staff expertise needed to implement these standards.

In addition, performance-driven contracting meets resistance from CBOs that read performance driven as "creaming." CBOs serving clients with the most serious barriers hope to see an alternate measure of success incorporated into performance-based contracting. That standard is "stabilization" as opposed to retention. Stabilization encompasses all the human service needs a client must address before they can succeed in the workplace. Homelessness, untreated mental illness, and simple transportation problems are typical of the problems that can destabilize an otherwise capable worker. The outcomes for these clients fall short of most performance measurement systems. However, if stabilization is a stepping stone to higher wages and increased retention, then achieving stabilization could be seen as achievement of a successful outcome, and should be built into performance measurement systems. Thus far, the contracting standards have not changed enough to incorporate this standard regularly and, therefore, some CBOs are harmed financially by serving the most needy, or they alter their service population to serve those with the highest likelihood of success.

To be sure, SJI and other organizations continue to try to create more standardization as well as cooperation on important programmatic issues. For instance, SJI holds conferences open to practitioners outside of their core group of CBOs. The goal is to bring professionals from a wide variety of service agencies, including agencies for the homeless or the mentally ill, together with experts in workforce training in order to create more effective, integrated workforce training programs.

The problem of implementing performance-driven, integrated workforce services is demonstrated by the lack of cooperation among SJI, SKCWDC, and KCJI on the measure of job retention. All three organizations use different measures of job retention, despite pledges over the years to work more cooperatively.

Significantly, the uneven implementation of appropriate outcome evaluation within the workforce system reflects the continuing tension between federal funding streams and local priority setting. The SKCWDC and many SJI affiliate CBOs are subject to very explicit performance standards set by the federal government. These standards are often not well suited to the local community context or individual client needs. Arguably, a hallmark of an effective, integrated workforce system is local priority setting regarding outcomes and performance. But to the extent that the federal government—and to a lesser extent the state government—retains control over the funding and the performance measures, this goal of local priority setting will remain unfulfilled, despite the concerted effort of local programs such as SJI and SKCWDC.

Finally, the implementation of outcomes-based programming is complicated by the internal dynamics of the CBOs, including their mission and financial situation. All of the CBOs are committed to training the disadvantaged for living-wage jobs and long-term job retention. This mission means working with job seekers over a sustained period of time. But CBOs receive payments for placements rather than long-term training. Thus, CBOs may provide training—due to their mission—but receive little or no compensation for their costs. This problem then creates cash-flow problems, especially for smaller, community agencies. Restructuring the contracts so that CBOs receive more money "up-front" reduces the incentive to reach specific performance or outcome targets. It is a very complex problem to solve given the undercapitalization of most community agencies. This issue will remain a very knotty, nettlesome problem, especially as funding for training and retention becomes scarcer.

RESOURCE ALLOCATION

One other measure of system change is shifts in funding flows. Funding from state and local government can be considered an indicator of local political and citizen support for workforce training. Thus, one could, at least theoretically, track funding over time to assay if funding is going up or down in response to the new initiatives such as SJI or SKCWDC. Some of this information is unavailable. The information that is available can be read quite differently. SJI, for example, was able to leverage the Annie E. Casey Foundation grant to obtain a $3 million annual appropriation from the city of Seattle. KCJI has received substantial job-training–related grants; however, funding for the SKCWDC is declining because of the gradual expiration of key federal grants that support their programs. Local foundation grants for workforce development programs have been quite limited; indeed, the modest initial interest in SJI and workforce training in general in the mid- to late 1990s appears to waning. Although representatives of business have often been supportive of improved work-force training programs, SJI, SKCWDC, and other workforce training programs have received scant funding from local businesses. In general, the key intermediary entities in workforce training in Seattle (i.e., SJI, SKCWDC, and KCJI) have been unable to leverage their initial funding to obtain a large amount of additional resources (with the exception of the city council appropriation for SJI).

One funding possibility for SJI is fee-for-service revenue such as the sale of products, including their well-regarded curricula. Other workforce programs are also investigating fee-based services. Given the competition for funds, however, it is also a challenge to generate substantial sums of money from fees; nevertheless, it may be an important supplementary source of income. The sale of new training products also serves to disseminate the message about integrated workforce development programs to a broader audience.

EVIDENCE OF A PERFORMANCE REGIME

The SKCWDC is in transition as it adjusts to a budget 20 percent smaller than the old PIC, and seeks new sources of funding to replace the previous revenue streams. In Stone's discussion of performance regimes relative to education reform, he states, "reform. . .requires more than discrediting of the old ways in favor of a fresh idea. It involves the difficult shift from a coalition built around distributive benefits to one built on a more complex set of factors" (Stone, 1998, 13). In the former PIC, decisions about service provision tended to be driven by funding streams. This arrangement, in turn, greatly influenced CBO service provision because the PIC subcontracted a portion of their grant money out to CBOs. This kind of decision making is in sharp contrast to the performance regime model Stone describes, in which diverse stakeholders create consensus about desired outcomes and the consensus drives program decisions and implementation.

SKCWDC and SJI represent a fresh approach to workforce training that embodies the vision of Stone's performance regime (Stone, 1989, 1999; Fitzgerald, 2002). SKCWDC embodies the reform vision of local policymakers, including King County Executive Ron Sims who decided to take the opportunity presented by the new WIA legislation to restructure the governing coalition of workforce development programs in King County. Consequently, the old PIC was essentially dissolved into its several parts with only a small percentage of the PIC staff being absorbed into the new SKCWDC.

In recent years, federal funding for the organization decreased due, in part, to welfare reform's retooling of employment services to decrease longer-term job training services in favor of short-term job placement assistance. In addition, the decrease was intended to encourage more investment from local businesses and service providers. This shift in the local coordinating body's access to resources and their overall policy direction trickled down to CBOs, forcing them to change their operations. CBOs were forced to seek new sources of funding, either because the shift away from training toward job placement meant they were no longer eligible for WDC contracts, or in some cases, the WDC's competitive contract process led to the loss of contracts because of unacceptably high costs or low performance. Interestingly, even as the budget decreased, WDC's target audience for services widened significantly because WIA required universal access to basic employment services through a local system of One-Stop Centers.

The previous relationship between CBOs and the PIC was plagued by a singular focus on qualifying for PIC money, which tended to distract from the larger social purpose of creating desired outcomes for clients. Larger, more established CBOs suffered the biggest losses when the transition to the WDC was made, because they had come to depend upon the PIC money. The changeover represented more than just changing the nameplate; indeed, many long-time PIC staff were replaced. As a consequence, CBOs no longer knew how to do business with the newly-constituted WDC. Indeed, many CBOs still are unclear about what services can be had at the One-Stop Centers. One notable effect of the administrative changes associated with the move from PIC to SKCWDC is the reorientation of CBOs relative to business. With PIC money gone, business is now seen as an untapped source of funding for pre-employment as well as on-the-job training.

SKCWDC's task of coordinating a fragmented system, rearranging funding streams to accommodate new priorities, and serving a wider, more diverse client pool is a wildly complicated goal, and one that continues to be problematic even as signs of progress appear. CBOs are still driven by funding opportunities, albeit to varying extents. SKCWDC lacks ongoing funds to support its core operations, and therefore, has to chase funding opportunities as well. Nonetheless, SKCWDC does put in place a structure that has the potential to institutionalize a new performance regime that is much more effective than the previous PIC regime.

SJI has certainly engaged new players in workforce development; however, it remains largely a staff-driven organization rather than one guided by a diverse cross-sectoral advisory board—although businesses are engaged at the sectoral training level (Fitzgerald, 2002). One goal for the upcoming years would be to engage more effectively the board and other relevant stakeholders in a coordinated approach to workforce training in Seattle.

LOCAL LEADERSHIP AND INITIATIVES

Meaningful systems change also hinges upon nurturing new leadership and encouraging local leaders to develop new programmatic strategies tailored to local circumstances. By this measure, some modest success is evident. For instance, one innovative local effort at system coordination is the Coordinated Funders Group formed in 1998 (Fitzgerald, 2002). This group applied for and secured a $5 million DOL grant to coordinate local employment services. Through this grant, the Funders Group hoped to create a comprehensive matrix of employment services in King County. When the creation of the SKCWDC made their organization's work redundant, the remaining DOL funds were folded into the WDC for use in similar attempts at coordination.

As another example of internal and external players collaborating to solve community problems, a group of human service agencies and social welfare advocates are working with transportation officials to better coordinate their respective work in order to create better outcomes for the low-income population. Transportation has been a particular problem in creating better opportunities for low-income workers who need reliable transportation to make connections to workplaces and child care centers.

Ride-share programs and free bus tokens to poor people have not been sufficient to address the full range of transportation needs of this diverse population. In the Seattle region, problems related to access to public transportation have been exacerbated by deep cuts in local transportation budgets. To date, this loose group of agencies and advocates has yet to obtain substantial new monies, but it has engaged key stakeholders in addressing problems vital to creating an effective workforce development system.

Another collaborative effort in place is called the Workforce Development Network comprised of representatives of human service providers in King County. The network's goal is to increase understanding of the WorkSource/One-Stop system and increase the ability of CBOs to partner with one another to coordinate their services. In particular, they are building a new matrix of all employment services available in King County. Their chair is the executive director of a CBO that was previously reliant on PIC funds for service provision. With the transition to the SKCWDC and the accompanying decrease in funding, they were forced to alter the services provided by the agency as well as develop previously untapped sources of funding. Because the changeover from PIC to SKCWDC presented many CBOs with this problem, some are still resistant to the way the SKCWDC does business. In spite of this opposition, a consensus among providers seems to be emerging that their agencies need to be more integrated with each other, and that they cannot ignore the SKCWDC's One-Stop Centers if they are to improve outcomes for their clients.

Elsewhere, a city of Seattle workgroup comprised of representatives from the city of Seattle, King County, the Community Colleges, SKCWDC, and CBOs is currently examining how to create "neutral brokers" to help coordinate services, by addressing the disincentives CBOs have to refer their clients away from their own agency. This is a very difficult problem to solve given the lack of core operating funding for CBOs. Many CBOs are also unaware of the actual services provided by other CBOs in the community; therefore, CBOs may be reluctant to refer clients elsewhere simply because they do not know that appropriate services exist at other agencies. Given the difficulty of this referral problem, the ultimate impact of this new Seattle workgroup remains to be determined.

In order to create a truly coordinated system, service providers must be in regular contact with public- and private-sector decision-makers. Indeed, as Stone observes, cross-sectoral participation from a broad spectrum of stakeholders is essential if civic capacity for change and reform is to be created (1999, 15). One aspect of participation that continues to be problematic in Seattle is the ongoing involvement of business and industry. Despite the strategic plans of every employment service provider in

Seattle to pursue close coordination with businesses and industries, the reality falls far short of the goal. There is little evidence of extensive employer involvement in strategic planning of job readiness and job training programs. Many CBOs currently regard the business community more as an opponent than an ally. CBOs and businesses have scant experience working with each other an ongoing basis; therefore, there is little existing "social capital" on which to draw. Moreover, businesses in Seattle are not creating an adequate number of living wage jobs that CBOs target as their ideal job. According to the Northwest Jobs Gap Study, there are five job seekers for every living wage job. The Seattle region also has a high concentration of very high-paying, high-skilled jobs and low-skilled, low-paying jobs with little in between.

Some of the economic trends that have been documented in other urban centers are clearly identifiable in Seattle as well. Manufacturing, with its higher-than-average wages, is in decline; retail trade and service industries, with their lower-than-average wages, are in ascendancy. Blue-collar jobs are declining and professional/technical jobs requiring post-secondary education and training are growing; part-time and temporary jobs are increasing (Watrus, 2000). For instance, hotel chains—a fast growing part of the local economy—are often willing to navigate the workforce development system to access referrals for low-wage workers. Although these jobs are abundant, they do not offer living wages or the promise of wage progression to a living wage job which is what CBOs seek for their disadvantaged clients. Consequently, CBOs are reluctant to actively cooperate with hotel chains.

THE ROLE OF BUSINESS IN PUBLIC WORKFORCE DEVELOPMENT

The WIA-mandated shift toward better, more extensive services to employers, and the institutional change of requiring a majority share of private representatives on the SKCWDC board have ushered in a new way of talking about services and clients. Clients are now primarily defined as employers rather than job seekers. There is a greater understanding now that, without job openings for job candidates, the system is missing a vital link. This shift is at least one indicator that the workforce development system is making the progress that will facilitate greater, more committed relationships with employers.

In spite of WIA's mandate to treat employers as the primary clients, there is still evidence of significant disconnects between the services business demands and those that providers are capable of and mandated to provide. An example of where the capability to provide a service falls short is in providing modular, competency-based skills training. Although community colleges are trying to adapt their services to the low-income, low-skilled population who only attend classes as they need additional occupational certifications, the administrative confines of the community college system conflict with the typical pace at which business makes decisions. Business moves quickly to fulfill an immediate need for workers as they try to maintain a maximum level of productivity. Community college funding cycles do not allow for that kind of quick turnaround on trainings offered. In fact, community colleges get their funding based on an FTE system, which consolidates the whole population of a college into FTEs and funds programs based on that calculation. The FTE system funds a standard level of administrative costs per "student" or FTE. In fact, however, a single FTE may be composed of many students, all of whom place varying levels of strain on the system and actually incur administrative costs to the college. This is one reason community colleges have a disincentive to focus on the modular, competency-based education that low-income, low-skilled people really need. It is quite simply more difficult and more costly to administer this type of program than the full-time two-year degree programs.

Not only is business asking for a level of services for which agencies may not be capable of providing, but business also is clearly interested in intensive screening of employees before they are referred for an open position. However, in the case of Employment Security, for example, this is outside their mandate. Agencies are funded to do only a very cursory screening of job seekers before they refer them to employers. The demand for intensively screened applicants appears multiple times in two recent local surveys of Washington businesses. The question for service providers is at what point are employers willing to pay for this kind of screening. Many programs offer the kind of general screening ESD provides, but real screening requires time and resources that would likely need to come in the form of fee-for-service. Service providers agree that before they can begin charging a reasonable fee for their services, they must first establish real credibility with business. Currently, business remains suspicious about how well the public workforce development system can meet its needs.

Although businesses point to problems with vocational and post-secondary training programs, CBOs claim that businesses do not invest in the training that low-skilled employees need to advance up the wage scale. Rather, CBOs contend that business' resources are directed at aiding their higher-skilled employees become even more highly skilled. For instance, a manufacturing company might pay for a middle manager to earn an MBA but refuse to pay for additional mechanical training for a technician. Without upfront employer investment in training, many service providers see living wage jobs as an unattainable goal that will be realized by very few low-skilled workers. If upfront investment in training is not available, the best way for a worker to advance is through employer-provided training. Although a 1999 Workforce Training and Education Coordinating Board survey of 10,739 (3,966 responded) Washington businesses finds that "almost half of all firms provide or pay for some classroom training," it is also true that provision is particularly high for managerial and technical staff.

If the local business world and the workforce development system do not work perfectly in concert, they at least are benefiting from better information. SJI collects and updates disaggregated economic data, which are shared with other local providers in the system, notably the SKCWDC and the community college districts. The data allow service providers to refer clients to training in industries with actual job openings rather than using a client's eligibility for training as the primary criteria for making a referral. Strategic thinking and improved information technology allowed this change to occur. In the past, labor statistics tended to be too outdated to be meaningfully connected to training decisions; hence, the service providers were more likely to be inertia-bound, continuing to do what had historically been done rather than responding to real data about the local economy.

Other positive signs exist regarding the engagement of business in workforce development. As noted, one problem with employer involvement in workforce development is the lack of a single entry point that provides access to a wide variety of potential employees. In response to this need, one of the One-Stop Centers is currently testing an internet-based database application that could significantly streamline its operations, allowing employers easy access to all of the state's workforce development resources. Called Services Knowledge and Information Exchange System (SKIES), this database replaces and consolidates data from two other systems, JobNet and DataFlex, which were each repositories of incomplete data, sometimes were duplicative, and both needed to be referenced to get a complete picture of services available. SKIES could be a significant step toward making the disjointed WorkSource Centers and the larger service provider network into a more integrated system of employers, job seekers, and service providers.

There is also evidence that the One-Stop Centers are better able to engage a wider variety of employers on a more regular basis at frequently scheduled on-site job fairs. However, it has been very difficult to discuss the One-Stop Centers as a group because the three One Stops and their affiliates in Seattle are operated with different governance structures with little coordination among them.

All three WorkSource Centers, the affiliate sites, and their co-located partners will be able to access DSHS, ESD, and other related program information using SKIES. Linking the agency data directly to the new database should prevent the problems that outdated information on program eligibility and other qualifying information can create. Employers can also access candidate referrals from all programs in this one database. This is a real step toward the "single point of entry" so consistently called for by employers.

The system is still being tested on a small scale with plans to implement it system wide as soon as possible. So, its functionality is as yet unproven, and some operational questions remain. Key among them is how much data sharing will there be with CBOs that are outside the network of WorkSource partners. SKIES would give a much more complete picture of the entire workforce development system if programs offered by Seattle–King County CBOs were also linked directly to the database. As yet, there are no plans for this level of incorporation of CBOs into SKIES. The system also suppresses certain information depending on the status of the viewer. For instance, some job listings will be able for viewing only at a WorkSource Center. Although the ability to suppress data in this way could make fee-for-service programs easier to administer (e.g., only paying clients can view the intensively screened job applicants), it could put CBOs at a competitive disadvantage if they cannot offer the same level of access that WorkSource offers.

SKIES potentially solves one of the most crippling problems of trying to engage business in workforce development: Access to a single repository of all the most important information. However, increasing the business community's degree of commitment to building pathways out of poverty is currently falling short of what service providers and SJI, in particular, want it to be, and developing SKIES as a resource will not simply wipe out the additional barriers to involvement. Linking low-income workers with the local economy is not a simple task.

There are many meaningful reasons for the lower-than-expected level of engagement SJI has seen thus far from the business community. Many of these reasons have been explored previously, but there is a subtle distinction to be made between a truly sectoral approach to engagement and the occupational clusters approach that it can be argued SJI has taken. This distinction may offer another piece of the answer as to why business involvement remains unexpectedly low. The difference between the approaches is subtle and is obscured partly because of the fact that SJI's literature refers to its outreach to employers as sectorally based. One of the key departures between sectoral and occupational clusters approaches is that sectoral engagement of business tends to take a long time to be successful and includes layers of relationship building that an occupational clusters approach does not require. Measurable results of a sectoral approach can take years to see. The depth of relationships built can be extremely valuable, especially in periods of economic slowdown. By building complex and varied relationships within several sectors, an agency can become a value-added actor over time. As a value-added actor, the agency—or the system as a whole—has more leverage with which to impact labor market practices to benefit the low-income, low-skilled population.

Arguably, SJI has taken an occupational cluster approach. The occupational cluster, with its more narrow focus, produces results much more quickly (e.g., job seekers trained, positions filled, and industry representatives consulted). Because public funding does not tolerate development cycles very well, it is a reasonable adjustment to shift to the longer maturing "sectoral" approach. This change, however, may limit business' potential for real, long-term, meaningful engagement in workforce development. It is interesting to note that the DOL has incorporated "sectoral" strategies into its workplans, clearly lifting the ideas and strategies from private foundations that pioneered them.

Currently, the most-skilled workers with the fewest barriers to employment success are already working due, in part, to a robust local economy. Thus, the unemployed are likely to be people with few skills and significant barriers to work, ranging from untreated mental health conditions to unreliable child care. In addition, many unseasoned employees do not have the communication skills or the understanding of workplace practices to negotiate the leave needed to address these problems; instead, they simply stop coming to work. Although basic skills training— interpersonal communication, problem solving, appropriate workplace conduct—is offered through many training programs, only 13 percent of all the employers that offer classroom training provided training in basic skills. If an employee does not come to the workplace "job ready," they are not likely to get formal instruction on managing their personal role in the workplace.

Businesses currently lack sufficient financial incentive to address the needs of this complicated population of unemployed. Without new financial incentives or dramatic changes in the structure of local workforce systems, the business involvement in the training needs of these workers will continue to fall far short of what is needed.

CONCLUSION

Workforce systems change in the Seattle–King County area is essentially a work in progress with many positive signs amidst the difficulties and challenges. The One-Stop Centers are creating new linkages and more effective partnerships among key stakeholders in local training programs. SJI continues to improve its programs, especially its sectoral training programs, and their reputation continues to grow as they extend their reach beyond serving clients and into the realm of systems change. Although business currently falls far short of expectations for funding or leadership, the downturn in the economy may increase the incentive of many local businesses to become more involved, and new strategies of engagement may help provide the basis for more sustained business participation. The investment in CBO infrastructure development, especially by SJI, may pay off in terms of increased organizational stability and improved relationships between CBOs and other key players in workforce training, including local businesses. Also, the community college system, though initially resistant to suggestions by SJI and others to actively participate in the development of a new, more effective workforce system, has recently signaled greater receptivity to a more coordinated approach to workforce development. The colleges have also increased operational efficiency as a result of changes in CBO's referral practices. Thus, the groundwork for better relationships created over the past few years may finally produce a new working relationship.

These steps toward a reformed workforce training system, however, will not be easily accomplished given the many organizations and politically influential individuals involved. In some respects, the PIC era of workforce training in Seattle was a more stable one—at least for a few years. The present system is more chaotic and uncertain. SJI, the OED, SKCWDC, KCJI, the One-Stop Centers, and the community colleges are just a few of the major organizations involved in workforce training. In principle, all of these organizations endorse integrated job training and close working relationships among service providers, businesses, foundations, and local government; however, creating and sustaining the cooperation necessary for this model of job training is a formidable challenge, especially in the absence of strong external pushes for collaboration and change. One of the challenges for policymakers in the coming years will be to develop new program models that build greater incentives for cooperation and service integration.

REFERENCES

Banfield, Edward. 1965. *Big City Politics*. New York: Random House.
Bardach, Eugene. 1977. *The Implementation Game*. Cambridge: Massachusetts Institute of Technology Press.
City of Seattle. 2003. Department of Neighborhoods. Available at www.cityof seattle.net/neighborhoods.

Cohen, Steven and Todd Eimicke. 1998. *Tools for Innovators*. New York: Wiley.

Donaldson, Susan. 2001. Personal interview.

Eskenazi, Stuart. 2001. "South King County: A Melting Pot of Cultures." *The Seattle Times* (April 11). Available at www.seattletimes.com.

Eskenazi, Stuart and Justin Mayo. 2002a. "Region's Poverty Shifting Outside the City of Seattle." *The Seattle Times* (July 23). Available at www.seattletimes.com.

Eskenazi, Stuart and Justin Mayo. 2002b. "In Dozens of Languages, Tukwila Now Means 'Home.'" *The Seattle Times* (May 11, 2002). Available at www.seattletimes.com.

Eskenazi, Stuart, Justin Mayo, and Tom Boyer. 2001. "Seattle Behind Other Cities When It Comes to Diversity." *The Seattle Times* (March 31). Available at www.seattletimes.com.

Fitzgerald, Joan. 2002. "Job Centered Economic Development: Linking Workforce and Local Economic Development." In *Economic Revitalization: Cases and Strategies for City and Suburb*, by Joan Fitzgerald and Nancey Green Leigh. Thousand Oaks, CA: Sage.

Giloth, Robert P. 2000. "Learning from the Field: Economic Growth and Workforce Development in the 1990s." *Economic Development Quarterly* 14(4)(November):340–359.

Imbroscio, D. L. 1997. *Reconstructing City Politics*. Thousand Oaks, CA: Sage Publications, Inc.

Jobs for the Future. 1999. *A Framework for Labor Market Systems Reform for Jobs Initiative Sites*. Boston: Jobs for the Future.

Katzenbach, Jon, and Douglas Smith. 1999. *The Wisdom of Teams*. New York: Plume.

King County Jobs Initiative (KCJI). 2000. *Program Reports*. Available at www.metrokc.gov/exec/orpp/kcji.

Klawitter, Marieka. 2000. *WorkFirst Report*. Unpublished.

Kotter, John. 1996. *Leading Change*. Boston: Harvard Business School Press.

Marris, Peter, and Martin Rein. 1982. *Dilemmas of Social Reform*. 2d ed. Chicago: University of Chicago Press.

Mazmanian, Daniel, and Paul Sabatier. 1983. *Implementation and Public Policy*. Glenview, IL: Scott Foresman.

Morone, James. 1990. *The Democratic Wish*. New York: Basic.

Pressman, Jeffrey. 1975. *Federal Policy and City Politics*. Berkeley: University of California Press.

Pressman, Jeffrey, and Aaron Wildavsky. 1979. *Implementation*. Berkeley: University of California Press.

Putnam, Robert D. 1993. *Making Democracy Work*. Princeton, NJ: Princeton University Press.

Schorr, Lisbeth. 1997. *Common Purpose*. New York: Harper.

Seattle Jobs Initiative (SJI). 2000. *Program Services*. Seattle: Seattle Jobs Initiative. Available at www.ci.seattle.wa.us/oed/sji/services.

Seattle King County Workforce Development Council (SKCWDC). 2000. *Unified Plan*. Seattle: SKCWDC. Available at www.seakingwdc.org/unifiedplan.

————. 2001. *Gap Analysis: Employer Services*. Seattle: SKCWDC (June).

Senge, Peter. 1990. *The Fifth Discipline*. New York: Doubleday.

Smith, Steven Rathgeb, and Michael Lipsky. 1993. *Nonprofits for Hire: The Welfare State in the Age of Contracting*. Cambridge, MA: Harvard University Press.

Stone, Clarence N. 1989. *Regime Politics: Governing Atlanta, 1946–1988*. Lawrence: University Press of Kansas.

————. 1998. *Changing Urban Education*. Lawrence: University Press of Kansas.

————. 1999. "The Dilemmas of Social Reform Revisited: Putting Civic Engagement in the Picture." Paper presented at the annual meeting of the American Political Science Association, Atlanta.

U. S. Bureau of the Census. 2000a. *Census 2000 Supplementary Survey Profile: King County*. Available at www.census.gov.

————. 2000b. *Census 2000, Supplementary Survey Profile: Seattle City*. Available at www.census.gov.

Vega, D. 1997. *Can Political Incorporation Help African Americans? A Case Study of Seattle*. Ph.D. diss., University of Washington.

Washington State Department of Employment Security. 2002a. *Long-Term Occupational Projections for Seattle-King County Workforce Development Area*. Available at www.wa.gov/esd/lmea/labrmrkt/occ/occ05.html.

————. 2002b. *High Growth and Declining Occupational Projections: Seattle-King County Workforce Development Area*. Available at www.wa.gov./esd/lmea/occdata/2yrhdd/king2yrhgd.html.

————. 2002c. *King County, Selected Economic Data*. Available at www.wa.gov/esd/lmea/labrmrkt/sed/kingsed.html.

Washington State Workforce Training and Education Coordinating Board Report. 1999. "Workforce Training Needs and Practices of Washington State Employers." (December).

Watrus, Bob. 2000. *CBOs, CDCs Vital to Workforce Development*. Unpublished manuscript.

Wilson, J. A. 1991. "Under the political rainbow: How candidates in Seattle clear the hurdles to political credibility." *Seattle Weekly* (July 31):34–35.

Scott Cummings, Allan Tomey, & Robert Flack

6   Workforce Development Policy
     in the St. Louis Metropolitan Region
     A Critical Overview and Assessment

FEDERAL WORKFORCE development initiatives have drawn considerable critical commentary from national policy analysts. According to
Fung and Zdrazil (2003) and others (Grubb et al., 1999), workforce development policies at the federal level, including the Comprehensive Employment and Training Act (CETA) and Job Training Partnership Act (JTPA),
have operated within separate spheres of activity with little overall vision
or managerial coordination. As a result, the programs created have tended
to be financially inefficient, because multiple objectives were often pursued
with little or no assessment of impact at the local level. Several policy analysts report that although the federal government has spent billions of dollars on workforce development interventions, the results have been
minimal, and program objectives are often incompatible, and at times,
contradictory (Grubb, 1996; LaLonde, 1995).

Fung and Zdrazil (2003) also contend that many programs have placed
too much emphasis on job seekers and have neglected the labor market
needs of local employers. Summarizing contemporary criticisms of workforce development policies, they observe that much of the research
describes, "a system that is a morass of problems and policies lacking an
overall strategy whose specifics are regularly re-negotiated through various administrative interaction among federal agencies, state governments,
and local governance bodies. . . This lack of coherence, comprehensive-
ness, and coordination has generated something of a consensus among
observers that the whole of workforce development policy and proactive
in the U.S. comprises a 'non-system' more than a system" (5).

In recognition of these problems, more economic development planners and policy analysts stress the importance of establishing a calculated
mix between regional and place-based strategies of workforce development reform (Parzen, 1997). The Workforce Investment Act (WIA),
passed in 1998, attempted to address many of these criticisms by promoting the consolidation of local programs through One-Stop Centers,
and by encouraging planning for workforce development activities at the
state level. WIA also made efforts to unify funding streams for programs

176

and encourage the participation of major employers in the planning enti-ties created—Workforce Investment Boards (WIBs)—to implement work-force development programs at the local level. Despite these reforms, local implementation is still largely shaped by the way in which federal workforce development policy has been historically delivered through a system of deeply entrenched, local political arrangements.

In contemporary policy circles, it is increasingly fashionable to argue that regional solutions to workforce development problems are prefer-able to place-specific interventions that are constrained heavily by local political culture (Orfield, 1997; Rusk, 1995, 1999). Regional solutions, according to advocates, are required in order to overcome local political arrangements that are inflexible and often conspire to undermine the changes necessary to reform local workforce development policy. Despite popular contentions about the need to adopt regional or statewide approaches to workforce development reform, our case study of St. Louis shows that local political culture and established political arrangements are much more rigid and resistant to change than much of the recent pol-icy literature suggests. In St. Louis, deindustrialization and disinvestment have created extreme geographic disparities in the regional economy. These extreme geographic disparities complicate policy interventions in the areas of regional transportation planning and workforce development and training programs. They also complicate the ability of workforce development leaders to mobilize corporate involvement across regional labor markets, promote equitable financial arrangements to pay for edu-cation and training, and coordinate the provision of services.

In St. Louis, regional development disparities and governmental frag-mentation also affect the ability of local policy leaders to address the spa-tial mismatch between job seekers and the locations in which employment opportunities are being created (Kasarda, 1989, 1993). Local policy lead-ers also have problems addressing the associated mismatch between the current skill levels of job seekers and the training required to compete for the types of jobs being created (Kasarda, 1988). Additional problems are derived from the inability of corporate leaders and economic development planners, public officials, and city managers, to agree upon the sectors that might be targeted for special workforce development initiatives. Because of uneven and mixed development across the St. Louis region, various sectors of the economy are expanding and contracting at differ-ent rates.

Our analysis shows that a clearer understanding of regional growth and development disparities, and their relationship to governmental frag-mentation, is needed in order to target geographic areas for policy inter-ventions, and to link and accurately match training programs to those sectors of the economy with the highest potential for continued growth and expansion (Birch, 1982; Jobs for the Future, 1999). The St. Louis case shows how local political arrangements and constraints often are highly resistant to reforms having origins at the federal level, and conspire to undermine implementation of policies promoting regional cooperation and coordination. In order to understand why the St. Louis region has proven highly resistant to workforce development reform, it is useful to place our case study within the framework of regime theory.

REGIME POLITICS, CAPACITY TO GOVERN, AND RESISTANCE TO REFORM

In his discussion about educational reform, Stone (1998) contends that major policy changes only occur if reformers adopt "a new set of political arrangements commensurate with the policy being advocated" (9). While elaborating his ideas about how a "durable performance regime" in support of educational reform might be created, Stone explains why changes that require an "alternative set of political arrangements" are often difficult to achieve. He reasons that while a region's civic capacity to promote major policy changes can be enhanced when various local stakeholders are mobilized behind a community-wide cause, coalitions premised upon a "social-purposive" political agenda are more fragile than those premised upon distributional motivations. According to Stone (1998), at least two factors shape a regime's civic capacity to govern: (1) The ability of local political leaders and stakeholders to overcome their differences, and (2) the external political constraints and circumstances to which local stakeholders must respond. Stone maintains that reform agendas—like educational or workforce development reform—are driven by a different set of political motives when compared with local issues organized around distributive goals and objectives.

Similar to Stone's argument about distributional politics, Molotch (1976) contends that major policy decisions in cities are usually dominated by growth coalitions that attempt to organize economic and political life in a manner that maximizes profitable business and land use activities. As explained more recently by Molotch (1988), this component of civic infrastructure, or capacity to govern, consists of

> nested interest groups with common stakes in development [who] use the institutional fabric, including the political and cultural apparatus, to intensify land use and make money. Coalitions with interests in growth of a particular place (large property holders, some financial institutions, the local newspaper) turn government into a vehicle to pursue their material goals. (31)

Molotch (1988) contends that because of the financial and civic resources that they command or that can be made available to various interest groups, local governments, councils of governments, and related political jurisdictions and entities can accurately be viewed in most cities as part of a powerful growth coalition.

Consistent with Stone's (1989) exposition of urban regimes, growth coalitions—if they are well organized—often exercise veto power in decision-making because it is not possible to govern without their active participation in local affairs. Logan and Molotch (1987) contend that members of growth coalitions must establish political relationships with elected local officials as part of their ongoing business activities. Growth entrepreneurs need building permits, changes in zoning regulations, infrastructure improvements, and tax abatements and concessions in order to pursue their economic and developmental interests. Likewise, elected officials must rely upon growth coalitions in order to stabilize tax revenues and to provide the services required by local residents. Their continuation in public office requires reliance upon the business community for financial and political support. Elected officials must also provide the developmental amenities and tax policies required to retain existing businesses and to attract new enterprises to the area.

The economic interests of growth elites and the political objectives of elected public officials reinforce the desire among localities to solve their own problems, and to perpetuate and protect existing political alliances and coalitions. According to Molotch (1988), "The doctrine of home rule implies that localities can best handle 'their own problems' and the vesting of land use regulation in local authorities, almost the only autonomous realm of governance remaining at this level, guides decision makers toward the development option for dealing with virtually any problem that manifests itself locally" (34). It is our contention that workforce development politics in the St. Louis region have been and continue to be heavily influenced by competing suburban development and downtown redevelopment interests and the desire for autonomy within the region's numerous governmental jurisdictions to pursue their developmental agendas separately and independently.

In order to meet the labor market and training needs of hometown employers, workforce development policies must be designed and implemented in a manner consistent with the private interests of local growth coalitions and mirror the business trends found in the regional economy. And, similar to policies that finance infrastructure improvements and underwrite development through tax abatements, the public sector is typically expected to subsidize the costs of the educational systems and programs needed to retrain or reorient the workforce. As Stone (1993) contends, however, some local growth coalitions and urban regimes do not always have the capacity to pursue their developmental interests. They do not always agree upon a common developmental agenda, and relations between the public and private sectors are not always devoid of tension, especially within reform regimes that represent the interests of minority and underclass populations. The absence of consensus within a regional growth coalition can be intensified under conditions in which multiple political jurisdictions are present within a metropolitan area.

What Stone (1993) calls the "capacity to govern" is an important element in shaping a local elite's ability to pursue its economic interests, and is an integral component of a region's civic infrastructure. In order to pursue a developmental agenda, including achieving consensus about how to change workforce development practices, a local regime must manifest the capacity to stimulate the cooperation of numerous private and public actors and be able to organize a governing coalition. According to Stone (1993), "Responding effectively to a challenge like economic restructuring means bringing about substantial change in established social and economic practices and that means drawing on nongovernmental resources and enlisting nongovernmental actors" (17).

Stone (1993) also observes that in order for a governing coalition to be politically viable, it must mobilize the resources that are commensurate with its primary policy agenda.

> Participation in governance, especially for those who are not public officials is based heavily on the goals they want to achieve. Participation may modify those goals, but participation is still purposeful. It follows that, if a coalition cannot deliver on the agenda that holds it together, then the members will disengage, leaving the coalition open to reconstitution. In the same manner, doable actions help secure commitments and perhaps attract others with similar or consistent aims. (17)

Stone explains that not all regimes have the capacity to organize a governing coalition or achieve the kinds of cooperation required to reach their developmental and political objectives. In a situation characterized by unstable and fragmented political alliances, a small group or constituency may dominate a particular policy outcome. If a policy issue produces a public response characterized by apathy and indifference, a small group of stakeholders may dominate the decision-making process. In such a situation, fragmentation may also lead to a stalemate in the policy formation process. A more interesting form of political fragmentation, however, is one characterized by differences of opinion within the coalition itself, or a situation in which a wide variety of stakeholders are unable to agree upon a common policy agenda. In this latter situation, resistance to change and a hardening of existing political alliances is a more likely outcome.

Molotch (1988) contends that some growth elites—and by implication, civic infrastructure itself—are rife with

> internal dissention, weighted down by incompetent leaders, or afflicted with diversionary agendas. Besides these idiosyncratic differences, the sediments of past historical conditions can have an impact on the effectiveness of a given growth elite. (32)

He maintains that growth elites and governing regimes have some degree of discretion to carry out their policy objectives but only within an established set of political constraints. He identifies several constraints that limit the ability of local elites to pursue their developmental objectives including: (1) Geographical and environmental constraints, (2) leadership fragmentation, (3) capital flight and disinvestment, (4) the talents of local political entrepreneurs, and (5) popular resistance to the developmental objectives of local growth elites.

Both Molotch and Stone maintain that policy formation at the local level is constrained by and embedded within an established set of political relationships. Members of a community's governing coalition maintain these established relationships and often promote organized resistance to change. Social change is pursued or prevented by members of the governing coalition, and the resources commanded by participants in the governing regime will determine how much influence these members can exert in pursuit of change. The political and economic relationships among members of a governing coalition are shaped by the developmental history of the geographic arena in which the regime operates, and reflects the political culture of the urban region in which the various coalitions are created, sustained, or undermined. All of these elements combine to form a region's civic infrastructure. In order to explain why systemic reform in workforce development policy in the St. Louis region has progressed so slowly, it is important to apply the observations of Molotch and Stone to the civic infrastructure found there, and to explain why local political arrangements have conspired to block workforce development reform.

Regional Disparities in St. Louis: Barriers Preventing Reform in Workforce Development Policy

There are three sets of historical and developmental forces strongly influencing the nature of regional politics in St. Louis; these forces constrain the likelihood of achieving systemic changes in workforce development policy in the region. The three areas of concern include: (1) Economic restructuring and regional development disparities, (2) extreme forms of racial inequality in the St. Louis region, and (3) governmental fragmentation within the region. We think that these factors contribute to an absence of consensus in the corporate and political communities over a workforce development agenda. Although these three areas of concern are reinforced by the sustained absence of coordination among existing federal and state programs that target workforce development and training as a primary objective, it is our contention that local political arrangements largely shape and constrain the way in which national policy is implemented in the St. Louis region. Each of these issues is elaborated in the following sections, and their impact on the region's civic infrastructure is explained.

Regional Development Disparities

Table 6.1 shows general population trends in the St. Louis region. The Metropolitan Statistical Area (MSA), which includes both Missouri and Illinois, has shown relatively little growth since 1970. Between 1970 and 2000, the region's population grew by less than 150,000 people. At the same time, dramatic population shifts took place within the St Louis MSA. The population of the city of St. Louis dropped from 856,796 residents in 1950 to 348,189 in 2000. During the same period, the suburban regions surrounding the city displayed remarkable population growth. Between 1950 and 2000, a relatively constant number of families and individuals spread across geographic space in a manner that produced extreme forms of suburban sprawl in the St. Louis region.

During this time frame, business and industry were significantly restructured and the city's dominant position in the region's economy was radically undermined. Data drawn from the County Business Patterns between 1951 and 1997 show the dramatic shifts that occurred in the region's employment base. Figure 6.1 shows the total number of employees found in the city of St. Louis and its four surrounding counties between 1951 and 1997. To maximize trend lines, the data points are aggregated in approximate five-year intervals.

In 1951, over 85 percent of the region's jobs were located in the city of St. Louis. Over the ensuing four decades, the dominance of the city over the region's economy steadily declined. By 1997, less than 30 percent of the region's jobs were located in the city of St. Louis. Not only did the city's relative economic position decline, but also its absolute position deteriorated. In 1951, approximately 419,813 employees were working in the city of St. Louis; by 1997, this figure was 276,542. During this same time frame, St. Louis County emerged as the dominant location of economic

Table 6.1 St. Louis Metropolitan Population by Decade from 1950 to 2000

County	Population (n)						Population Change 1950–2000 (n)	Population Change 1950–2000 (%)
	1950	1960	1970	1980	1990	2000		
Missouri								
Franklin	36,046	44,566	55,116	71,233	80,603	93,807	57,761	160.2
Jefferson	38,007	66,377	105,248	146,183	171,380	198,099	160,092	421.2
Lincoln	13,478	14,783	18,041	22,193	28,892	38,944	25,466	188.9
St. Charles	29,834	52,970	92,954	144,107	212,907	283,883	254,049	851.5
St. Louis	406,349	703,532	951,353	973,896	993,529	1,016,315	609,966	150.1
City of St. Louis	856,796	750,026	622,236	452,085	396,685	348,189	(508,607)	−59.4
	7,666	8,750	9,699	14,900	19,534	24,525	16,859	219.9
Total	1,388,176	1,641,004	1,854,647	1,824,597	1,903,530	2,003,762	615,586	44.3
Illinois								
Clinton	22,594	24,069	28,315	32,617	33,944	35,535	12,941	57.3
Jersey	15,264	17,023	18,492	20,538	20,539	21,668	6,404	42.0
Madison	182,307	224,689	250,934	247,691	249,238	258,941	76,634	42.0
Monroe	13,282	15,507	18,831	20,117	22,422	27,619	14,337	107.9
St. Clair	205,995	262,509	285,176	267,531	262,852	256,082	50,087	24.3
Total	439,442	543,797	601,748	588,494	588,995	599,845	160,403	36.5
Metropolitan Statistical Area	1,827,618	2,184,801	2,456,395	2,413,091	2,492,525	2,603,607	775,989	42.5

SOURCE: Laslo (2001).

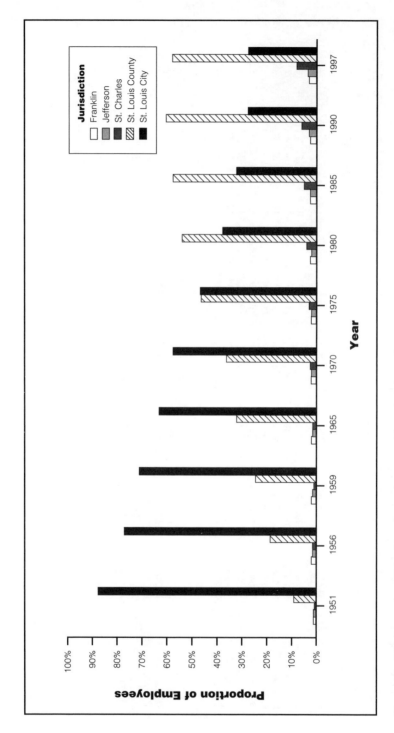

Figure 6.1   The Proportion of Total Employees Categorized by Political Jurisdiction

activity in the St. Louis region. In 1951, less than 10 percent of the region's workforce was located in St. Louis County; by 1997, nearly 60 percent of region's workforce was located there. In 1997, approximately 580,200 individuals were employed in St. Louis County, a figure substantially greater than that reported by the city at its peak economic capacity in 1951.

Similar trend lines are revealed in a comparable analysis of the total number of firms located in the St. Louis region. In 1951, over 80 percent of all firms were located in the city. By 1997, less than 20 percent of the region's firms were located in St. Louis City. Similar to the data presented in Figure 6.1, the relative economic position of St. Louis County gradually surpassed that held by the city during the decade of the 1970s. By 1997, the county was home to nearly 60 percent of the region's firms. Also similar to the data in Figure 6.1, the analysis of firms shows that the county housed more firms in 1997 (30,314) than did the city in 1951 (23,427).

Analysis of earnings also confirms the gradual erosion of St. Louis City's domination of the region's payroll. In 1951, the city accounted for over 85 percent of the region's first-quarter payroll. By 1997, only 30 percent of the region's first-quarter payroll was being earned in the city of St. Louis. Conversely, about 60 percent of the region's payroll was being earned in St. Louis County by 1997. A small trend line between 1990 and 1997 suggests that the relative income in St. Charles County was increasing at the expense of St. Louis County. These trends will likely continue as business moves deeper into the region's suburbs. Between 1970 and 1990, St. Louis City lost approximately 82,061 manufacturing jobs. During this same time frame, the counties surrounding the city gained more than 44,000 manufacturing jobs; the bulk of these jobs (35,229) appeared in St. Louis County.

Racial Disparities in the St. Louis Region

Giloth (2000a) makes a strong case in support of analytical paradigms that include racial inequality as a major factor shaping reforms in workforce development policy. The St. Louis region is characterized by sharp differences in racial inequality and extremely high levels of concentrated poverty in the city, especially in its northern communities and neighborhoods. Racial polarization has undermined the region's civic capacity, and continues to influence local debate over workforce development policy. High levels of concentrated poverty among African Americans are now beginning to appear in the inner-ring suburbs of St. Louis County. Our analysis suggests that the racial inequities and disparities in the region will likely continue to be integral components of any successful effort to promote systemic changes in workforce development practices in St. Louis (Manning, 1998). Racial inequality is a pervasive, underlying factor shaping a wide variety of political issues in the St. Louis region, thereby amplifying the importance of Giloth's observations.

Consistent with Wilson's (1987) analysis of structural inequalities found in Chicago's urban economy, poverty and racial disparity in St. Louis are among the most severe in the nation. The size of the urban underclass in St. Louis represents one of the most pressing challenges to those leaders and political constituencies who are attempting to promote changes in workforce development policy in the region's labor markets. According to Checkoway (1992), St. Louis is one of the poorest and most distressed cities in the nation. Similar patterns of racial inequality are found in East St. Louis (Shaw, 2000). According to 1990 census figures, almost one in four of St. Louis City's residents live in poverty, and over 55 percent of its children reside in poverty (Jargowsky, 1997). The St. Louis public school system reports that over 80 percent of its students fall below the official poverty level, and that public school teachers can expect an approximate 40 percent turnover of students enrolled in their classes each year. Over 70 percent of students were eligible for free or reduced-price lunches in 1998. Approximately 40 percent of students enrolled in the St. Louis public schools in 1997 did not complete high school and contribute to an average dropout rate of 16.2 percent—one of the highest in the nation.

Although the St. Louis region is less segregated now than it was in 1970 (Farley, 2001), it remains among the most segregated cities in the nation. Not only has the African American population become increasingly concentrated in the city and in the older suburbs of St. Louis County, income disparities between black and white residents appear to have increased. In 1990, a black family's median income was about 53.5 percent of that found among white families (Manning, 1998). In 1970, however, the median income of black families was about 60 percent of that found among white families. A recent study reported that that the poverty rate in the city increased from 19.9 percent of the total population in 1970 to about 24 percent living in poverty in 1990 (Manning, 1998). Most significantly, according to the study, the disparity rates between African American and white poverty found in St. Louis were among the five highest of the cities studied. Those African Americans living in St. Louis City in 1990 reported the lowest average personal income ($7,154) in comparison with those living in the four counties surrounding the city. In the four-county area, white residents consistently claimed more than 90 percent of total aggregate personal income.

Data also show that in 1990, African Americans lagged considerably behind whites in educational attainment levels in both the city and county. Although African Americans residing in the county revealed higher graduation rates from colleges than those reported by black residents of the city, both populations were considerably behind the proportion of whites graduating from institutions of higher education. Census data show that rates of formal education among the African American population have changed little over time. In 1970, about 20.8 percent of the city's African American population reported that they had graduated from high school; in 1990, this figure had increased to only 27.3 percent. In the county, approximately 25 percent of African Americans reported that they had graduated from high school in 1970; by 1990, this figure increased to only 26.6 percent. The lowest levels of educational attainment were found among African American males living in St. Louis City, thereby emphasizing the importance of targeting this population in workforce development initiatives (Giloth, 2000a).

Based upon these data, it is clear that the population in greatest need of training and workforce assistance is African Americans living in the city and county. In terms of sheer numbers, however, many white residents also report low levels of formal education. Approximately 46,287 African-American and 47,687 white residents of the city reported having less than a high school education in 1990. In the county, 19,230 African Americans and 96,163 whites reported having less than a high school education. Overall, therefore, about 68.7 percent of the total population who reported having less than a high school education in St. Louis City and St. Louis County are white, and 31.3 percent are African American. Although it is probably erroneous to assume that levels of formal education can determine eligibility for workforce development and training programs, the data do reveal the political dilemmas involved in targeting only the African-American population (Wilson, 1999).

Many of the neighborhoods now populated by African Americans were occupied by working- and middle-class whites during the post-war period of industrial and manufacturing prosperity in St. Louis. Middle- and working-class white residents left these neighborhoods partly in response to the economic restructuring of the region and the layoffs that followed in its wake. Although white flight and racial antagonism surely contributed to the sweeping demographic changes that occurred in St. Louis during the 1970s and 1980s, disinvestment and deindustrialization also undermined the economic vitality of the city's neighborhoods and severely compromised its ability to sustain the delivery of urban services, especially public education (Bluestone and Harrison, 1984). More significantly, the white working and middle classes of St. Louis were directly affected by economic restructuring because it was this population that disproportionately occupied the higher-paying union jobs found in the city's declining manufacturing and industrial sectors.

188   SCOTT CUMMINGS, ALLAN TOMEY, & ROBERT FLACK

Our analysis suggests that current workforce development activities in St. Louis have not addressed adequately the underlying racial component of program interventions. Although current initiatives have made effective efforts to enfranchise community organizations and agencies—especially the African-American political constituency—we do not think these efforts reflect a strategic mix of regional and place-based policy interventions. Racial politics remain an explicit, albeit unstated, component of much of the strategic maneuverings surrounding workforce development politics in the region. Moving beyond a racially targeted initiative, however, will not be easy, and will likely entail skillful negotiation over difficult and controversial programmatic tradeoffs (Wilson, 1996, 1999).

Although more African Americans now live in St. Louis County (193,306) than in the city (153,565), they compose only around 19 percent of the county's total population, and a much lower proportion of the region's population. African Americans, therefore, are more of a political force in city as opposed to county and regional politics. Nonetheless, low turnout among African-American voters reduces their influence at the polls. And, although St. Louis is now a predominantly African-American city, whites of voting age still outnumber blacks eligible to vote in city elections. The consequences of these political demographics were seen when Francis Slay was elected in the last mayoral race. Slay, a white candidate, defeated two African-American candidates for the Democratic nomination, largely because of bloc voting among whites and widespread support for his candidacy among the downtown corporate community.

Racial politics—directly or indirectly—dominate many public policy issues facing the city and region. Many suburban residents view St. Louis City and East St. Louis as having intractable racial problems. Although no public official would likely admit to such a proposition, the counties and political jurisdictions surrounding these two cities would prefer to keep racial issues and problems confined to the city. Yet, this agenda is not at all compatible with those elements of the local growth coalition that are aggressively promoting the transformation of the downtown area. An absence of consensus among downtown and suburban development interests often undermines the capacity of the St. Louis regime to govern, to wield power in an efficient and strategic manner, and to agree upon a common workforce development agenda. These problems reflect the observations of Stone about a regime's capacity to govern and reveal the difficulties entailed in organizing a performance regime around an agenda like workforce development reform.

Moreover, black political figures in the city and county must still cater to the white corporate community and to those business interests that are attempting to revitalize the downtown, construct a new stadium for the

St. Louis Cardinals, and increase tourism in the central city. Two recent black mayors in St. Louis could ill afford to alienate the white business community, and had to balance the tradeoffs involved in satisfying a progressive agenda supported by African American community groups (Lauria, Whelan, and Young, 1994; Newman, 1994), with the development agenda being pursued by the local business elite. Consistent with Stone's (1988) observations, the stability of a progressive regime is often undermined under these circumstances, and pressure upon minority politicians often compels them to become more conservative than their voting constituency would prefer (Banks, 2000).

To the extent that workforce development policy in St. Louis continues to be perceived as a "black issue" or a "black program," it is likely that political debate over the matter will mirror the class and racial divisions that split city and suburban interests in the region. It is important to note that suburban interests in St. Louis have benefited from economic restructuring. As noted earlier, suburban St. Louis has managed to attract 44,000 manufacturing jobs since 1970. Suburban Wentzville, for example, was able to retain the General Motors assembly plant after the company had threatened to leave the region altogether in the late 1980s. As a result, suburban political interests have been much more responsive to workforce development issues related to displaced workers. As was observed by an informant interviewed for this report, "White union members vote; minorities living in St. Louis don't." According to the informant, suburban elected officials and business leaders have been lukewarm about transportation strategies to bring inner-city residents to suburban jobs, or to modify housing and land-use policies that might result in creating more racial and social class diversity in the suburbs.

Political Fragmentation and Workforce Development Policy in St. Louis

Even advocates of a regional approach to workforce development policy acknowledge the difficulties involved in organizing political support across urban and suburban governmental jurisdictions (Orfield, 1997). These formal political barriers are even more difficult to overcome when extreme geographic disparities in wealth and income across metropolitan regions are institutionalized in the form of separate political jurisdictions and governments. In St. Louis, political fragmentation, racial inequality, and development disparities are integral components of a highly contentious and competitive political environment.

The political fragmentation in the St. Louis MSA, although extreme, simply reflects existing disparities of wealth and power across the region. Jones (2000) reports no less than ninety-two separate political jurisdictions

in the St. Louis metropolitan region. In St. Louis County alone, local government service delivery is divided among more than 150 political jurisdictions. The state of Missouri, St. Louis County government, ninety-two
municipalities, and a large number of special districts levy taxes separately
and provide services directly to residents of the county. According to Jones
(2000), these separate governments insulate the wealthy from the myriad
urban problems left behind in St. Louis City. For all practical purposes,
upper- and middle-income whites can create political and legal barriers
between themselves and the African American poor living in the city by
maintaining strict building codes and restricting land-use policies within
their separate suburban jurisdictions.

Political fragmentation within the formal structures of city and county
government is also mirrored in the organization of public education.
According to an East-West Gateway report (2001), the region's public
school system

> is one of the most fractured in the nation. In 1992, there were 119 differ-
> ent public school districts in the St. Louis metropolitan area. With 4.7
> school districts per 100,000 people, St. Louis is only surpassed by Okla-
> homa City and Portland in the number of these governmental entities per
> capita. (2)

When it comes to workforce development policies and politics, the perceived and actual interests of city and suburban residents in the St. Louis
region are not easily reconciled. These observations are illustrated partly
by the number of individuals who currently work in St. Louis City but live
outside its boundaries. In 1960, 84.1 percent of the city's residents also
worked in St. Louis; by 1990, this figure had dropped to 65.7 percent. In
1960, 58.7 percent of all city workers also lived in St. Louis; by 1990, this
proportion dropped to 32.9 percent. In 1960, only 30.9 percent of city
workers lived in St. Louis County; by 1990, 42.7 percent of the city's
workforce was living in St. Louis County. Reflecting the widespread patterns of deindustrialization that occurred during the 1970s and early
1980s, 33.9 percent of the city's manufacturing workforce also lived in
St. Louis in 1960. By 1990, this proportion dropped to 13.3 percent. The
data also show, however, that the proportion of the city's professional
workforce living in St. Louis increased from 12.4 percent in 1960 to 30
percent in 1990.

The disjuncture between location of residence and location of work,
the racial composition of the suburbs, and the governmental structures
that parallel these disparities make it difficult for city and suburban residents to agree upon a common workforce development agenda (Nicklaus,
2000). Ironically, the inability to agree upon a common regional agenda

conspires to align both suburban whites and urban blacks behind place-specific strategies of workforce development like those being promoted by the Initiative for a Competitive Inner City (ICIC, 2000; Porter, 1998a, 1998b, 2000). ICIC's proposal to revitalize St. Louis City's economy was well received by African American political interests, and those elements of the corporate community committed to revitalizing the downtown (Nicklaus, 2000; "Real Strategy," 2000). More significant, however, is the fragmented and competitive manner in which the various political jurisdictions in the region have historically responded to federal workforce development policies.

Workforce Development Politics in Action: An Unauthorized Political History

As part of this case study, we conducted in-depth interviews with key individuals who have been, and continue to be involved, in workforce politics in the region. All respondents were pledged confidentially in return for their candid commentary. Their comments about the history of workforce development in St. Louis and their prognoses about the potential for long-term systems reform are consistent with the critical observations about workforce development policy summarized by Fung and Zdrazil (2003). They also illustrate the critical observations of Stone about the factors that undermine civic capacity and curtail reform. As explained by one official interviewed, each political jurisdiction within the region has its own set of interests to protect and its own position on what constitutes the best course of action for workforce development policy. When reflecting upon how the region implemented prior workforce policies, he observed that each jurisdiction had its own "pot of money" and had considerable latitude on how to spend it: "That is why they don't give money to mayors and county executives anymore; that's the primary reason why the CETA days are over; the mayors and county executives spent it on what they wanted to."

Consistent with his colleague, another informant commented that in the late 1970s

> at the end of CETA, there were millions of dollars coming into St Louis County, which at the time was considered a very rich county. And there was money that was coming in for public-service employment, which was the thing that eventually killed CETA. The money was flowing in for youth programs. The "feds" were pouring all kinds of money into the region to try and have people try different things. Well, at that time, nobody stuck their nose into anyone's business because they had more than enough money to deal with it. With public-service employment dollars there were years when they would come out and say, "Here is 8 million dollars; it is yours and you

will spend it by the end of the year." Each one of the jurisdictions had their own separate pot of money and it was more than they could spend. The city had probably twice as much as St. Louis County and everybody else had their own good-sized pot as well.

With the replacement of the CETA by the JTPA in 1982, workforce development policy at the local level became increasingly tied to various community-based organizations (CBOs). Nonetheless, these legislative changes and reforms, according to our informants, did little to alter the delivery of services through a system of deeply entrenched political relationships at the local level. The St. Louis pattern is consistent with that explained by Fung and Zdrazil (2003): "For those local networks of CBOs, neighborhood associations, and the various possible relationships and politics among them often emerge as 'armies of resistance' to policy changes, denying program implementation or remolding it to local conditions, traditions, and advantages" (7).

Although JTPA was designed partly to weaken the control of workforce development funds by local elected officials, all of our informants contended that JTPA did little to alter the fragmented and politicized manner in which the St. Louis region responded to workforce development issues. According to one informant:

> In 1982, when JTPA came in, and just prior to the end of CETA, they had something called Title 7, which created the private industry councils [PICs]. The PICs had a little control over some of the funds. JTPA came in and said that the PICs are no longer advisory councils but are full partners with the elected officials. So, no workforce development budget could be approved unless it was approved by the PIC. The PIC had to be 51 percent business, and it had to have representatives from community-based organizations, social security offices, and education, social services, and DVR [Division of Vocation Rehabilitation]. But each of the major jurisdictions in the region had their own PIC, and the elected officials always found ways to stack the PICs and control the funds.

In the St. Louis region, according to informants, each government responded to workforce development policy as a separate political entity, thereby reflecting the fragmented set of political relationships that characterizes its formal governments. For a short time during the early phases of JTPA, a regional PIC was formed between St. Louis City and St. Louis County. All of the other counties, including the Illinois component of the St. Louis MSA, established their own PICs. The joint city and county PIC, however, did not prove to be a sustainable partnership. The competitive forces that undermined this effort mirrored the larger internal conflict of interests between the city and the suburbs.

As explained by one interviewee, the initial collaboration between the city and county was made possible because the two directors of the programs established a good working relationship with each other, "and at the time it made sense to try to keep things together." What really made the relationship work, according to the informant, is the fact that "they were sitting on their own separate pots of money; the city and the county had their own pots of money; from a planning standpoint, they could go along with a single PIC as long as they controlled their money."

According to another informant, what eventually undermined the joint PIC was the intrusion of the Regional Commerce and Growth Association (RCGA), and its effort to assume leadership over workforce development policy in the area. RCGA has since emerged as a high profile, regional economic development entity in the St. Louis MSA (Jones, 2000). At the time, however, much of its activities were directed toward city and county issues. What was viewed as a "power play" on the part of RCGA, according to one informant, ultimately undermined cooperative relations between the city and county, and eventually reinforced the fragmented manner in which the region responded to workforce development policy. Ironically, according to this informant, the involvement of RCGA was initiated because the city and county PIC had poor representation on the part of the private sector.

Another individual interviewed suggested that private-sector representation and participation gradually drifted toward RCGA efforts to establish administrative and financial control over workforce development initiatives. Initially, both the city and county had separate directors of their respective PICs. In addition, each had a separate staff and an independent budget. A third individual was hired by RCGA who

> was pretty well on the same line as the directors of the city and county PICs, but he was an employee of the RCGA. He tried a power play and we all assumed that he took his direction from his employer. He tried to remove the joint council. He was not a director but it apparently was his thought that everything should report to him—that his office should be the ultimate power and the program directors should report to him. He tried that sweep but it didn't work.

Those interviewed thought that the internal political dispute over control of the city and county PIC, and presumably the funds potentially associated with it, eventually undermined one of the few early efforts at regional planning in workforce development in the St. Louis region. A key event that apparently intensified the controversy was the erosion of funds that accompanied the introduction of JTPA into the workforce development policy arena. According to one former official,

> When JTPA came in we lost probably 25 percent to 30 percent of our work-
> force funds off the top; the feds just cut it out; mostly they were employ-
> ment dollars; we lasted about a year or so and everybody knew there was
> going to be a power play to take control of the remaining budget; many of
> the staffers and directors expected the RCGA group to say, "you will no
> longer have this budget; I will take yours and the city's budget and put it
> together as mine."

Fearing loss of administrative and financial control, several administrative officials within the workforce development establishment lobbied
elected officials to retrench and secure their respective budgets. Independent of what political forces were behind a regional planning effort, or
their level of credibility, elected officials apparently did not see the political wisdom of surrendering budget control of their respective workforce
development dollars. And, private interests saw little to be gained by taking sides in what was essentially a struggle within the formal political and
governmental arena. At a meeting at which a formal vote was to be taken
on the RCGA consolidation scheme, city and county representatives made
it clear that they did not support the plan. The elected officials from the
city and county sent their executive officers to the meeting to indicate that
their CEOs were strongly opposed to the consolidation plan.

At that point, according to one participant whom we interviewed "it
became very political and clear to the private industry people that a major
problem was brewing and most did not see the point in starting a full-
scale fight with those in political power; and so when they brought it up
for a vote it lost."

In line with city and suburban interests, and independent of what was
viewed as a "power play" on the part of the RCGA, there were other reasons why the joint city and county PIC was undermined so easily. As one
interviewee explained,

> Many of the county players thought, although they would not admit it pub-
> licly, that there was no need to take county dollars and deal with city issues,
> and vice versa. The inner city had its own issues and we didn't want the PIC
> staff to end up pitting one set of interests against another. There are com-
> pletely different issues in the county in comparison to the inner city; and
> people in the county have to deal with suburban issues.

What followed in the wake of the split between the two PICs was a
loose confederation of PIC directorship partners. The separate directors
from the city and county, and from Jefferson, Franklin, and St. Charles
counties, and Madison and St. Clair counties in Illinois, would meet quarterly to coordinate what they were doing and then report back to their
respective constituencies. One participant explained that the loose

collaboration would continue through the directors meeting with each other, each reporting that information back to their respective PIC; and that is how it has stayed for the past several years. Each jurisdiction has been more or less left on its own—the employment and training group, they did their thing—took the federal money that was flowing through to them and went into the community and served those that needed to be served.

According to one individual, the degree of local autonomy exercised prior to the passage of WIA rivals that found during the CETA era. Explaining that many elected county and city officials did not even like the request for proposal (RFP) process through which JTPA required workforce development funds to be allocated. He contended that most elected officials and administrators "wanted to take the money and direct it more. They wanted to have more control as to who would get those dollars—who will get it and what agency will get it." Explaining that the political process really drove the allocation of workforce dollars, he observed that "we really didn't have a straight RFP process. It was really a 'somebody looking over your shoulder' RFP process. It was really pretty interesting how information was disseminated about what funds were available—and who ended up with funds."

The economic restructuring of the metropolis appears to have had a major impact on how workforce development policy was implemented in the St. Louis region. During the mid-1980s, many local corporations started downsizing and initiated mass layoffs. During this time period, one individual reported that

> Title 3 of JTPA really kicked in for the dislocated workers and because there were mass layoffs in the region we started working together again. Some of the officials said "OK, we've got McDonald Douglas cutting back and St. Louis County had to recognize that there was a major component that was in St. Charles so they gave part of that grant to St. Charles." It really made more sense for them to be dealing with the problems out of their area.

Interestingly, economic crisis produced a degree of workforce development cooperation and coordination that could not be obtained through the established political process.

> We were all working together to deal with the layoffs, either assigning staff or assigning resources; but, again there were big dollars that became available. There were federal dollars through Title 3 for displaced GM workers and there were big bucks from state money as well. Everybody had respect for everybody else. We built relationships that we knew would work and we had to organize things faster because a lot of people were effected and in trouble.

Informants indicated that during most of this period, the East-West Gateway Coordinating Council, the region's transportation Metropolitan Planning Organization (MPO), was not involved in local or regional workforce development politics or program activities. In 1995, however, a major grant from the Annie E. Casey Foundation (n.d., 2001) elevated East-West Gateway as a prime time player in local workforce development politics. One interviewee stated, "East-West was nowhere in the game. They were not in the game until around the early 1990s when they went after a grant called *Bridges to Work*. East-West got money to do a study and set up a program that was designed to get people to the same areas where the jobs were being created." As the regional transportation entity, the East-West program was consistent with their mandate and addressed an increasingly popular approach to the spatial mismatch formulation of workforce development policy.

The program was based on the idea that jobs were not in the same area as the people who might fill them. According to those interviewed, East-West's intention was to develop a program to take inner-city people out to where jobs were being created. Chesterfield, a far western suburb of St. Louis, was selected as the target community. Although there were service-sector jobs in Chesterfield, there was only one bus that served the area: "The bus apparently went out to Chesterfield one time in the morning and another returned one time at night. Most of the time, the bus stopped only at the mall and didn't go further into the valley." A grant was obtained with the assistance of various participating entities, and East-West "made the pitch that it should be the one to administer the program due to prior experience with regional transportation issues."

According to some individuals interviewed, the *Bridges to Work* initiative served as the springboard from which East-West Gateway attempted to expand its sphere of influence from regional transportation to workforce development policy. Based upon one respondent's version of local history, in the mid-1990s East-West Gateway made efforts to mobilize political support behind the idea of assuming leadership of workforce development policy in the region, attempting to promote and resurrect the idea of a regional PIC. A formal proposal was circulated that outlined plans for an area-wide initiative that would be structured like a regional PIC. One informant recalls,

> that is when everybody in the community went into a defensive posture. Some individuals at East-West were lobbying hard to get people back to the table and consolidate or at least attempt to secure a new position for itself in workforce development.

Another informant believed that this occurred at

right about the time that Casey showed up in town and they were probably impressed by what East-West was attempting to do; Casey came in at the prime time for East-West because they really had no history in this area and had never done anything in workforce development before.

Independent of their previous accomplishments and considerable credibility as a regional planning entity, there appears to exist some level of resentment over the selection of East-West Gateway as the development intermediary for the Annie E. Casey Foundation project. Although all interviewed conceded that workforce development policy in the region has not been implemented in an exemplary manner, and funds have not been expended in the most efficient way, a distinctly adversarial tone toward East-West Gateway was evident in nearly all of the interviews conducted during the study.

Explaining the competitive dynamics driving workforce development politics in the St. Louis region, one informant contended:

The whole workforce development program has always been just a cash cow. If the elected officials can get the money coming in and they can do some things with it, then that's all right but they really don't want to deal with the real political issues. I can't say this and you can't quote me but the people who really need the help don't vote and they are poor. They are not invested in the community and they can't play in the political game. So, the incentive is to carry out the program and don't pay any attention to the clients. They are poor so just take the money. It is just for poor blacks and there are no political costs if you don't accomplish anything. This is the real political side of it but I can't prove it and no one will admit to it.

Elaborating on his political analysis, the informant explained,

You can ask "Will this program help or will it make sense?" But it's all right if nothing really happens. We'll do this and we'll do that and if we can get a special grant to deal with something like the McDonald Douglas crisis, well that's great. I can stand next to Sandy McDonald or some other political or labor big wigs and everyone can claim they did something positive. And most important, the elected officials can show what they did in their next campaign. See what we did. Look at what we did. That's the only time that workforce development stuff has any real sex appeal.

According to another observer, youth programs do not generate much political capital or interest among elected officials either.

As JTPA went along, we watched the funding move into youth programs and eventually into other areas. But Title 3 for dislocated workers just rose astronomically. Take it back to its basic political points: "Do kids vote? *Nope.* Do dislocated workers vote? Probably, and most likely. *Yes*. And will I lose a base of political support if they leave my town?" So, there is a lot more reason to fight and there's a lot more bang for the political buck if I'm front and center showing that I'm fighting for dislocated workers. That's a vote for me.

According to several of those who have been involved in workforce development politics in St. Louis, it is not entirely clear how recent reforms accompanying the WIA will interface with established political practices and institutions. Some local observers, however, contend that existing agencies and established organizations will simply "morph" into whatever is being required by the new policies and reforms. One example identified is the Cornerstone Partnership. Modeled after Detroit's FOCUS Hope, Cornerstone was initially created by the St. Louis County Economic Council. The original plan was to provide metal manufacturing training through programs run by the St. Louis Community College District and the Rankin Technical College. The program did not reach the expected levels of service activity achieved by FOCUS Hope, nor was community and business involvement very high. As the Cornerstone Partnership evolved, more traditional training courses such as construction and computers were added and the initiative ultimately "morphed" into the Metropolitan Employment and Training Center (MET Center).

Most contend that "PICs will simply become WIBs, and the same players will be around the table." One informant was bolder in his prognoses.

> This is where the real cynic comes in. The clowns that developed this and who think that WIBs are really a control point in the system are in an ivory tower and don't know the real world. Because of the way they set it up a PIC and now a WIB are appointed by the chief elected official. The appointment is certified by the governor but the only thing that anyone is going to change is if the members are all white males from big companies. That might be fixed but otherwise you still have the local officials in charge and money is still coming right to them; the WIB is supposed to control the process but the elected officials still control who is on the WIB or the PIC, or whatever.

Based upon our interviews and general observations, we are comfortable concluding that workforce development policy has been and continues to be shaped largely by the way in which local politics have been and will probably continue to be practiced in the St. Louis region. Workforce development reformers must operate in a local political climate that is highly contentious, adversarial, and competitive (Walsh, 2000). Based upon this conclusion, we can offer several observations about current workforce development activities in St. Louis, and speculate about the future of workforce development reform in the St. Louis region.

St. Louis Is a Tough Place: Local Resistance to National Reform

The fragmentation of local government, racial disparities and inequities in the region, and the restructuring of the regional economy all conspire to make St. Louis a contentious and difficult political environment in which to operate. One of our informants explained, "St. Louis is a tough place to play the political game." Workforce development policies in the region have typically been implemented with an eye toward jurisdictional budget control, and within the confines of existing political relationships and alliances. Local implementation has been reinforced by the fragmented and uncoordinated manner in which federal workforce policy has evolved. Despite the policy innovations accompanying the passage of the WIA, local interests have been busy adapting prior institutional arrangements and political alliances to the latest round of federal requirements. Smart money is betting that the established players in the workforce development arena will make a smooth transition from the old to the new policy landscape.

In order to illustrate the complicated and fragmented nature of current workforce development activities in St. Louis, Figure 6.2 depicts current revenue flows into the region. The various funding streams present a partial profile of the total amount invested in workforce development. For example, federal funds from the Department of Education do not appear in the figure, nor do private funds and charitable donations from sources like the United Way or local foundations. The primary sources of federal funds are, however, included. These funds are received from the Department of Labor and from Health and Human Services. These funds are directly targeted for workforce development programs and welfare reform, respectively. Figure 6.2 also depicts the recent grant from the Annie E. Casey Foundation (Abt Associates, n.d., 1997, 2000).

Within the St. Louis metropolitan area, which includes East St. Louis, two state governments are involved in the implementation of welfare reform and workforce development policy: Illinois and Missouri. As a result, the political dynamics of two state governments and their respective agencies complicate the delivery of services and programs to the target populations. Within the bi-state target area, a wide variety of entities deliver training and workforce development services to the client population, including organized labor, community colleges, private for-profit training institutions, nonprofit CBOs, and business and industry.

As noted in our discussion of fragmentation within the formal governmental sector, the existing system of service providers is highly fractured and competitive. As the current Director of Policy and Programming at

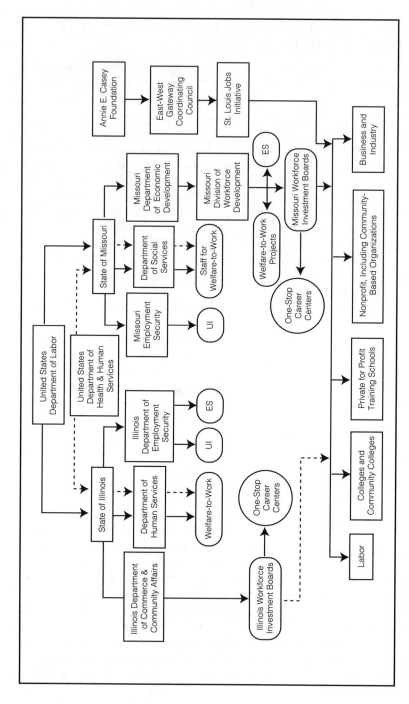

Figure 6.2 Workforce Development Funding Streams

East-West Gateway explains it, "There are 114 public and two major denominational school districts serving children, youth, and (in some instances) adults throughout the region. The region has nine major technical and vocational schools, nine two-year and community colleges, three public colleges and universities, and nine independent colleges and universities. Approximately, 170 nonprofit organizations provide some form of employment/job training services." Her observations are further illustrated by the difficulties entailed in coordinating training services through the region's community college system.

The region's community colleges are important providers of workforce development training and placement services. The St. Louis Community College District serves residents of St. Louis City and County. They provide job search assistance and coordinate private sector on-the-job training efforts under contract through the Center for Industry, Business, and Labor (CIBL). Separate community colleges, financed through a separate funding stream, however, serve the Illinois side of the St. Louis metropolitan area. Additionally, on the Missouri side of the metropolitan region, separate community college districts in St. Charles, Franklin, and Jefferson Counties operate independently, and are less involved in workforce development activities.

The United Way of Greater St. Louis has recently identified no less than 267 organizational entities that offer some type of workforce development and training program in the metropolitan region. These entities vary widely in the type of services provided and in the number of clients served. Although some of these entities are part of larger administrative operations (e.g., city and county government, community colleges, Veteran's Administration, etc.), it is clear that there are many interests competing for workforce development market shares in the St. Louis region. These market shares include not only clients but also subcontracts and contracts with private companies, foundations, and federal, state, and local governments to provide workforce development and training services.

The extensive service provider infrastructure is funded by a variety of dedicated local tax revenues, private donations, fee-for-service arrangements, as well as state and federal appropriations. Reflecting the fragmented nature of the St. Louis region, the federal funds for workforce development activities are administered through six separate WIBs—four in Missouri and two in Illinois. Each of the WIBs is linked to a political jurisdiction. In Missouri, the jurisdictions include St. Louis City, St. Louis County, St. Charles County, and the Jefferson and Franklin County consortium. In Illinois, the several counties included are Jersey and Madison, and Bond, St. Clair, and Monroe.

Table 6.2   Workforce Investment Act Program Allocations for the St. Louis Metropolitan Statistical Area from 2001 to 2002

County	Total	Allocation ($)		
		Adult Programs	Workers Programs	Dislocated Youth Programs
Illinois				
Jersey	$1,900,180	$679,096	$500,770	$720,314
Madison and Bond	$2,246,045	$745,992	$657,820	$842,233
St. Clair and Monroe	$3,892,969	$1,420,740	$805,323	$1,666,906
Total	$8,039,194	$2,845,828	$1,963,913	$3,229,453
Missouri				
St. Louis City	$8,020,375	$3,108,646	$1,079,553	$3,832,176
St. Louis County	$3,989,302	$1,373,099	$947,393	$1,668,810
St. Charles	$399,955	$53,579	$267,290	$76,086
Jefferson and Franklin	$487,082	$111,361	$241,303	$134,418
Total	$12,896,714	$4,646,685	$2,535,539	$5,711,490

Source: Data provided by individual Workforce Investment Boards in Illinois and Missouri.

Table 6.2 illustrates the current WIA allocations targeted for the St. Louis metropolitan area. Federal funds are still allocated to and are reported within governmental jurisdictions, thereby reinforcing administrative and political processes that undermine and frustrate regional planning efforts. Moreover, the amounts allocated are substantial, especially for St. Louis City, St. Louis County, and East St. Louis. Although the amounts may be small in comparison to the dollars available during the CETA era, it is not reasonable to assume that any political jurisdiction or its elected and administrative officials will relinquish fiscal control over a shrinking supply of federal funds to their competing political or regional planning entity. It would not be surprising to learn, therefore, that city and county interests may be even less willing under WIA to engage in regional planning efforts over workforce development policy, especially if their respective budgets appear threatened.

Table 6.3 indicates the allocation of total state dollars invested in workforce development programs for the St. Louis MSA. The amounts invested parallel the proportions appearing in Table 6.2. St. Louis City and St. Louis County receive the bulk of funds in Missouri. In Illinois, the bulk of funds are invested in Monroe and St. Clair Counties, which include East St. Louis. Both tables indicate that public funds continue to be invested in and reported by political jurisdictions, and that programs continue to be implemented by these same governmental entities in tandem with the WIBs associated with those entities.

Table 6.3   Allocation of Total State Dollars Spent on Workforce Development in the
St. Louis Metropolitan Statistical Area

County	Federal Workforce Development Funds Received (%)	Assumed Allocation ($) 2001	Assumed Allocation ($) 2000
Illinois			
Clinton	1.832	$3,203,881	$1,941,232
Jersey	1.832	$3,203,881	$1,941,232
Madison	2.166	$3,787,042	$2,294,569
Monroe	3.754	$6,563,910	$3,977,074
St. Clair	3.754	$6,563,910	$3,977,074
Missouri			
Franklin	1.060	$728,513	$677,920
Jefferson	1.060	$728,513	$677,920
Lincoln	1.060	$728,513	$677,920
St. Charles	0.510	$350,496	$326,155
St. Louis City	29.590	$20,335,644	$18,923,408
St. Louis County	13.070	$6,982,304	$8,358,518
Warren	1.060	$728,513	$677,920
Total		$53,905,120	$44,450,942

SOURCE: Data provided by individual Workforce Investment Boards in Illinois and Missouri.

Several interviewees explained that it is in the political interest of elected public officials to control the composition of the WIB operating within their jurisdiction. Each WIB, therefore, is subject to the influence of established political figures and coalitions who have a direct stake in workforce development policies. More often than not, the network of political relationships is confined within specific governmental jurisdictions and the geographic space associated with them. Fung and Zdrazil (2003) refer to these spatially bounded political arrangements as "workforce development ecologies." Similar observations can be applied to the political processes that result in contractual relationships between governmental entities and the numerous organizations and agencies who provide workforce development services. Some informants contend that contractual relationships with providers are typically confined within political jurisdictions. In the case of the St. Louis metropolitan region, there are numerous jurisdictions involved.

Reflecting the racial disparities described elsewhere in this study, the selection of target service areas and the specification of eligibility for program participation are also influenced by the social and political composition of the multiple jurisdictions within the St. Louis metropolitan area. Because minorities were largely underserved through previous initiatives, the Annie E. Casey Foundation encouraged the Jobs Initiative program to target African-American males. African-American political interests in St. Louis City and in East St. Louis have been highly critical of previous workforce development initiatives. In 1999, a group of protesters shut down Interstate Highway 70, demanding increased opportunities for minorities in the construction industry (Kee and Leiser, 2000). The protest resulted in the establishment of the Construction Training School at the MET Center in St. Louis.

Selection of appropriate target areas and constituencies for workforce development initiatives is seldom devoid of racial conflict and controversy. An East-West Gateway spokesperson explained that the selection of appropriate CBOs and community agencies to implement the Jobs Initiative program within the target area was initially contentious. During interviews, East-West Gateway officials also acknowledged that because the Jobs Initiative program makes a strong effort to target an African American constituency, its potential appeal to county residents and officials is limited.

The Annie E. Casey Foundation, the East-West Gateway Coordinating Council, and the Jobs Initiative are depicted as part of a separate funding stream in Figure 6.2. The leadership challenges facing East-West Gateway are significant and illustrate the obstacles discussed by Stone that sometimes frustrate the emergence of a performance regime. As the region's transportation MPO, East-West controls significant transportation funds from the federal government. Transportation funds have been pivotal to the development of the suburbs in the St. Louis region. Although emphasis had been placed on the need to transport inner-city residents to the job-rich nodes of suburban economic activity via public transportation and light rail services, the primary beneficiaries of freeway construction are regional developers, real estate entrepreneurs, and the mortgage industry. The strategic position of East-West Gateway in regional transportation politics, therefore, ensures that suburban jurisdictions will pursue cooperative relations with them. Despite the potential significance of using public transportation to move inner-city residents to the suburbs to pursue job opportunities, the movement of East-West Gateway into the workforce development arena has not been altogether smooth—a fact that further reflects the contentious nature of the St. Louis political environment.

In its capacity as the regional council of governments (COG), East-West has cultivated and established an important service relationship with the political jurisdictions in its service area. It has also cultivated and obtained cooperative relationships across two state governments. Nonetheless, East-West's movement into workforce development politics through the *Bridges to Work* program, and more recently through the

Casey-sponsored Jobs Initiative program, is apparently viewed with suspicion within some political quarters. Several individuals interviewed contended that East-West Gateway would continue to encounter stiff resistance to any effort to consolidate workforce development planning under its managerial auspices. Some individuals expressed cynicism about the "imperialistic" and "expansionistic" motives of East-West Gateway in the workforce development arena. They were especially concerned about any efforts to, in their words, "control workforce dollars" and to "consolidate planning" under East-West's existing operations. Although we are not in a position to determine the magnitude or severity of these political obstacles, it does seem clear that Stone's observations about the numerous barriers preventing the emergence of a reform agenda are potentially very significant for the St. Louis region.

As Stone observed, and our analysis suggests, the adversarial nature of St. Louis politics will probably limit and constrain the possibility of longer-term system reforms in workforce development policies. In light of the barriers described previously in this chapter, it is significant to note that some individuals who are affiliated with the St. Louis Regional Jobs Initiative—the program funded by the Annie E. Casey Foundation—were candid about the difficulties involved in seeking and promoting progressive change in workforce development policy in the region. Nonetheless, they are aggressively pursuing a reform agenda and attempting to exercise leadership in a region that has a well-established reputation for sustaining a contentious and competitive political culture. As articulated by the Director of Planning and Programming for East-West Gateway, the "capacity for systems reform in the St. Louis region" is being built through a collaborative effort between East-West Gateway and the RCGA that was launched during the spring of 2001.

In order to promote longer-term systems reform and regional workforce planning, a thirty-eight member policy group called the St. Louis Regional Workforce Development Policy Group has been organized. The group currently consists of fourteen business leaders, eight elected officials, twelve educational figures and administrators, two labor leaders, and the respective heads of East-West Gateway and RCGA. The mission statement adopted by the Policy Group is ambitious, and includes the recommendations derived from a series of focus group interviews conducted by state and private-sector consultants. As determined from interviews, personal correspondences, and comments made by various committee members, the agenda being proffered by the Policy Group is regional in nature, and identifies important but very difficult to achieve goals and objectives, such as:
(1) Identify and monitor the skills, aptitudes, and attitudes needed in the workforce and work with all levels of public education to ensure these

qualities are included in the curriculum; (2) develop linkages between businesses and educational institutions that are "market driven" and "responsive;" (3) "encourage business" to use existing training systems and to encourage them to raise the skill levels of mid- and entry-level workers; (4) create a research presence among local universities in the workforce development arena; (5) develop and market a "regional workforce intelligence system" capable of linking workforce demands with appropriate business retention and recruitment strategies; (6) link planning and decision-making so that private and public investment strategies can be coordinated with regional development strategies; and (7) coordinate private and public resources behind a regional workforce development strategy.

In addition to the larger policy group, the regional initiative being promoted by East-West Gateway and RCGA also includes three separate workforce development strategy committees. These three initial committees have been organized around three of the most important policy goals. Invited to participate in the various committees are individuals who are active in local workforce development activities in both Missouri and Illinois, including WIB directors, administrators from One-Stop Centers like the one administered by the St. Louis Agency on Training and Employment (SLATE), local entrepreneurs, community activists, and those involved in the implementation of welfare reform. On paper, the list of participants creates a positive impression of widespread involvement and commitment to an ambitious regional policy and planning agenda.

This impression is positively marketed and strategically promoted by the East-West Gateway Coordinating Council and the RCGA. According to an East-West Gateway official, "This is the only interstate workforce development policy planning effort in the nation." The planning effort is portrayed as having substantial and widespread support not only among elected officials, business leaders, and workforce development functionaries, but also from the governors of Illinois and Missouri. An East-West official contended that, "As of July 2002, the flow of funds to local workforce boards in the St. Louis area will be contingent upon local plans being in alignment with regional policy and strategy as articulated in the evolving plan of the St. Louis Regional Workforce Development Policy Group." In light of the adversarial political culture in the St. Louis region, this objective—although ambitious—could prove to be a bold approach by the Policy Group leadership. More significantly, it could be interpreted as confirmation of the fears expressed by some informants that a regional planning agenda could potentially undermine the budget control most political jurisdictions are seeking to maintain.

Closer examination of the current regional policy initiative, as described by East-West Gateway officials, reveals a number of important issues. It is not clear how this ambitious policy initiative will be funded, nor is it clear how the various institutional sectors, governmental entities, and political constituencies identified will be brought into compliance with the goals and objectives that are articulated in the plan. For example, although it might be desirable to alter current public school curriculum, and involve local universities and community colleges in workforce development research and planning activities, it is not likely that these matters will be easily influenced by an informal committee structure that is organized by a regional transportation entity and a regional chamber of commerce. Nor is it clear why regional business entities would alter their hiring and personnel policies, or change their private investment and expansions decisions in response to a statement of objectives issued by an ad hoc policy group.

These observations and issues are magnified when combined with the social and political cleavages that shape conflict and competition in the St. Louis metropolitan area. The Regional Policy Group has no legal or corporate standing, and no set of formal mechanisms through which the public may hold it accountable. And, unless this group eventually controls workforce development funds, it will have little political power. As a result, the Regional Policy Group will have questionable legitimacy within the local political arena. Nonetheless, the ad hoc policy group could potentially become an important and influential force in local workforce politics. On paper, the base of participation appears broad, and includes several important elected officials, educational administrators, and community activists. Noticeably absent from the list of committee members, however, are representatives from the major employers in the region. The top 100 corporations in the region, are sparsely represented at best among the list of participants and in the committee portfolios distributed by East-West Gateway. Without the major corporate players, developers, financial institutions, and local foundations around St. Louis's latest workforce development policy table, it is probably not likely that the Policy Group will evolve beyond a planning exercise among a loose confederation of individuals and organizations whose primary responsibilities, political allegiances, and professional obligations lie elsewhere.

The longer-term success of the Regional Policy Group will largely depend upon the political and organizational skills of its two sponsors: East-West Gateway and RCGA. Both entities, however, possess considerable influence in the region, and have aggressively pursued regional solutions to the public policy issues that face the metropolitan area. As Molotch and Stone observed, however, unless members of St. Louis' governing regime support a reform agenda that is compatible with their economic interests, the possibility of longer-term changes in workforce development policy is probably not high. The most immediate challenge facing the Regional Policy Group is how to mobilize regime members and a diverse group of political and financial interests behind a common agenda, build a coalition behind that reform agenda, and sustain the coalition over time.

In St. Louis, the specific challenge is to mobilize a variety of diverse constituencies and stakeholders behind a common workforce development reform agenda (Giloth, 2000b). As Stone (1998) explains, achieving reforms and policy changes usually "requires more than the discrediting of the old ways in favor of a fresh idea. It involves the difficult shift from a coalition built around distributive benefits to one built on a more complex set of factors" (13). His observations nicely summarize the difficult set of responsibilities facing the groups and political interests who are promoting workforce development reform in the St. Louis region. Historically, workforce development funding streams in the St. Louis region mirror a distributional system that is shaped by the way in which local government is organized and operated, and reinforced by well-established political alliances and relationships.

References

Abt Associates, Inc. and The New School for Social Research. n.d. *Evaluation of the AECF Jobs Initiative (Planning Phase: 1995–1997)*. Baltimore: Annie E. Casey Foundation.

———. 1997. *Evaluation of the Jobs Initiative: First Annual/Cross-Site Report*. Baltimore: Annie E. Casey Foundation (September).

———. 2000. *Evaluation Report on the Capacity Building Phase (March 1997–March 2000)*. Baltimore: Annie E. Casey Foundation (November).

Annie E. Casey Foundation. n.d. *Stronger Links: New Ways to Connect Low-Skilled Workers to Better Jobs*. Baltimore: Annie E. Casey Foundation.

Annie E. Casey Foundation. 2001. *Jobs and Race*. Baltimore: Annie E. Casey Foundation.

Banks, Manley Elliott. 2000. "A Changing Electorate in a Majority Black City: The Emergence of a Neo-Conservative Black Urban Regime in Contemporary Atlanta." *Journal of Urban Affairs* 22(3).

Birch, David L. 1982. "Who Creates Jobs?" In *A forum for small businesses*. Transcription of presentation, November 3, Louisville, KY, Greater Louisville, Inc.

Bluestone, Barry, and Bennett Harrison. 1984. *The Deindustrialization of America*. New York: Basic Books.

Checkoway, Barry. 1992. "Revitalizing an Urban Neighborhood: A St. Louis Case Study." In *The Metropolitan Midwest: Policy Problems and Prospects for Change*, edited by Barry Checkoway and Carl V. Patton. Urbana and Chicago: University of Illinois Press.

East-West Gateway. 2001. "Public Education in the St. Louis Region." *Where We Stand*. St. Louis: East-West Gateway.

Farley, John E. 2001. *Racial Housing Segregation in the St. Louis Metropolitan Area, 2000*. Presented at SIUE Institute for Urban Research symposium, June 19, 2001, East St. Louis, Illinois.

Fung, Archon, and Scott Zdrazil. 2003. *Ecologies of Workforce Development: Patterns of Interaction and Prospects for Reform in Milwaukee, Wisconsin*. Baltimore: Annie E. Casey Foundation.

Giloth, Robert P. 2000a. "Learning from the Field: Economic Growth and Workforce Development in the 1990s." *Economic Development Quarterly*, 14(4):340–359.

Giloth, Robert P. 2000b. "Workforce Systems Change." Annie E. Casey Foundation, Interoffice Memorandum, August 7.

Grubb, W. Norton. 1996. *Learning to Work: The Case for Reintegrating Job Training and Education*. New York: Russell Sage Foundation.

Grubb, W. Norton, Norena Badway, Denise Bell, Bernadette Chi, Chris King, Julie Herr, Heath Prince, Richard Kazis, Lisa Hicks, and Judith Combes Taylor. 1999. *Toward Order from Chaos: State Efforts to Reform Workforce Development Systems*. Berkeley, CA: National Center for Research in Vocational Education.

Initiative for a Competitive Inner City (ICIC). 2000. *St. Louis Inner City Competitive Assessment and Strategy Project: Creating Jobs, Income, and Wealth in the Inner City*. St. Louis: Initiative for a Competitive Inner City (September).

Jargowsky, Paul A. 1997. *Poverty and Place: Ghettos, Barrios, and the American City*. New York: Russell Sage Foundation.

Jobs for the Future and On Purpose Associates. 1999. *A Framework for Labor Market Systems Reform for Jobs Initiative Sites*. Baltimore: Annie E. Casey Foundation (May 5).

Jones, E. Terrence. 2000. *Fragmented by Design*. St. Louis: Palmerston and Reed Publishing Co.

Kasarda, John. 1988. "Jobs, Migration and Emerging Urban Mismatches." In *Urban Change and Poverty*, edited by L. E. Lynn, Jr., and Michael G. H. McGeary. Washington, DC: National Academy Press.

———. 1989. "Urban Industrial Transition and the Urban Underclass." *Annals of the American Academy of Political and Social Sciences* 501:26–47.

———. 1993. "Inner-city Poverty and Economic Access." In *Rediscovering Urban America: Perspectives on the 1980s*, edited by J. Sommer and D. A. Hicks. Washington, DC: Office of Housing Policy Research, U.S. Department of Housing and Urban Development.

Kee, Lorraine, and Ken Leiser. 2000. "Interstate 70 Sit-in Reaped Rewards for Minorities in Construction, Some Call the Protest a Watershed Event for Black Empowerment Here: Effects Are Still Unfolding." *St. Louis Post-Dispatch* (July 9):A1.

LaLonde, Robert J. 1995. "The Promise of Public Sector-Sponsored Training Programs." *Journal of Economic Perspectives* 9:149–168.

Laslo, David. 2001. "A Brief Demographic and Spatial History of the St. Louis

Region: 1950–2000." St. Louis, MO: Public Policy Research Center, University of Missouri–St. Louis.

Lauria, Mickey, Robert Whelan, and Alma Young. 1994. "Urban Regimes and Racial Politics." *Journal of Urban Affairs* 16(1):1–36.

Logan, John, and Harvey Molotch. 1987. *Urban Fortunes.* Berkeley: University of California Press.

Manning, Margie. 1998. "Lost Souls, Lost Dollars." *St. Louis Business Journal* (July 17). Available at stlouis.bcentral.com/stlouis/stories/1998/07/20/story2.html; accessed on April 20, 2001.

Molotch, Harvey. 1976. "The City as a Growth Machine." *American Journal of Sociology* 82(2):309–330.

———. 1988. "Strategies and Constraints of Growth Elites." In *Business Elites and Urban Development,* edited by S. Cummings, 25–47. Albany: State University of New York Press.

Newman, Harvey. 1994. "Black Clergy and Urban Regimes: The Role of Atlanta's Concerned Black Clergy." *Journal of Urban Affairs* 16(1):22–33.

Nicklaus, David. 2000. "Inner City Presents Exciting Possibilities to Noted 'Thinker.'" *St. Louis Post-Dispatch* (September 13):C1-3.

Orfield, Myron W. 1997. *Metropolitics: A Regional Agenda for Community and Stability.* Washington, DC: Brookings Institution.

Parzen, Julia. 1997. *Learning from the Regions.* A National Strategy Session of the Metropolitan Initiative. Brookings Institution Center for Urban and Metropolitan Policy. Available at http://info.cnt.org/mi/dc_notes.html; accessed on March 22, 2001.

Porter, Michael E. 1998a. *Competitive Strategy: Techniques for Analyzing Industries and Competitors.* New York: Free Press.

———. 1998b. *Competitive Advantage: Creating and Sustaining Superior Performance.* New York: Free Press.

———. 2000. "Regional Prosperity Depends on Prosperity that Benefits Our Inner City." *St. Louis Post-Dispatch* (September 17):B4.

Real Strategy for City Development. 2000. *St. Louis Business Journal* (September 15).

Rusk, David. 1995. *Cities without Suburbs.* Washington, DC: Woodrow Wilson Center Press.

———. 1999. *Inside Game/Outside Game: Winning Strategies for Saving Urban America.* Washington, DC: Brookings Institution.

Shaw, Wendy. 2000. *A Tale of Two Cities: The Best of Times, the Worst of Times. Inequality in St. Louis's Metro East.* Available at www.siue.edu/~wshaw/esl.htm; accessed on July 2, 2001.

Stone, Clarence N. 1989. *Regime Politics: Governing Atlanta.* Lawrence: University Press of Kansas.

———. 1993. "Urban Regimes and the Capacity to Govern: A Political Economy Approach." *Journal of Urban Affairs* 15:1–28.

———. 1998. *Changing Urban Education.* Lawrence: University Press of Kansas.

Walsh, Joan. 2000. *The Eye of the Storm.* Baltimore: Annie E. Casey Foundation.

Wilson, William Julius. 1987. *The Truly Disadvantaged: The Inner City, the Underclass, and Public Policy.* Chicago: University of Chicago Press.

———. 1996. *When Work Disappears: The World of the New Urban Poor.* New York: Alfred A. Knopf.

———. 1999. *The Bridge over the Racial Divide: Rising Inequality and Coalition Politics.* Berkeley and Los Angeles: University of California Press.

Robert P. Giloth

7 Comparative Local Workforce Politics in Six Cities

Theory and Action

Investing in the human capital and career development of low-income, low-skilled workers has been a staple of U.S. social policy for many years. Since the 1960s, billions of public dollars have been invested in "workforce development": The latest manifestation is the Workforce Investment Act (WIA) of 1998. At its best, this approach—frequently called employment and training—has promised benefits for workers and businesses as well as contributed to the health and well-being of families, neighborhoods, and cities.

These aspirations and investments, however, have not delivered the desired results. Evaluation studies question the effectiveness of most employment and training efforts. Government programs have created a complicated "non-system" of programs and institutions that are uncoordinated and disconnected from labor markets. Given that there are millions of Americans without the skills and work experience to move ahead (Grubb, 1996), these efforts demonstrate that political leaders and civic coalitions rarely have made workforce development a priority.

Nevertheless, the 1990s witnessed renewed attention to workforce development. Labor shortages, particularly skill shortages, prompted employers to make workforce development a top priority. The national political consensus placed "work" at the center of social policy, as demonstrated by the welfare reform legislation of 1996. Local economic development officials realized that their cities could not competitively attract new businesses and projects without a skilled and ready workforce. Furthermore, many community advocates realized that new partnerships and policies were needed if low-income and low-skilled families were to become self-sufficient.

Today's economy is less supportive of workforce development in some respects because of slow growth and layoffs. There are, however, still labor shortages in sectors such as health care, and the re-employment and dislocated worker retraining challenge remains substantial. Moreover, how to advance in the labor market remains an elusive goal for many working Americans.

This book includes chapters from a diverse set of authors who explore the meaning of local workforce development politics in five quite different cities—Denver, Milwaukee, Philadelphia, St. Louis, and Seattle. A case study of New Orleans, not included in this book, is drawn upon for the discussions in this chapter (Whelan, Gladstone, and Hirsh, 2003). All of these cities participated in the Jobs Initiative of the Annie E. Casey Foundation, an effort to support workforce innovations and system reforms. The initial charge to the authors was to write theoretically informed case studies—not just descriptions of workforce funding streams and institutions, or prescriptions for how these dysfunctional and disconnected systems could be better aligned.

The common starting point for the chapters was Clarence Stone's concepts of employment and performance regimes, in which, in the former case, the inertia and resistance of existing workforce organizations lead to institutional survival rather than reform strategies. Performance regimes, in contrast, represent a network of stakeholders—inside and outside of workforce systems—who adopt a common set of problem definitions, goals, strategies, and performance criteria against which to hold workforce investments accountable.

One important performance goal is the retention and advancement of low-income, low-skilled workers in the labor market and in good jobs. Achieving this goal requires a systemic change agenda that promotes good jobs and career ladders, information, support services, vertical linkages from kindergarten through twelfth grade to career advancement, and business engagement at all steps along the way. To make progress toward achieving these system reforms (i.e., performance regimes), Stone et al. have argued that civic capacity—relationships, networks, leadership, and beliefs—must be identified, mobilized, expanded, and focused on a systemic agenda for changing workforce systems.

This chapter explores what can be learned about local workforce politics by looking across these case study and background chapters in a comparative fashion. Although not included in this book, a paper by Plastrik, Seltzer, and Taylor (2003) provided background material for this chapter. This paper presents the overall strategic framework adopted by the Jobs Initiative to guide system reform investments. Comparing theories, city conditions, and workforce systems and performance enriches our overall understanding of workforce systems. For example:

- What can be learned by applying different theoretical lenses to cities and workforce development?
- What issues receive attention and what issues are ignored?

- What collective picture of workforce systems emerges from the six case studies?
- Why are some features of workforce systems more important or relevant for specific theories or data collection?
- How do these theoretical perspectives complement each other in contributing to a more comprehensive account of how workforce systems are constituted, behave, change, and adopt performance goals?

Although a small sample, the six cities discussed in this book represent different combinations of civic capacity, economic context and incentives, institutional infrastructure, and government leadership. Which of these features are salient for understanding and distinguishing workforce politics in the six cities? Are there other factors? Moreover, what environmental or civic conditions support emerging performance politics? What features prevent or undermine such a politics? What is left unexplained? These case studies provide a modest—but unique until now—opportunity to address these questions.

The final comparative task for this chapter is to discuss in more depth common issues raised by authors in their case study and background chapters. These issues include the resources, structure, and governance of workforce systems; the importance of ideas in workforce development; contrasting definitions of performance; sources of civic capacity; strategies for workforce systems change; and the value of the performance regime metaphor for understanding local workforce systems and politics. Perspectives on each of these critical issues are placed in broader program and policy contexts.

What is the feasibility for a local politics of workforce development that focuses on ambitious goals for low-income, low-skilled workers? A pessimistic scenario raises serious questions about whether durable coalitions for workforce change can be built around small, fragmented institutions in the context of major inequities and considerable organizational inertia and resistance. A more optimistic scenario portrays substantial resources in workforce systems that do not produce the right outcomes. Progress toward performance regimes depends upon social capital, effective government, talent, and minimal problems. But many other types of cities, as well as rural regions and small towns, may achieve reform in smaller ways by changing the rules of the game that constitute workforce systems and behavior, and by building civic intermediaries that bring together workforce allies to advocate for and achieve important workforce results.

The chapter's initial discussion of theory and human capital politics is followed by a more specific discussion of the theories and conceptual frameworks used by authors in their case study and background chapters. Case study materials are then presented for each of the cities that focus on economic and demographic contexts, workforce systems funding and institutions, and evidence of workforce change and performance. Jobs Initiative results are an additional indicator of workforce performance for the six cities. Workforce systems change in the six cities is then analyzed in relation to the patterns of social capital, poverty, segregation, economic change, and public policy across the cities, metropolitan areas, and states. The chapter concludes with a discussion of five critical issues—resources, ideas and strategies, barriers, performance, and civic capacity—and the conceptual strength of regime theory for making sense of workforce systems and reform strategies.

Theoretical Orientations

Why is theory and theorizing important for an inquiry into the practice and potential of a local politics of workforce development that is organized around achieving more ambitious outcomes, such as career advancement and family self-sufficiency? Will an exploration of theory take us far afield from the context and practicalities of local workforce programs and institutional arrangements? There is one compelling answer, with two parts, to both questions.

First, the design and implementation of workforce policies and programs have repeatedly failed to help families move along a pathway to self-sufficiency and career development. Second, most analyses of workforce program failures rarely go deeper than articulating the predictable litany of human and bureaucratic constraints and missteps. Little in-depth attention is given to the environment in which implementation occurs, or to the civic capacity required to do it differently. Attention to theory is one way of conceptualizing those factors and conditions that affect the implementation of workforce policies and programs.

The authors in this volume adopt theoretical perspectives about how governing coalitions produce cooperation, how systems change and evolve, and the barriers to cooperation, system change, and performance. Explanatory and normative theories identify the component parts of workforce systems and how they are connected to each other and to other systems, and the relationships among environmental factors, system behaviors, and outcomes. Theories help invent new explanations or solutions to problems, and help explain differences among variables. Summarizing and comparing these approaches contributes to developing a more comprehensive account of the possibilities of a performance-oriented local politics and the conditions under which performance behavior can—or cannot—emerge, grow, and take root.

That discussion itself is a contribution to the workforce field. Moreover, each theoretical lens illuminates different aspects of workforce systems and processes as well as the political–economic dimensions of the local and regional environment. The exploration of workforce systems and policies from multiple perspectives enables a more textured and complete empirical account of their constraints and opportunities.

Regime theory has served as an initial conceptual framework for commissioning these chapters about workforce development politics. Although regime theory is a relatively new body of theory compared with pluralist or elite political theory, it is distinguished by its focus on the "social production" of informal governmental and nongovernmental arrangements and governing coalitions for achieving common goals (Stoker, 1995).

This set of arrangements, though taking many forms and evolving over time, bridges state and market, and builds upon the collective social capital of places. Attention to the social production of durable coalitions makes regime theory sensitive to the issues of social and institutional fragmentation, collective action problems, rewards and incentives, structures of authority, definitions of problems and purposes, and civic capacity and mobilization. The conceptual continuum of employment and performance regimes provides an analytic as well as a normative construct for examining systems change in specific places (Stone, 1998).

Regime theory has drawbacks when used to investigate multifaceted workforce systems. Regime theory's assumptions about the organization of stakeholders and authority structures may be too restrictive in its emphasis on central authority and resources. Regime theory may also be ill suited to comprehend and give guidance to strategies that are part of private markets, such as those institutions involved in labor markets. The employment/performance framework is helpful in its contrasting features, but it may mask some of the contested terrain between these poles. On the other hand, regime theory's understanding of the barriers to forming new civic arrangements is quite applicable to the non-system of workforce development.

Structure and Function of Workforce Systems

Many knowledgeable observers have a difficult time agreeing whether workforce development comprises a system, systems, subsystem, or non-system. Moreover, analysts also differ in thought about the central forces that produce the various institutional patterns that comprise the landscape of workforce development.

Workforce, or second chance, systems are a loosely-organized, highly-independent set of actors with little hierarchy or shared authority and meager resources according to Clarence Stone and Donn Worgs (Chapter 8). In this sense, workforce systems comprise a policy subsystem. Governance of these loosely connected actors requires a common understanding of problems and solutions; however, too many conflicting definitions of the problem are at play in the workforce field. Resources used to solve the workforce problem—whatever its definition—must be roughly commensurate with the problem under consideration. Vast disparities exist between available workforce resources and the population in need; not enough public commitment exists to build performance regimes.

A systems approach to defining workforce systems derives from organization and planning studies. This theory emphasizes the challenges of understanding complexity and "wholes"—the structures and mental models underlying complex situations—and how to identify high-leverage change strategies. In contrast to Stone and Worgs, Peter Plastrik, Marlene Seltzer, and Judith Combes Taylor (2003) identify regional labor markets as the appropriate unit of analysis, rather than public funding streams.

Focusing on labor markets requires an understanding of its supply, demand, and intermediary components; the dual-customer nature of labor market interactions; the importance of regions as the appropriate geography; the complexity and dynamics of labor markets; and the functions and activities of workforce development, from recruitment to career advancement. A systems approach calls attention to the connections between labor markets and other systems, such as education and welfare; the importance of strategic plans rather than laundry lists of reforms; the requirement for stakeholders to understand the "big picture" of labor market dynamics; and the outcomes of scale and sustainability.

A fundamental component of a systems approach to labor market change is "drivers." Drivers represent strategic resources that provide underlying order to complex and chaotic labor markets, shaping the way labor markets operate, and, in particular, the effectiveness of workforce interventions. Drivers include financial resources, policies and regulations, information, competencies and norms, and political and civic will.

Alternatively, Archon Fung and Scott Zdrazil (Chapter 3) offer Norton Long's concept of "ecology of games" as a better metaphor for local workforce policies and institutions—an approach characterized by "slippage and chaos." Ecology suggests distinctive niches as well as competition, and perhaps succession, among niches. In the realm of politics, competition occurs over various requirements and prizes (e.g., contracts, jobs), and is shaped by the constituent rules that shape niches.

The workforce system(s) is really a "non-system" made up of myriad labor market intermediaries (LMIs) that integrate supply and demand for labor, federal and local workforce investments, and employers and training institutions. Examples include community colleges, workforce service providers, workforce boards, and employer partnerships. LMIs are shaped by policy and market imperatives, and pass these influences and constraints on to their immediate partners and stakeholders. Public policies, for example, constitute LMIs and establish legal constraints and obligations, incentives and rewards, and workforce development strategies. As a result of these influences, each LMI demonstrates a distinctive pattern of governance, organizational arrangements, and outcomes.

Fung and Zdrazil conceptualize five "ideal type" workforce ecologies, each potentially including multiple and distinctive LMIs. As ideal types, these are abstract pictures of LMIs; in fact, though, the boundaries among these different types are unclear and constantly changing. The value of the ideal type is that it underscores the composite features of different parts of the workforce non-system. The "minimalist neoliberal" ecology represents minimal public investment in workforce development infrastructure or programs. The message is: Let the labor market function. In the "laissez-faire rent seeking" ecology, substantial funding is available in the context of few rules and permissive governance. LMIs may proliferate, but it is as likely that they will seek to exploit these arrangements rather than push their limits of performance.

A "privatized bureaucracy" ecology embodies an industrial model of top-down specification of production functions and performance targets. An "innovation" ecology is also well funded and has substantial discretion. What distinguishes this type of ecology is that within it, LMIs are subject to rigorous performance monitoring on behalf of continuous improvement and the generation of new and best practices.

Finally the "coordination" ecology is one in which linkages and productive integration among key workforce development institutions are forged on behalf of improving outcomes.

Impediments to Workforce Systems Change

Clarence Stone's concept of employment regime suggests an almost immovable pattern of internally focused organizational self-interest, concerned with protecting the status quo and its associated jobs and contracts. Stone further argues that changing employment to performance regimes requires substantial civic capacity combined with footholds of authority, resources, and opportunities. Unfortunately, key stakeholders for workforce development, such as business and job seekers/workers, are not mobilized sufficiently and supported to play effective advocacy and governing roles for changing workforce systems.

David Bartelt (Chapter 4) identifies a "contested terrain" for the interplay of performance and the old ways of doing business. That is, given weak civic and political institutions, the "lashed up arrangements" of the past (i.e., machine politics) produce a dualism, at best, of new performance behaviors coexisting with employment regimes. It is not a matter of one or the other, although Bartelt acknowledges that the funding streams that supported the employment regimes of the past are quickly diminishing.

External investors, civic intermediaries, and other local actors introduce performance criteria into this contested terrain. In the arena of workforce development, two metaphors describe this contested terrain as either a "bowl of spaghetti" or as "too many tables, with too many cooks," giving a sense of multiple and disconnected ideas, stakeholders, and institutions. Workforce funding streams, for example, arrive with their own definitions of the problem, favored solutions, and performance metrics. Moreover, performance itself is contested as many cities have experienced "performance-driven" failures, as has been the case in many school reform efforts.

The complicated and disconnected nature of workforce development is reinforced by multiple and, frequently, contradictory civic conversations about workforce development. These conversations reflect real intellectual, political, and implementation problems and dilemmas, which inhibit consensus building around strategic focus and, at worst, produce paralysis of action. These dilemmas include:

- Small-scale projects that address employer demand for skilled employees versus system-wide changes
- Real needs for job readiness training versus the use of "soft skills" as a way to mask racial stereotyping and discrimination
- Simple welfare-to-work versus a more robust system for supporting families as they move toward economic self-sufficiency
- Place-based community organizations as access points to and supporters of neighborhood residents versus community organizations as political support organizations that have become stalwart members of employment regimes

Scott Cummings, Allan Tomey, and Robert Flack (Chapter 6) add a political economy dimension to understanding the persistence of employment regimes in obstructing performance-oriented workforce development. Three political-economic processes exacerbate the disparities between city and suburb. The first is economic restructuring—the structural shift to services and the spatial shift of economic activity to the suburbs and ex-urbs.

The second is extreme racial polarization in the region as evidenced by residence, business location, family and neighborhood poverty, and political power. The third factor is government fragmentation.

This landscape of disparity exacerbates competition among subgroups and subplaces in the region as well as resistance to regional solutions that infringe upon local autonomy, however defined. Growth coalition politics is not homogeneous across regions, but focuses on nodes, whether downtowns, airports, edge cities, suburban counties, or small jurisdictions. Divisions and tensions exist within the coalition members and groups that come together in some fashion with different specific interests. When government fragmentation is added to the equation, resistance and parochialism are built into regional political and institutional dynamics.

Regional solutions and attempts to transform employment regimes frequently flounder in this environment. Stalemate and dissension prevail, rather than agreement and change. Civic capacity is weak, or small groups with narrow solutions capture agendas. Capturing an agenda, however, does not indicate that progress is achieved, or that other stakeholders concede. In fact, this is when the culture and "lashed up" arrangements of current politics and institutions resist regional solutions. Cummings, Tomey, and Flack illustrate how regional solutions often meet the same fate as top-down federal initiatives parachuted in from elsewhere; they have a short life and fail to take root. Meanwhile, the disparities generated by economic change, fragmentation, and exclusion continue.

Durable coalitions, according to Susan E. Clarke (Chapter 2), require long-term leadership, resource commitments, and successes. They can start small, but a trajectory of growth and results is needed if stakeholders are to stay at the table.

Sustaining mobilization around workforce systems performance has proven difficult in the context of competing reforms, such as schools, making work pay, and family self-sufficiency agendas. Even natural allies take sides when only so many agendas can be pursued at once. Moreover, competition and conflict around performance, geography, and systems reform goals contribute to a weakening rather than strengthening of emerging coalitions. Coalitions need "glue" to maintain levels of interest and coordination; yet, these are the most difficult resources to attain and have a habit of drying up before the work is done.

Is there a minimal threshold of civic capacity required for pursuing performance regimes related to workforce development? Robert Whelan, David Gladstone, and Trisha Hirth (2003) raise this provocative question, and their answer is yes.

Legacies of exclusion and weak public institutions contribute to the persistence of patronage, weak government institutions, and poor service delivery. In these situations, public and civic leaders are preoccupied with the basics of delivering competent and predictable services, such as police protection and public safety. Most public systems are broken. There is no better example of these broken systems than public education.

Whelan, Gladstone, and Hirth (2003) identify two other issues that contribute to this situation. The first relates to the legacy of racism, frequently expressed in divisive relationships between central cities and surrounding counties. The second issue relates to limited social capital—bonding among insider groups but little capacity to bridge among diverse groups.

Finally, Stone and Worgs argue that a "two worlds" problem seriously impedes workforce system change. A profound disconnection exists between inner-city—frequently minority—job seekers, workers, families, and young people and the economic mainstream. This disconnection is expressed in lack of job readiness, loss of hope and increased cynicism, underinvestment in education, discrimination and relocation of firms, and neighborhood poverty.

Change Strategies for Workforce Systems

What strategies for pursuing workforce systems change are plausible given the breadth and depth of these political impediments? Are some contexts more favorable for change than others? Are different scales of change possible in different contexts?

The failures and false starts of the social programs of the 1960s haunt today's social reform, whether workforce development or community rebuilding. Steven Rathgeb Smith and Susan Davis (Chapter 5) draw lessons from this history of failure and articulate an alternative, normative theory of social intervention for implementing successful performance-oriented initiatives. Programs should not be "parachuted" into cities and neighborhoods in a top-down fashion. Rather, program design and implementation should be approached like political development, with a strategic focus on relationship building. Implementation must emphasize "creative problem solving"—the capacity to invent new solutions in a bottom-up fashion as programs and the environment evolve.

The environment in which the implementation of social programs now occurs has changed dramatically since the 1960s. A diverse and dynamic nonprofit sector exists that has developed effective solutions to tough social issues on a small scale. Many of these nonprofits, however, are not connected to each other—an outcome of individual rather than cooperative incentives. At the same time, funding streams developed to support social programs since the 1960s have ossified into funding "silos" that prohibit or undermine collaborative solutions. Consequently, Smith and Davis identify collaboration and system reform as key, strategic elements for this new, bottom-up theory of program design and implementation. Stand-alone programs are not sufficient to make or sustain change.

Under what conditions might this theory of social intervention prove effective? Can it be applied in all cities and across all issue types? Lack of sprawl and social and racial polarization are important factors in promoting community cohesion. And, a robust economy with low unemployment rates and many opportunities for wealth creation supports workforce innovation. Moreover, municipal budget investments are both an indicator of and a catalyst for systems change. A local political culture in which many different stakeholders can achieve their goals and reduce transaction costs and social frictions through formal and informal arrangements, supports the change process.

Fung and Zdrazil criticize the limits of top-down policies, program designs, and implementation. In the workforce development arena, they point to the repeated failure of national efforts to consolidate, simplify, and coordinate workforce investments and institutions. This top-down approach represents the "rational model" of policymaking, which so often has failed as a tool for solving complex social problems.

Changing workforce ecologies requires municipal, regional, and state leadership to redefine the constitutive rules that shape the behavior of LMIs. A broad consensus about strategic directions is a first step, starting with a civic conversation about the nature of "fair and effective" workforce development. Transforming and aligning the metrics for measuring the outcomes of LMIs to reflect such a consensus would be an important first step. These strategic reforms can provide a foundation for constructing innovation and coordination ecologies.

System change strategies transform the drivers of workforce systems— information, resources, power, relationships, and competencies—so that they better support the job retention and career advancement of low-income, low-skilled workers. Plastrik, Seltzer, and Taylor (2003) identify seven strategy areas that offer high-leverage opportunities to change these drivers, including adopting skills standards and credentials, linking economic and workforce development, and organizing employers. In other words, when underlying strategic resources are reformed, change ripples through labor markets, and, if strong enough, produces scale and sustainable impacts.

Clarke concludes that although performance regimes related to workforce development are unlikely to form in American cities given the privileged position of urban growth, economic and demographic factors will keep workforce issues on the table. The challenge is not one of initial mobilization but of transforming opportunities and leadership into sustainable and durable coalitions that stay the course in order to achieve ambitious workforce outcomes. A consensus exists about the management strategies required for governance under these conditions. The challenge is how to mobilize stakeholders with weak incentives to participate, sustain their involvement in the face of competing agendas, and institutionalize interests in durable coalitions with a focus on common performance goals.

In the end, Stone and Worgs argue that workforce development change should be a part of broader efforts to redefine community development— a movement based on "shared aims, not deficits." Such a movement should attack a broader array of issues, build citizen leadership, and engage in political advocacy. Project QUEST and the COPS/Metro congregation-based organizing coalition, of which QUEST is a part, is one example of this approach.

Summary

All chapters in this book test the regime theory conceptual framework as they explore local workforce politics and search for evidence of performance regimes. How helpful this conceptual framework is for understanding workforce systems is a salient issue that is addressed at the conclusion of this chapter. At this stage, it is worth noting the additional theoretical lenses that the authors have adopted and why they felt these additional perspectives were needed. There are three additional theoretical lenses.

First, systems theory and the ecology of games metaphor offer different conceptual approaches for understanding the dynamics of loosely-structured, decentralized workforce institutions. Second, other theories help explain the barriers to a performance-oriented workforce politics, such as growth coalitions and the "private city." In a more general way, the "two worlds" challenge calls attention to the profound separation of inner-city neighborhoods from the economic mainstream. Third, lack of clarity or competition of ideas in workforce development contributes to the lack of progress in building effective performance-oriented coalitions.

Top-down, rational models for workforce reform have not worked and have, in many cases, made things worse. Implementation of new designs and reform agendas must be approached like political development, investing in how cooperation and coalitions can be produced in a durable fashion. Regime theory underscores this challenge of producing cooperation. Building civic capacity is needed whether one wants to alter workforce ecologies, change the systemic drivers that shape labor markets, or build civic, workforce intermediaries.

The experiences of the six cities are now considered: Their economic, policy, and institutional environments; and the elements of performance that are emerging and taking root.

WHAT THE CASES REVEAL

The six case study chapters answer comparative questions about the local politics of workforce development. A first set of questions relates to common factors, such as economic change, that affect workforce systems and local performance politics. For example, does economic growth or decline affect local workforce politics? Does the suburbanization of employment location affect workforce politics? Does the growth or decline of specific sectors, such as manufacturing or health care, affect workforce politics?

A second set of questions focuses on the relationships between cities, regional, and state attributes and the emergence of performance politics. That is, if performance-oriented workforce politics is the dependent variable, what independent variables contribute to its strength, weakness, or nonexistence? Explanatory variables might include the intensity of local social capital, municipal government performance, racial segregation, poverty, and economic change.

Local workforce politics occurs within specific contexts. The case studies have drawn upon available information and key informant interviews about workforce development. Cross-site analysis, however, has limits because the case studies are not completely consistent in the data that they have collected or the issues they have addressed. Comparative analysis, even given these qualifications, is nonetheless important because it suggests what variables and composites of factors have an effect under different conditions. Deindustrialization is a salient factor, but not in all cities. The geographic shift of economic activities to the suburbs is critically important, but it occurs at different rates, and in combination with both city growth and decline. In terms of workforce systems, city descriptions are quite similar in the institutions that they identify, but investment levels and the role of intermediary organizations vary considerably. Workforce outcomes and evidence of emerging and potential performance politics also vary across the cities.

Denver

Denver is a growing city in a growing state. The city's population reached 559,836 in 2000, up 87,026 from 1990, whereas Colorado grew by one-third in the 1990s, reaching 4.3 million in 2000. In Denver, the Latino population has grown to become 23 percent of the total population; the white, non-Hispanic population declined to 52 percent. Denver is also unusual in that it remains a growing job center with 459,000 jobs and 35 percent of all metropolitan businesses. Forty-one percent of these jobs are in the service sector. Since 1991, the metropolitan area added 77,000 new jobs. Consequently, Denver did not experience the problems of spatial mismatch between job seekers and employers that occurred in many other cities. On the other hand, continuing population and economic growth in the city has produced rising housing prices and, subsequently, an affordable housing challenge for the working poor.

Denver's economic and political environments appear favorable for meeting these challenges. It has a dynamic economy and political leaders have emphasized workforce development and the investment in public infrastructure for two decades, since the regime change in the early 1980s signaled by the mayoral election of Fredrico Pena. In terms of mobilizing stakeholders, public recognition of the working poor and the challenges that they face—in all aspects of their lives—increased during the 1990s. At the same time, business interest has been episodic, advocates are fragmented, and the state role is weak. External initiatives dominate in mobilizing local interests, but current Mayor Wellington Webb has asserted an ambitious workforce and economic opportunity agenda in the last years of his mayoralty, revamping his workforce office and launching a local Earned Income Tax Credit (EITC) funded with Temporary Assistance for Needy Families (TANF) surplus resources.

Workforce systems in Denver are characterized by a weak state role related to policy, resources, and implementation; most welfare and workforce activities are devolved to the consolidated city/county of Denver. The Mayor's Office of Workforce Development (MOWD) underwent a change of leadership in 2000, and administers about $23 million in workforce-related funds targeted to youth and welfare-to-work clients, as well as to other residents who require training. MOWD operates seven neighborhood One-Stop Centers, involving 132 staff, thirteen public agencies, and thirty-nine community-based providers.

The Community College of Denver is nationally known for innovation and quality education. It has an independent budget from the state as well as its own constituencies and governance, and is motivated to create a pipeline for new college students rather than a partnership with external employment institutions that have different goals. Their Essential Skills program, however, has received wide recognition for its occupational career ladders, and the employment rate of its graduates.

Denver recently allocated $22 million of TANF surplus dollars to support a local EITC—one of the few locally-funded EITC programs in the nation. An estimated 28,000 families who are eligible for the federal EITC would also be eligible for the local EITC. In the eyes of some local stakeholders, the local EITC was a way to circumvent turf battles and funding bottlenecks in order to better support the working poor.

The Denver Workforce Initiative (DWI), the Annie E. Casey Foundation-funded Jobs Initiative effort, garnered widespread interest, but its jobs project strategies ultimately failed to have significant wage and income impacts on the residents it had placed. At the time of its withdrawal from the Jobs Initiative because of performance questions and priorities, DWI had established a stakeholder's forum that brought together a wide range of workforce players to identify strategic systems reforms.

Durable coalitions require long-term leadership, resource commitments, and successes. They can start small, but a trajectory of growth and results is needed if stakeholders are to stay at the table. In Denver, the opportunity to move such an agenda is related to the economy, mayoral leadership, and the role of Denver City/County in funding welfare reform. These resources and opportunities, however, may dry up as the mayor ends his final term, staff churns, the economy tanks, and welfare dollars become scarce. In a broader sense, the attractiveness of regional solutions easily gives way to maintaining the preserves of jurisdictions and fragmented bureaucracies.

Milwaukee

Milwaukee's population of 596,974 experienced slight declines in the 1990s compared with a 13 percent growth in the suburbs. Most new job growth is in the suburbs, which accounts for 43 percent of the job openings. Three of five job openings require post-secondary skills. Although Milwaukee has experienced an overall decline in manufacturing jobs, a disproportionate number of its residents still hold manufacturing jobs.

The Milwaukee case study explores five LMIs through the lens of workforce ecologies. The authors examine the W-2 welfare-to-work agencies in Milwaukee, the joint Milwaukee City/County Workforce Investment Board, the Milwaukee Area Technical College (MATC), and the Wisconsin Regional Training Partnership (WRTP). It is only in the last example that they find elements of innovation and coordination ecologies that emphasize "fair and effective" workforce system performance and attention to long-run retention and job advancement.

According to Fung and Zdrazil, approximately $500 million is spent annually on workforce development in the greater Milwaukee area by federal, state, local, and philanthropic sources. The state of Wisconsin's Department of Workforce Development, which oversees both welfare and workforce investments, spent $171 million in Milwaukee on its W-2, welfare-to-work program, contracting out to five agencies.

The Milwaukee Workforce Investment Board, jointly administered by the city and county, has an annual budget of $26 million. The MATC has an annual budget of $200 million; suburban technical colleges spend an additional $60 million. Foundation investments and the local expenditure of federal Community Development Block Grant (CDBG) dollars amount to almost $4 million each year.

The W-2 program provided substantial financial incentives for its five contractors to move welfare recipients into unsubsidized employment as soon as possible. At stake for W-2 contractors were substantial profits, in the range of $28 million, and approximately $19 million to reinvest in client services. Although the state imposed a variety of bureaucratic rules on implementation, contractors had considerable discretion. Renegotiation of these contracts from 2000–2001 introduced new goals and incentives to promote retention, advancement, and workforce innovations.

Several organizations invest in employment and training services. Milwaukee's Private Industry Council (PIC) (or WIB) has the potential to promote innovative workforce strategies by the ways it invests in subcontracted services for education and training. Its review process for contracts, however, experiences great pressures to fund favored neighborhood organizations with political constituencies. MATC is the largest provider of education and training in Milwaukee. At least 20 percent of its employed graduates are economically disadvantaged or come from low-income neighborhoods. Although MATC has developed effective training models, customized and short-term training are not seen as priorities.

The WRTP promotes both workforce innovation and coordination of workforce investors and stakeholders, although it is by far the smallest of the major labor market intermediaries in Milwaukee. It derives its credibility from its partnership of employers and unions, a track record in modernization and workplace learning, and its more recent experience in placing 1,500 low-income residents in good-paying jobs. WRTP has state and local PIC funding, and has used MATC as a training provider.

New Orleans

The New Orleans region of eight parishes had 1.3 million residents in 2000, whereas Orleans Parish's population of 484,674 declined 2.5 percent from 1990 (Whelan, Gladstone, and Hirth, 2003). Seventy percent of the region's population is concentrated in Orleans and Jefferson parishes. Two thirds of the city population is African American compared with 75 percent of the suburban population, which is white. New Orleans experiences higher poverty and child poverty rates than most cities.

New Orleans had 788 fewer jobs in 1997 than in 1977, compared with 1.46 percent job growth in the surrounding region for the same period. The bulk of new employment has taken place in the suburbs. Jobs losses have occurred in port-related businesses and in manufacturing, whereas health care employment has increased. With little overall earnings growth, the New Orleans economy has become increasingly bifurcated; the top end of the labor market increased its earnings while the lower end stagnated.

New Orleans only recently evolved from a caretaker regime to a corporate regime. The legacy of exclusion and weak public institutions, however, is evident in the persistence of patronage, weak government, and poor service delivery. Recent mayors have been preoccupied with the basics of delivering competent and predictable services, such as police protection and public safety. Most public systems are broken. There is no better example of these broken systems than public education, a doubly important issue because of the very low levels of education and literacy among most New Orleans residents.

Although the authors dispel misconceptions about the unique disadvantage of the New Orleans economy, economic development remains the chief issue that brings stakeholders together. When workforce development shows up, it is primarily related to training incumbent workers for existing and new firms; hence, it is less concerned with investment in low-skilled workers. In short, too many competing agendas for change crowd out workforce development from public and civic attention.

The workforce system in the New Orleans region has eight colleges and universities, three community colleges, five public technical colleges, numerous proprietary schools, and four Workforce Investment Boards (WIBs). Delgado Community College, located in New Orleans, is the largest community college and provider of associate degrees and customized training. The Orleans Private Industry Council (OPIC), now the New Orleans WIB, oversees federal workforce dollars, whereas the Office of Family Services oversees welfare-to-work activities and TANF.

In the past, OPIC had strained relationships with all levels of government; the federal Department of Labor forced OPIC to pay back $4.5 million, and issued a letter for corrective action on another occasion because of questions concerning expenditures. In 2000, Orleans received $6.4 million in federal workforce resources and the region received $12.7 million. At the same time, Orleans received $5.1 million in welfare-to-work resources and the region received $7 million.

Louisiana has primarily invested in incumbent worker training—upgrade training for existing workers. It initially allocated $6 million from its unemployment insurance pool for this training; the state recently expanded this funding pool to an annual $50 million investment. In general, investments in existing workers do not reach unskilled or low-income workers.

Other key New Orleans workforce actors include the MetroVision Economic Development Partnership (the regional chamber) and the New Orleans Jobs Initiative. Both of these groups have provided better information about labor market opportunities, models and innovative programs, and forums for developing cross-sectoral and regional partnerships. So far, the results of these efforts have been modest.

Philadelphia

Philadelphia is the largest city and metropolitan area of the six case study cities. It has experienced slow population growth, at best, and a decline in its working population of workers between the ages of 16–64. The region was slow to recover from the last recession in the 1990s; the number of city jobs only returned to 606,000 in 2000 compared with 620,000 in 1989. The city accounts for 27 percent of the jobs in the region and manufacturing has declined dramatically. Growth clusters include professional services, data intensive services, health care, hospitality, and advanced manufacturing.

Philadelphia workforce systems comprise uneasy relationships between state government and the city. As reported by the Regional Workforce Partnership, there are five state agencies investing in workforce and training, twenty-two WIBs, and forty-nine job training and education programs. State and federal funding for these workforce development activities totals more than $1.2 billion, and this does not include a number of other federal, state, and local funding streams. Most of these resources are unmeasured, and report on different goals and outcomes. That is, welfare-to-work has, until recently, focused on welfare caseload reduction, whereas workforce development investments have measured job placement and retention.

Although both workforce and welfare are administered by the same state agency, this has not fostered cooperation nor reduced conflict. For instance, the spatial organization of these services greatly differs; there are seventeen welfare offices and one One-Stop, workforce center. Jurisdictions defeated an effort to create a regional WIB early on, but individual WIBs have signed on to a cooperative arrangement.

Four civic intermediaries play important roles in promoting outcome-focused workforce development. Greater Philadelphia First and the Regional Workforce Partnership are business partnerships that have advocated to focus workforce investment resources in growth clusters. The Latino Workforce Development Taskforce has recently developed program strategies and outcomes that consider the unique assets and barriers of the city's Latino community. Finally, The Reinvestment Fund (TRF), the Annie E. Casey Foundation's Jobs Initiative intermediary, has incubated new performance-driven workforce projects, and linked workforce development and economic development in its venture financing for small, growing companies.

Philadelphia's governing coalition is too weak, divided, and loosely connected to effectively advocate for workforce development and economic revitalization. It has limited effectiveness and it focuses episodically on specific "deals." It is reminiscent of what Sam Bass Warner called the "private city." What is lacking is regime authority or a "transcendent purpose" to guide the nurturing of a broader public interest. In this sense, Bartelt questions whether the concept of "regime" even makes sense.

Seattle

The population of King County, which contains Seattle, grew from 1,507,305 to 1,737,034 in 2000, an increase of 15.2 percent. Seattle's population was 563,000 in 2000. Although the number of people living in poverty (60,000) remained about the same in Seattle, this population grew by 70 percent (78,500) in King County, which is just outside of Seattle proper. Seattle's minority population is not growing, largely because people are being pushed out of the city, or are bypassing the city for cheaper housing in King County.

Service-sector employment grew substantially in King County during the 1990s, whereas manufacturing declined. Only 25,000 manufacturing jobs remained in Seattle as of 2000. Although the Seattle region has been hit hard by the recession, projections are strong for high-tech occupations and service-sector growth in the future.

Seattle is a "progressive regime" in which good government is combined with a legacy of reform. This regime emerged in the late 1960s and has remained through the terms of multiple Seattle mayors. Under this regime, no one elite "calls the shots;" advocates of projects and reforms make their cases within and across a diversity of forums, stakeholders, and constituencies. The business community is marginalized under this regime according to Smith and Davis, or has simply adopted the Seattle process of reform to get things done. The point is that many different stakeholders have achieved their goals and reduced transaction costs and social frictions through the formal and informal arrangements of Seattle's progressive regime.

Workforce systems in Seattle and in the state of Washington have received above average marks. The state has linked economic development with workforce and investment in wage progression strategies, and it has encouraged local areas to pursue unified plans for WIBs that bring together welfare, community colleges, and vocational education on a voluntary basis. Shoreline Community College is an outstanding example of a community college investing in employer-driven, short-term training. Outsiders viewed the former Seattle PIC, in spite of its shortcomings, as fairly effective. And, a number of workforce intermediaries have grown up in Seattle, including Port Jobs and the Seattle Jobs Initiative, which is the intermediary funded by the Casey Foundation.

The state invests substantial resources in workforce development in the Seattle region each year. Four agencies oversee its Workfirst program—the Department of Health and Human Services, the Employment Security Department, the State Board of Technical and Community Colleges, and the Department of Trade and Commerce. The Seattle King County Workforce Development Council invests several million dollars annually in workforce development. The Seattle Jobs Initiative has a budget of $4 million to $5 million each year, with at least $3 million coming from municipal funds. One hundred and fifty million dollars is invested in local technical and community colleges.

In the early and mid-1990s, PIC dominated the workforce system in Seattle. As a direct service provider, PIC—a creature of the JTPA—competed with community-based organizations and spent little effort on business engagement or on integration with other workforce players, such as community colleges. The focus was on pre-employment skills and job placement, not on job retention and career advancement.

A number of changes occurred from the mid-1990s on that made the Seattle workforce system look and function quite differently. Seattle's mayor formed the Seattle Jobs Initiative (SJI) as an intermediary organization that would focus on system reform, rather than direct services, by building relationships with community-based organizations, employers, and community colleges. SJI advocated a rethinking of PIC's role under the new WIA of 1998. Ultimately, the city/county replaced PIC with the Seattle King County Workforce Development Council (SKCWDC), a new organization that does not provide direct services but invests in One-Stop Centers and community organizations, and undertakes research and strategic planning. As the city of Seattle formed SJI, welfare reform brought about the competing strategy of "work first," which pressured community organization finances and referral networks.

Seattle's community college district, containing five colleges, has an uneven record in serving low-skilled workers. The incentives for these colleges encourage a focus on easier-to-serve individuals and on regular degree programs. The Seattle Vocational Institute (SVI) is the one college that focuses entirely on low-skilled workers, and SVI has formed a strong partnership with SJI in several occupational areas, and in its long-term strategic plan.

Smith and Davis identify progress toward institutionalizing performance as a priority, but more progress is needed. SJI, SKCWDC, and community-based organizations have formed new relationships and partnerships, although evidence shows continuing competition and duplication as well. SJI and SKCWDC have also embraced outcome measurement, but they have different measurement metrics. Moreover, community-based organizations are struggling with performance contracts that weaken their financial well-being by loading payments on the back end. Except for SJI, financial resources for job training and education are not growing—and are even declining. Finally, the business community remains largely unengaged in workforce reform efforts.

St. Louis

St. Louis has undergone massive population and economic changes in the past fifty years. Its population declined from 856,796 in 1950 to 348,189 in 2000, losing 50,000 residents in the 1990s. At the same time, the Missouri portion of the metropolitan area grew by 100,000 people, mostly in the outlying counties, and the entire Missouri/Illinois Metropolitan Statistical Area (MSA) grew by about 110,000. Economic changes mirrored population declines. In 1951, St. Louis had 85 percent (419,813) of the metropolitan jobs compared with only 30 percent (276,542) in 1997.

Only 20 percent of all metro businesses are located in St. Louis. St. Louis County surpassed St. Louis in economic activity by 1970; between 1970 and 1990, St. Louis lost 82,061 manufacturing jobs, whereas St. Louis County gained 44,000 manufacturing jobs. This poor and distressed city is the most racially diverse of the six case study cities with a population of 153,565 African Americans in 2000.

Workforce systems are quite complicated in the St. Louis metropolitan area because of the multiple levels of governance in two states, St. Louis City and St. Louis County, and smaller jurisdictions. By one estimate, there are ninety-two political jurisdictions, 114 public and two denominational school districts, nine major technical and vocational schools, nine two-year or community colleges, three public universities, nine independent colleges, and 170 nonprofits providing some type of employment service. The United Way identified 267 organizations in the metropolitan area that provide employment and training services. Six separate WIBs administer federal workforce funds in the St. Louis metropolitan area, four in Missouri and two in Illinois, each linked to an individual or a consortium of political jurisdictions.

Through its Department of Human Services, the state of Missouri has taken an outcomes-focused approach to its investment in welfare-to-work, and has invested in education and training as well as "work first" activities. The WIBs vary in performance. The St. Louis County WIB has assembled the Metropolitan Employment and Training Center, which combines a One-Stop Center with a variety of high-performing workforce providers, such as WorkLink. SLATE is the city's WIB, and under new leadership is investing in more innovative jobs strategies. East-West Gateway Coordinating Council, the Jobs Initiative intermediary, is the regional Council of Governments and the Metropolitan Planning Organization. It has invested in innovative jobs programs, such as WorkLink, and proposed regional workforce cooperation through a variety of mechanisms and incentives, including the allocation of transportation funds. It has worked in partnership with the Regional Commerce and Growth Association in this effort to promote regional cooperation. In the context of regional competition and fragmentation, these activities have engendered considerable ill will. East-West Gateway has also partnered with the Initiative for a Competitive Inner City's (ICIC) effort to identify economic growth clusters in the St. Louis region and to link them to effective workforce programs.

Jobs Initiative Results

These chapters are not intended to provide another evaluation of the Jobs Initiative (JI) sites. Evaluation of the Annie E. Casey Foundation's JI is the concern of the evaluators—Abt Associates and the New School University (Abt, 2002). Rather, this book describes the practice and potential of performance-oriented workforce politics in JI cities, regions, and states, drawing—when possible—upon the rich and varied lessons of JI partners.

Nevertheless, JI performance represents an additional, and arguably important, data point about workforce systems change and performance. Indeed, the underlying premise of the JI was to contribute to changing the way workforce systems operated through investing in outcome-focused jobs projects and system reforms. JI performance is briefly presented as a way of providing additional confirming or contrary evidence about the six cities and regions.

Table 7.1 portrays JI site performance in relation to jobs projects and system reforms. Jobs project performance is a composite of the number of job placements, wage levels, retention and advancement, and matched and leveraged funds. System reforms refer to the impact, leverage, and influence of early JI system reforms as well as explicit system reform investments.

Because the initiative remains a work in progress, these rankings are preliminary. This ranking of sites is not an entirely new discovery that emerged during implementation; it was evident early in implementation, if not in the selection process for sites at the beginning of the JI.

The one anomaly is Denver. Denver withdrew from the JI in 2001 after failing to improve performance and develop plausible and compelling system reform investments. Paradoxically, it was a front-runner early in the initiative and, in fact, the prior workforce investments of the Piton Foun-

Table 7.1   Project Performance Ratings of the Annie E. Casey Foundation Job Initiative

Cities	Job Placements[2] (n)	Return on Investment[3]	Leverage of Public and Private Resources[4]
Denver[1]	872	Low	Low
Milwaukee	1433	High	Medium
New Orleans	377	Very low	Low
Philadelphia	705	Low	Medium
Seattle	2692	Medium	High
St. Louis	1351	Medium	Medium

SOURCES: Data from AECF (2002), Mueller and Schwartz (2002), and Abt Associates (2002).
[1]Denver withdrew from the Jobs Initiative in June 2001.
[2]As of June 30, 2002, AECF Quarterly Jobs Initiative Results.
[3]Calculation based upon placements, retention, starting wage, pre-JI wages, and public subsidies.
[4]Assessment based upon matched and leveraged public and private resources.

dation, Denver's JI intermediary, had served as a model for JI's "development intermediary" role.

Two JI sites are high performers—Seattle and Milwaukee. Seattle, the overall leader of the sites, which was initially led by Mayor Norman Rice, has placed 2,692 participants, leveraged at least $25 million in resources, and has system reform investments that affect the role and capacity of community-based organizations and community colleges. Milwaukee has principally supported the development of one of the nation's most ambitious and effective workforce intermediaries—the WRTP, which engages 100 employers and unions in a variety of industries. WRTP has placed 1,433 participants, and helped design a $20-million state advancement fund.

Two JI sites are medium performers. The St. Louis JI is a project of the East-West Gateway Coordinating Council, a respected regional transportation and planning organization, which has placed 1,351 participants in jobs and leveraged unusual state investment in employment and training projects. East-West Gateway has invested in an effective job readiness and placement program named WorkLink, a consortium of workforce providers named Workforce Partners, and an ongoing effort to create an effective pipeline for minorities to enter the building trades. TRF, one of the top community development financial institutions in the country, oversees the Philadelphia site. TRF and its jobs projects have placed 705 participants in jobs, and have launched jobs projects for customer service jobs and as a complement to their venture investments in growing small companies. The Regional Workforce Partnership is an effective voice for employers in workforce policy arenas.

New Orleans was always the high-risk site for the JI, even during site selection. It did not have a strong civic infrastructure related to poverty alleviation, and it is the only city that had to build a new intermediary organization to implement the initiative. Starting from scratch has meant not only a longer development timetable, but also fewer job placements and lower retention rates. New Orleans has placed 377 participants as of 2002, with relatively low starting wages and support services. Although the New Orleans Jobs Initiative (NOJI) has obtained some public funding for its projects, it is the most dependent on Casey funding.

As discussed earlier, Denver withdrew from the JI in 2001. Under the auspices of the Piton Foundation, a business-oriented operating foundation, Denver placed 872 participants in jobs as of 2001. Unfortunately, Denver experienced very low job retention rates and wage progression, and it leveraged few funds from the public and private sectors. Their system reform investments never got off the ground.

Explaining Performance

This chapter has discussed the theories that case study authors used to make sense of varying performance changes in workforce systems. The task now is to ask comparative questions about the six cities as a group.

- What factors seem to account for more emphasis on workforce reform and performance?
- What factors impede a performance politics?
- What combination of factors is most powerful?

Answering these questions contributes to a better conceptual understanding of the politics of workforce development, rather than simply confirming or disconfirming specific causal relationships.

Table 7.2 arrays preconditions or indicators of heightened or lowered emphasis on performance-oriented workforce politics. Other factors are certainly at work, but these factors represent important economic, social, institutional, and policy variables.

The first is a measure of statewide social capital developed by Putnam (2000); it measures the density of memberships and networks, and is suggestive of a propensity to develop cooperative arrangements and solutions.

Elasticity is an indicator developed by Rusk (1993) that measures the integration of metropolitan regions in terms of annexation, race, and incomes, and is suggestive of the intensity of social problems and a propensity for regional solutions.

Governing Magazine (2000) develops local government performance measures on an annual basis. Overall scores demonstrate government capacity, knowledge about results planning, and the potential priority of more complex quality of life issues, such as workforce development.

The percentage of low-birth-weight babies who are born to mothers with less than twelve years of education is a measure of the prevalence

Table 7.2 City, Metro, and State Performance Indicators

	Social Capital	Elasticity	Government Performance Average Grade	Managing for Results	Percent Low Birth Weight/Less 12 yrs School	Metro Segregation Index 2002	Metro/State Ranking New Economy Index 2002	State Development Report Card 2002	Index of Distress 1970–1980	Education Preparation 2002	Asset Report Card Mean Net Worth State Ranking	School Aid as % of Tax Capacity
Denver Colorado	Medium +	Medium	B-	B-	34.7	62	7 / 4	A	2.219	B	24	14
Milwaukee Wisconsin	Medium +	Zero	B	A-	34.9	82	40 / 40	A	0.196	A-	16	51
New Orleans Louisiana	Very Low	Low	C-	D+	27.01	69	38 / 45	F	-2.189	F	41	*
Philadelphia Pennsylvania	Low	Zero	B	B	26.5	72	18 / 19	B	-3.56	B-	21	26
Seattle Washington	High	Low	B	B	11	50	3 / 2	A	0.187	B-	8	16
St. Louis Missouri	Low +	Zero	*	*	32.2	74	27 / 4	C	-6.4	B-	28	39

Sources: For social capital source is Putnam (2000). For elasticity, Rusk (1993). For government performance, Governing Magazine (2002). For low birth weight/less 12 years school, AECF (2001). For Metro Segregation Index 2002, Mumford Center (2001). For Metro/State New Economy Index 2002, Progressive Policy Institute (2001). For Index of Distress 1970—1980, Wolman, Ford, and Hill (1992). For State Development Report Card 2002, Corporation for Enterprise Development (2001). For Education Preparation 2002, National Center for Public Policy and Higher Education (2002). For Asset Report Card mean net worth, Corporation for Enterprise Development (2002). For school aid as % of tax capacity, Orfield (2002).

*Data not available.

and likely persistence of workforce challenges related to lower skills levels (AECF, 2001).

Metropolitan segregation indices measure the number of people who would have to be spatially moved to achieve integration that reflects the overall percentages of specific subgroups, such as African Americans and Hispanics (Mumford Center, 2002). This measure indicates levels of integration and separation by race across city landscapes.

The Metro/State New Economy Indices (Progressive Policy Institute, 2000; 2001) capture competitive economic features, such as number of people holding bachelor degrees, and are suggestive of how particular regions are likely to fare in a technological, skill-driven economy.

The State Development Report Card measures how supportive states are of entrepreneurial approaches to economic development (Corporation for Enterprise Development, 2001).

Harold Wolman, Coit Cook Ford, and Edward Hill (1992) developed an Index of Distress for major cities in the early 1990s that incorporated a variety of population, economic, and employment variables. Although they used this index as a way of exploring perceptions of revitalization, it is also useful in this context because it gives a sense of what was happening in our six cities in prior decades.

Measuring Up 2002 provides a variety of state-level measures for educational performance. The preparation measure encompasses a number of indicators related to high school credentials, testing, and upper-level courses attended (National Center for Public Policy and Higher Education, 2002).

The Asset Report Card reports on outcome and policy performance related to building assets and wealth. Mean net worth state ranking is one of a number of outcome variables that capture current levels of asset disparities categorized by state (Corporation for Enterprise Development, 2002).

Finally, School Aid as a Percentage of Tax Capacity categorized by city/metro area captures the size of local property tax base and school aid (Orfield, 2002). This approach answers questions such as: To what extent are schools supported from local revenues? How much school aid is transferred?

The case study insights and the data in Tables 7.1 and 7.2 suggest several groupings of cities and performance. Figure 7.1 suggests a preliminary ranking of the six cities by their relative degree of performance-oriented workforce development politics as it has been described in this book. These groupings comprise two "no brainers," three "mixed bags," and one anomaly. Analysis of these groupings is suggestive of the preconditions and indicators of "civic capacity"—that set of factors identified by Stone as so important for building performance regimes.

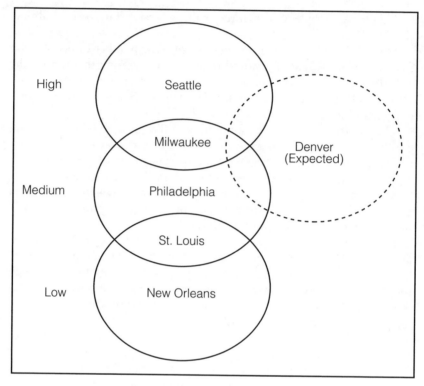

Figure 7.1   Workforce Performance in Six Cities

The "no brainers" are Seattle and New Orleans—the sites at either end of the performance continuum. It is not surprising that Seattle would take on workforce reform, although, the mayoral leadership of Norman Rice and unprecedented budget surpluses are the stuff of great timing. Seattle is a good government performer in a state with social capital and policies and economic and demographic characteristics supportive of economic and social development. Moreover, its poverty and low-skilled worker problem is relatively small.

New Orleans, in contrast, is a city of low government performance in a state of low social capital and a poor set of policies and attributes supportive of economic and social development. Nevertheless, segregation is lower and elasticity is higher in New Orleans than in several of the better performers.

The "mixed bag" cities are truly mixed. Milwaukee is a city with government capacity in a state with higher social capital and good policies for entrepreneurship. It is, however, a highly segregated metropolitan area with a large low-skilled worker problem and disadvantages relative to the new economy. Philadelphia's local government is rated good, although Pennsylvania social capital is low. It is a segregated region with zero elasticity, but has positive economic, demographic, and policy features relative to the new and entrepreneurial economies. St. Louis has generally lower performance levels across the indicators; the Jobs Initiative in St. Louis performed better than would have been expected.

The anomaly is Denver. It has good government performance in a state with medium social capital and high levels of economic, demographic, and policy factors for new and entrepreneurial economies. It has one of the highest levels of low-birth-weight babies born to mothers with less than twelve years of education. Although performing poorly in the JI, Clarke suggests Denver is doing well in relation to workforce development, the recognition of working poor issues, mayoral leadership, the local EITC, community college performance, and even the deliberations of the DWI in its last year. Clarke also reports that Denver demonstrated rather low "civic capacity" in its school reform efforts.

This comparative analysis of cities suggests that building civic capacity to change workforce systems is complicated, challenging, and not always a first civic priority. Even Seattle, where conditions supported change strategies, made only modest progress, and competition among stakeholders and systems remained. In other cities, such as New Orleans and St. Louis, the legacy of the past weighed heavily, whether it was a history of patronage or regional equity disparities. And, even when conditions seemed propitious for supporting performance-oriented change, timing, strategy, and commitment make a difference, as in the Denver case.

WORKFORCE SYSTEMS CHANGE ISSUES

Each chapter has used a variety of theoretical lenses and empirical methods to describe and analyze how workforce systems are structured, their component parts, barriers to change, and reform strategies. Regime theory has guided this inquiry, helping to identify emerging workforce performance and the composite of factors that may be important preconditions for workforce systems change.

A critical reading of these cases reveals five salient issues about how to think about workforce systems and the politics of workforce development: Resources; ideas and strategies; barriers; performance, and civic capacity. Addressing these issues leads to a reflection on the strengths and weaknesses of regime theory as applied to workforce development.

Resources

For Stone, the "iron law" of regime theory is that available resources must be commensurate with the policy problem at hand if sustained change is to occur (Stone, 1998). Stone and Worgs (Chapter 8) conclude that insufficient financial resources exist in the workforce arena given the overall need in the population for skills and career development. This conclusion certainly describes the limits of the WIA, which is the most explicit federal workforce policy and invests $6 billion nationally and up to $20 million to $30 million in each of the case study sites.

The situation is different, however, when community colleges and welfare (i.e., TANF) are viewed as a part of workforce systems; their funding streams amount to as much as $200 million to $500 million per metropolitan area. Sufficient financial resources are available; they are simply misaligned.

This larger estimate of workforce development financial resources poses several problems. First, it embodies broader definitions of target populations and types of workforce strategies. Community college participants, for example, are generally easier to serve, even when they are low income, and TANF resources largely serve welfare moms and emphasize "work first" rather than employment and training strategies. Second, a broader definition of workforce systems exacerbates fragmentation, funding silos, and dispersed authority. In the case of community colleges, autonomy is matched with goals and a mission, all of which are conflicted about whether even to provide short-term training for the low-skilled students. Although welfare programs and workforce development are frequently overseen by the same state agency , TANF differs from workforce investments in terms of strategy, organizational culture, outcomes, and service delivery. Nevertheless, total workforce development resources are substantial at the local and state levels. The question remains: How well are these resources spent and for what outcomes?

Financial resources, however, are only one type of resource required to support workforce systems change. Leadership, relationships, and networks make up a large portion of civic capacity. Smith and Davis point to the role of Mayor Norman Rice as key to forming and supporting the SJI. Moreover, they describe a "progressive regime" lasting over three mayoral administrations, which enabled multiple tables for policy discussions and decision-making. A number of authors also call attention to the civic, business, union, and religious institutions that supported the emergence of civic intermediaries, such as Project QUEST in San Antonio. More broadly, Plastrik, Seltzer, and Taylor (2003) suggest that authority, information, relationships, and competencies comprise strategic resources as well as financial resources.

Finally, Stone and Worgs depict a "two worlds" problem of inner-city job seekers/workers disconnected from the economic mainstream. Anyone who can organize either side of the labor market—or both sides—to reach out and connect with the other will have managed to tap a powerful resource for change.

Ideas and Strategies

Ideas shape workforce problem definitions, systemic change strategies, and coalition building. Clarke, for example, traced the escalating number of references to the "working poor" in the Denver media in the late 1990s—an indicator of growing public awareness. The challenge for workforce development is that there are contending ideas about effective workforce strategies—derived from evaluations, ideology, and beliefs—not just one overarching idea. Indeed, some workforce experts claim that "work first"—rather than human capital investment—is the only real contender for an overarching idea in developing workforce strategies.

Ideas shape the social purposes and goals around which civic capacity, coalitions, and performance regimes are organized. If common ideas are not possible, common purposes and common strategic actions are unlikely to emerge for changing the politics of workforce development. Fung and Zdrazil show how multiple ideas are built into the constitutive rules governing different workforce ecologies (e.g., reducing welfare caseloads, retention and advancement, or dual-customer strategies). Civic agreement about more performance-oriented ideas could lead to a change in the rules and incentives of workforce ecologies, and in turn, encourage more innovation and coordination on behalf of career advancement and family economic self-sufficiency. Bartelt, however, reports on multiple and conflicting "civic conversations" that underscore differences of understanding and strategic direction: Targeted versus universal workforce investments; whether employers or job seekers have soft skills deficits; work first versus human capital investment; and community organizations as points of access and support or "agents of resistance" to change. Stone and Worgs broaden the debate about workforce development in their characterization of a "two worlds" problem that divides inner-city communities and the economic mainstream. As Clarke shows, competing ideas can become competing agendas for public attention and resources: A local EITC—a "making work pay" strategy—may bring immediate benefits to the working poor in contrast to the long-run hopes of investment in human capital.

Barriers

Performance-oriented politics of workforce development is difficult to achieve and maintain. Stakeholders can be mobilized, Clarke argues, but sustaining and institutionalizing their interest is the challenge. According to Stone, regimes form when those with control over resources come to a common table to pursue a common purpose (Stone, 1998). Stone and Worgs conclude that insufficient authority exists at the center of workforce development around which to cultivate durable performance coalitions.

Workforce systems are complicated, fragmented, and confusing. Bartelt speaks of multiple workforce development tables, cooks, and conversations: Workforce development is like a "bowl of spaghetti." Smith and Davis describe the current workforce landscape as "more chaotic and unstable," particularly given the heightened participation of community-based organizations as workforce providers. Fung and Zdrazil describe this workforce situation as a "non-system."

There are several alternative ways to look at the apparent chaos and lack of authority at the center of workforce development. Plastrik, Seltzer, and Taylor (2003) argue that workforce development is embedded in largely private regional labor markets, which are made up of voluntary transactions with supply, demand, and intermediary components. They adopt a "systems approach" to examine the functioning of these markets. Fung and Zdrazil offer the conceptual framework of "workforce ecologies" to describe the patterned but decentralized niches that cluster inter-related workforce activities around different LMIs. A combination of policies, incentives and rewards, and strategies constitute their five "ideal type" workforce ecologies.

Employment regimes represent more than preserving jobs, contracts, and organizational inertia. Cummings et al., point out how regional disparities create and reproduce regional fragmentation that preserves its bureaucratic autonomy, not simply as a matter of employment, but of governmental and growth coalition discretion that is often motivated by protecting racial exclusion. Bartelt emphasizes the "lashed up arrangements" of machine politics and the "private city," as expressed in the culture of the deal.

Two big issues received uneven attention in the case study cities. Sustained business voice is missing in many workforce systems debates. Yet, employers are definitely present in the discussions in Philadelphia, New Orleans, and Milwaukee. Stone and Worgs, Whelan et al., and Cummings et al. identify racism and racial divisions as requiring sustained attention beyond the scope of workforce development.

Performance

The performance of performance regime is not a uniformly understood or embraced goal. Most observers agree that workforce development has not produced powerful outcomes related to income gains and poverty alleviation. This perceived failure at producing impacts feeds the dynamic of multiple ideas and strategies—performance as reducing welfare rolls, work first, making work pay, or career advancement. Also, what is meant by first job, good job, or wage progression?

Performance-driven reform processes and investments have not always produced positive change, however. Bartelt cites the school reform effort in Philadelphia called Children Achieving as an example of this concept. In their pursuit of performance, Workforce programs, such as JTPA and WIA, have frequently encouraged providers to "cream" the easiest-to-serve job seekers, leaving the harder-to-employ without assistance. Alternatively, Fung and Zdrazil argue that because welfare-to-work efforts in Milwaukee have failed to reach the people most in need, or help families move out of poverty, more productive discussions have begun about how to connect welfare-to-work and employer-driven training and retention.

Performance-driven contracts may squash innovation and actual long-term performance because of the onerous demands they place on workforce providers. Smith and Davis, as well as Clarke, confirm this problem for community organizations that increasingly provide workforce service. They have lean budgets and meager working capital and hence are vulnerable to cash-flow problems. Consequently, these organizations are sometimes unable to reach performance targets.

Bartelt, however, does identify some community organizations as opposed to performance; paradoxically, these organizations become a part of employment regimes. Some discipline is required to disrupt the pattern of non-performance and the lack of innovation, but there is no doubt that these changes present major challenges. Public investors in workforce development have not determined how to grow and replicate effective programs.

The either/or of employment versus performance regimes may obfuscate the "contested terrain" of performance. That is, at any point in time in most cities, elements of performance and non-performance coexist in workforce development systems and practice. The question becomes not one of wholesale change, but of incrementally increasing credibility and favorable conditions for enhancing workforce performance.

Civic Capacity

Stone et al. argue that civic capacity and civic mobilization are necessary to build durable coalitions that overcome barriers and address common problems and purposes, such as reforming urban education (Stone et al., 2001). What they mean by civic capacity is a form of collective social capital—relationships and networks configured around common ideas and purposes. Workforce development requires civic capacity to bridge its many components; yet, this fragmented and geographically dispersed non-system may not have natural constituencies to build such capacity beyond those it employs.

Recognizing the need for this civic capacity, the Annie E. Casey Foundation looked for cities that demonstrated evidence of a "civic infrastructure" to participate in its Jobs Initiative. Evidence of civic capacity, however, includes many dimensions. Whelan et al. (2003) observe that New Orleans is known for "bonding versus bridging" social capital; that is, citizens are able to form inclusive groups but are unable to connect to other, different groups.

Clarke discusses the broad spectrum of civic actors engaged in workforce development, such as advocates, bureaucrats, community organizations, and the public, and how they are connected, if at all. Smith and Davis identify changed relationships among key stakeholders as an indicator of systems change in Seattle, although they note that persistent competition remains among these same actors. Moreover, Seattle's "progressive regime" indicates that no one table at which decisions are made exists; rather there are multiple, connected tables.

Civic intermediaries bridge parts of workforce systems, organize stakeholders, identify common purposes, and advocate strategic directions. These partnerships build civic capacity as a matter of their day-to-day work, and the nature of their stakeholders and credibility are expressions of civic capacity at the same time. Four civic intermediaries in Philadelphia play this role, particularly in relation to articulating business perspectives on workforce development. Fung and Zdrazil point to the Wisconsin Regional Training Partnership as an example of a "coordination ecology," which brings together parts of workforce systems to achieve performance objectives. Smith and Davis characterize the Seattle Jobs Initiative as an intermediary devoted to systems reform that organizes the parts of the workforce system around ambitious purposes and outcomes.

Regime Theory

The conceptual framework of regime theory facilitates these case studies and comparative reflections, even acknowledging the tensions and issues raised by this approach. Regime theory provides a framework of analysis that focuses on public and private coalitions formed around common purposes, and the conditions under which such coalitions emerge and are sustained. Hence, it is an explanatory theory of why workforce systems are not performing, and a normative theory about building civic capacity to support performance-oriented local politics.

Too often workforce reform has emanated from top-down initiatives that ultimately have failed because of rational planning assumptions about the way the world works. Regime theory is not about command and control organizations, but instead is about the social production of cooperative arrangements. Not all situations, however, have the requisite financial resources and authority mandates to build durable coalitions. Three significant barriers prevent the building of performance regimes: Contending ideas, competing agendas, and divisive political, regional, and racial legacies. Conditions are not propitious, several authors argue, for building performance regimes around workforce development.

Should this conclusion be accepted? Is regime theory helpful for explaining loosely connected systems? Regime theory's assumptions may omit almost any policy arena except economic development promotion and mega-development projects. Two chapters offer alternative conceptions: Labor markets as systems or as workforce "ecologies." Both accept, even support, the decentralized aspects of workforce systems. Both approaches make sense of this complexity, and identify leveraging points that have the potential for changing the functioning of markets or ecologies in the direction of performance outcomes.

What these alternative conceptions do not provide, however, is an answer to the question of how strategic leveraging points or rules and incentives can be changed. How can capacity and focus be built among stakeholders to take incremental steps toward reform, much less build durable coalitions? These alternative conceptions of workforce development politics clarify the structure and functioning of workforce systems. Regime theory, however, remains critical in its emphasis on inquiring about the sources of civic capacity and leadership to pursue reform agendas.

CONCLUSION

This chapter has taken a comparative perspective on the six case studies and two background chapters. The goal of the chapter has been to describe and understand workforce systems, discuss relevant theories used to understand local politics of workforce development, reflect on regime theory, and discuss crosscutting themes and approaches that promote or impede workforce reform strategies. The diversity of the six cities and the intellectual perspectives of the authors have made this a rich and engaging enterprise.

Two broad conclusions derive from this synthesis. A pessimistic conclusion is that workforce development serves few in need, frequently fails to make a difference, is a part of fragmented public systems with little authority, is divided by competing ideas and agendas, and takes place in a political and institutional environment that is hostile to building real career pathways for low-skilled workers and communities. Paradoxically, conservatives and the left-of-center share aspects of this conclusion. The former focus on the waste of government money for ineffective interventions; the latter argue that the problem is a matter of the lack of good jobs or a real public commitment.

A contrasting conclusion is more optimistic. Considerable money is spent by a variety of public institutions on aspects of workforce development—$200 million to $500 million a year in some medium-sized metro areas. And, there are examples of workforce development producing results; these examples bring together good jobs, employers, a mix of hard and soft skills, and retention supports. Intermediaries in many cities—partnerships of employers, unions, community organizations, and the public sector—are building these models one by one and changing workforce systems at the same time.

There is no one rational reorganization plan for workforce development systems. What is needed is the right statement of purposes, strategies, and accountability measures at the top, and entrepreneurial civic intermediaries building up solutions from the bottom that explicitly take into account political development and continuous improvement. This approach requires the right mix of civic capacity, economic strengths, and leadership, but it is possible to start small and make a difference.

What if we were able to build and nurture enough civic intermediaries and model projects to met the needs of a wide range of workforce stakeholders? This would still not meet some of the objections stated in the first conclusion. Are there enough good jobs? How can we reach 15 million to 50 million workers who need skills upgrading? And, the "two worlds" divide between inner-city communities of color and the economic mainstream remains persistent and deep. A much broader coalition must be built under a larger banner than workforce development.

Regime theory has focused our attention on the strategies and barriers that are relevant to the social production of durable coalitions necessary to pursue a more performance-oriented approach to workforce development. Regime theory has stumbled, to a degree, on workforce systems, markets, and fragmented non-systems at the same time. It has been difficult to identify the areas of agreement and strategic leverage necessary to move workforce systems from employment to performance regimes. At the same time, weak local capacity, regional disparities, and a legacy of patronage politics have obstructed even modest reform efforts.

Nevertheless, regime theory points us in the direction of building civic capacity, perhaps in the form of civic intermediaries. This strategy will not yield immediate regime change, but it may help cities make incremental progress toward performance on a "contested terrain."

REFERENCES

Abt Associates and The New School University. 2002. *AECF Jobs Initiative: Evaluation of the Capacity Building Phase, April 1997–March 2000.* Cambridge, MA: Abt Associates.

Annie E. Casey Foundation (AECF). 2001. *The Right Start: City Trends—Conditions of Babies and Their Families in America's Largest Cities (1990–1998).* Baltimore: Annie E. Casey Foundation.

———. 2002a. *AECF Jobs Initiative Quarterly Report (June).* Baltimore: Annie E. Casey Foundation.

Corporation for Enterprise Development. 2001. *Development Report Card.* Washington, DC: Corporation for Enterprise Development.

———. 2002b. *Asset Report Card.* Washington, DC: Corporation for Enterprise Development.

Judge, David, Gerry Stoker, and Harold Wolman. 1995. *Theories of Urban Politics.* Thousand Oaks, CA: Sage Publications.

Governing Magazine. 2000. *The Government Performance Project.* Washington, DC: Congressional Quarterly, Inc. Available at www.governing.com.

Grubb, W. Norton. 1996. *Learning to Work: The Case for Reintegrating Job Training and Education.* New York: Russell Sage Publications.

Mueller, Elizabeth, and Alex Schwartz. 2002. *Creating Change: Pushing Workforce Systems to Focus on Family Economic Success.* Cambridge, MA: Abt Associates.

Mumford Center. 2002. *Ethnic Diversity Grows: Neighborhood Integration Lags Behind.* Albany, NY: Mumford Center, State University of New York. Available at www.albany.edu/mumford/census.

National Center for Public Policy and Higher Education. 2002. *Measuring Up 2002.* Washington, DC: National Center for Public Policy and Higher Education.

Orfield, Myron. 2002. *American Metropolitics.* Washington, DC: Brookings Institution.

Plastrik, Peter, Marlene Seltzer, and Judith Combes Taylor. 2003. *Changing Labor Markets: A Systems Approach to Reform.* Boston: Jobs for the Future.

Progressive Policy Institute. 2001. *New Economy Metropolitan Index.* Washington, DC: Progressive Policy Institute. Available at www.ppionline.org.

———. 2000. *New Economy State Index.* Washington, DC: Progressive Policy Institute. Available at www.ppionline.org.

Putnam, Robert. 2000. *Bowling Alone: The Collapse and Revival of American Community.* New York: Simon and Schuster.

Rusk, David. 1993. *Cities Without Suburbs.* Baltimore: Johns Hopkins University Press.

Stoker, Gerry. 1995. "Regime Theory and Urban Politics." In *Theories of Urban Politics,* edited by Judge, Stoker, and Wolman, 54–71. Thousand Oaks, CA: Sage Publications.

Stone, Clarence. 1998. *Changing Urban Education.* Lawrence: University Press of Kansas.

Stone, Clarence, Jeffrey Henig, Bryan Jones, and Carol Pierannunzi. 2001. *Building Civic Capacity: The Politics of Reforming Urban Schools*. Lawrence: University Press of Kansas.

Whelan, Robert, David Gladstone, and Trisha Hirth. 2003. *Building a Workforce Development System in New Orleans*. New Orleans: University of New Orleans.

Wolman, Harold, Coit Cook Ford, and Edward Hill. 1992. *Evaluating the Success of Urban Success Stories*. Research conference of the Association of Public Policy and Management, October 29–31, Denver Colorado.

8   Poverty and the Workforce Challenge

By all accounts big-city schools fail half or more of their students from lower-income backgrounds. Dropout rates are high, and even many students who graduate possess only a modest level of academic skills. Some of the students who dropout manage to acquire GEDs on their own and find their way into the job market. Even students with high school diplomas, however, have difficulty entering the mainstream economy of steady work at good pay. Additional training or, more broadly, workforce development offers a possible chance for individuals who had a bad start to recover and attain a decent-paying job.

Some companies provide on-the-job training for entry-level workers, but that is a small opening for a large pool of potential applicants. Responsibility falls mainly on the government, with assistance from the nonprofit sector, to knit together the means by which the labor market is addressed to afford a second chance to those who have missed entry into the mainstream economy. The problem runs deep. Racial stereotyping, inadequate skills, spatial mismatch, inadequacies in information networks, and particular features of low-wage work combine to make access to family-supporting jobs difficult for a large segment of the urban population.

In the eyes of some on the political right, welfare is the logical beginning point for addressing the issue of poverty; to them the world went awry in the 1960s with a large expansion in the welfare system. However, to believe that poverty or urban problems date from that time is to look at the inner city with a foreshortened understanding of history. Economic marginality runs far back into the nation's past, and urban schools have a long history of being unable to overcome that heritage.

Urban education began to decline in the 1930s, when the Great Depression undercut teenage employment (Mirel, 1993). After a brief interval of full employment during World War II, high schools became holding operations for many individuals who had nowhere else to go. Although deindustrialization reached a peak in the 1970s, work began to disappear earlier than that time (Wilson, 1996). By the 1950s, school superintendents in big cities had already made a plea for help (Marris and Rein, 1967, 1973). Despite a response in the form of the Ford Foundation's Gray Areas project and subsequent federal initiatives, schools were left to cope as best they could, and many embraced the "shopping mall" solution of minimal demands on students (Powell, Farrar, and Cohen, 1985). That strategy did not minimize a high dropout rate, and it contributed to the weak academic achievements of many students who did graduate. A heritage of faltering urban schools has bequeathed a huge population who are in need of a "second chance" to enter the mainstream economy.

Workforce development affords second chances, but it is a complex and not well-synchronized system. Unlike public school districts with their hierarchical structures, the workforce development system is diffuse and loosely organized. The most problem-laden connection in workforce development is the link between a low-skilled labor pool, concentrated in the central city, and a body of employers spread over a still expanding metropolitan region. These employers have changing needs that are increasingly tilted toward a higher order of skills. At one level, then, the workforce challenge consists of a skills and location mismatch. Therefore, the solution appears to be a matter of improved placement that includes breaking down employer stereotypes, appropriate training before placement on-the-job, better transportation, and sufficient child care and support services. However, if the problem is this simple, why does it persist? The discussions below attempt to answer that question and sketch a multipart strategy for addressing the problem. First, we offer a brief sketch of key elements in the "second chance" system.

THE ACTORS AND RELATIONSHIPS IN THE SECOND CHANCE SYSTEM

A major goal of the workforce development system is to link unemployed and underemployed individuals from high-poverty communities with *available* jobs that pay a family-sustaining wage.[1] That task has proved to be deceptively complicated even in times of tight labor markets—with low unemployment. Under seemingly favorable conditions, it has proved difficult both to move large numbers of unemployed individuals from low-income communities into the active labor force, and also to make substantial progress in moving low-wage workers into better jobs.

To gain a clearer perspective on this system, we consider the major players in the "second chance" system and the relationships among these actors that facilitate or impede the movement of low-income individuals into well-paying jobs. Key actors are the target population of low-income and unemployed individuals, the array of organizations that provide training and job preparation, labor market intermediaries, employers, and government officials (local, state, and federal government).

Target Population

The individuals who make up the *target population* share certain characteristics, but are by no means homogeneous. They differ in educational background, previous work experience, race and cultural traditions as well as in the "soft skills" employers often point to as critical for sustaining employment. Of special importance, the target population varies along a continuum of employability, which corresponds to their particular circumstances and the obstacles affecting their preparedness for work. Individuals facing the fewest obstacles are usually the ones who take advantage of the available opportunities. This is not necessarily to say that those who serve the target population are engaged in "creaming," because they are working with people in need (but see Lafer, 2002). It simply emphasizes the point that some individuals are harder to serve than others, and those hardest to serve are also least likely to get attention.

Consider Project QUEST in San Antonio. This program has reaped well-deserved acclaim for facilitating the transition of low-income individuals into decent jobs (Warren, 2001). Project QUEST, however, has substantial entry requirements that include possession of a high school diploma or GED. Applicants begin the intake process by attending an outreach meeting. Ultimately, approximately 20 percent of those who attend the meeting end up in the program (Osterman and Lautsch, 1996). Those who gain entry are quite likely to be those with the smallest number of hurdles in their path. This is a recurring story in low-income communities: Those surrounded by the fewest obstacles are the most likely to be placed in jobs, whereas those encountering the greatest obstacles are often neglected. Although there is no clear line of demarcation, it is helpful to think of the target population in terms of "the easier to employ" versus "the hard to employ." This distinction allows us to consider the extent to which interventions can reach those who are most difficult to integrate into the mainstream economy.

The Training Providers

The institutions that provide training to the target population are diverse and vary in their effectiveness, but they are central in the process of moving individuals from the target population to jobs that pay family-sustaining wages. Local school systems are charged with being the primary training providers, but the failures of this "first chance" system are what make the task of the "second chance" system so massive. The details of "how and why" the first chance system performs badly need not be dealt with here.

We also do not need to spend much of our efforts considering the four-year colleges because the workforce development system has delegated the responsibilities for training in such a manner that four-year institutions are rarely called upon to facilitate the transition of low-income adults to well-paying jobs. That responsibility has fallen primarily to four kinds of institutions: Specific job training and placement organizations that may have important community links, community colleges, public post-secondary technical centers, and proprietary schools. There is a scattering of other programs, some run by labor unions, for example; however, most of the training to which low-income populations have access comes through one of the four institutions above.

The main responsibility for training the low-income population falls on the variety of *local job training* and *preparation programs*, including the array of welfare-to-work programs and others. Researchers have found that the job-training sector has demonstrated mixed results, with many having little long-term impact on the individuals they serve; they too rarely place these individuals in well-paying jobs. Consequently, their clients who do achieve employment often end up in dead-end, low-paying jobs. For the welfare population, "work first" programs are especially likely to yield minimum-wage jobs. A recent evaluation of welfare-to-work programs concluded that, although programs did move people into employment, the programs failed to meet the goal "of making people materially better off" (Hamilton, 2002, 62).

Community colleges tend to have strong relationships with employers, but are not major trainers of low-income individuals, although they do train some through both their regular certificate and degree programs, and through contract agreements with nonprofit organizations or federal, state, or local government policies. Community colleges have a history of contracting to train individuals through federal programs (e.g., CETA, JTPA) as well as nonprofit organizations (e.g., Project QUEST in San Antonio).

The community colleges' link to employers is illustrated in the growth of contract training over the last two decades. Currently, 90 percent of community colleges offer some form of contract training (Dougherty and Bakia, 2000). Contract students comprise 17–18 percent of all students enrolled in the schools. Some of this growth was a result of government programs or nonprofit organizations, but most has come from increased demand from the private sector. The reasons are familiar—the perceived increasing skill demands and perceived shortages in trained workers. A key factor in this growth has been the cost effectiveness of contracting with community colleges compared with training in house. State subsidies have aided this growth; for example, some states subsidize training as an economic development strategy (Dougherty and Bakia, 2000, 213). Community colleges also benefit from their responsiveness to the needs of the contracting client as well as from the perception that they are more academic than vocational schools, and more reliable than proprietary schools.

Although the community colleges are often very effective as training providers, low-income individuals enrolling in these schools sometimes face obstacles, ranging from entry requirements (e.g., a high school diploma or GED) to scheduling issues (e.g., program length and the times at which courses are offered). Those who do enroll often need remedial courses that offer no credit. This limits the availability of student aid, which requires a minimum number of credits for eligibility. Furthermore, the "work first" orientation of welfare reform and the Workforce Investment Act (WIA), thus far, discourage individuals who pursue training at community colleges.

The point is that community colleges have a capacity to offer training, and do provide a significant amount of training for employment in decent jobs through both contract training as well as through their regular certificate and degree programs. Although there are barriers that limit the access of poverty populations to this channel into employment, steps could be taken to enhance access. Except for the contract training for community organizations or government programs, community colleges have not been a major vehicle for the impoverished.

Public post-secondary vocational schools have much in common with community colleges. They too engage in significant contract training and are supported by public subsidies. They differ in that they may be slightly more responsive to employer desires because of their ostensible mission to prepare workers. These institutions are not as ubiquitous as community colleges, but have a significant presence in certain states. Tennessee, for example, has a system of Technology Centers throughout the state. These centers played a significant role in the administration of federal training programs, and are poised to be key in the training supported by the WIA.

Another significant set of institutions that serve low-income individuals is the *proprietary schools*. There are more than 5,000 proprietary schools serving over one million students, including many who are economically disadvantaged. These schools have the potential to be important factors in the reformation of local workforce systems. The schools in this category vary tremendously, from barber "colleges" to for-profit universities, but the sector deserves consideration because these schools provide much of the training to which low-income individuals have access. Although many of these schools may be effective, as a group they have a dismal record. Proprietary schools garnered much national attention during the early 1990s when Congress concluded that these schools were participating in fraud and abuse of the federal student aid system. As one General Accounting Office (GAO) official stated, "Some proprietary school operators have enriched themselves at the expense of the economically disadvantaged students while providing little or no education in return" (Blanchette, 1996). All many students received for their efforts were large loan debts—on which they often defaulted. In 1990, the default rate peaked at 41 percent of loans entering repayment, whereas the average for all post-secondary students was 22 percent. The schools accounted for 35 percent of loans entering repayment during 1991 and 1992, but accounted for 71 percent of those who defaulted during those years.

As a result of the high default rates, Congress passed legislation mandating that schools could not receive more than 85 percent of their revenue from Title IV funds, which are primarily federally-subsidized student loans and Pell grants. A GAO study of the impact of this legislation found that schools that relied the most on Title IV funds had poorer outcomes; students had lower completion rates, lower placement rates, and higher default rates. Another report found that these schools were spending millions of federal education dollars to prepare students for occupations that were already oversupplied.[2] Though proprietary schools have serious drawbacks, they represent a significant segment of the available training resources for the populations upon which we are focused (U.S. General Accounting Office, 1997a; 1997b).

Intermediaries

Labor market intermediaries have come to play an increasingly important role over the last decade. In fact, they have increased significantly in number. Richard Kazis has argued that the growth of intermediaries has been a reaction to the increasing "uncertainty and risk of the open labor market" (Kazis, 1998, 5). These intermediaries take various forms: Trade associations and employer organizations, labor unions, temporary agencies, community-based organizations, and government entities (e.g., particular agencies or workforce investment boards). As Kazis points out, these intermediaries generally focus on one of the following approaches, though they may not be limited to a single strategy:

- Accept the labor market as a given and try to improve the efficiency of the *job matching process*
- Accept employer demand as a given and work to improve the ability of the supply-side *workforce development* institutions to meet employer needs
- Try to *change employer demand for labor* in ways that reduce inefficiencies and inequalities in wages, benefits, job security, and advancement (Kazis, 13)

These organizations try to connect the labor supply to employers. They vary in determining whom they view as their primary client and what their priorities are. Thus, community-based organizations that serve as intermediaries likely have an objective of placing low-income individuals in good positions, whereas industry organizations have a priority of meeting the employment needs of their members or sector. The divergent priorities suggest different levels of willingness to sustain costs necessary to meet either objective. Intermediaries also vary greatly in size, with small ones sometimes serving as subcontractors for larger ones (Fung and Zdrazil, 2001).

Employers

In considering the employer's role in the workforce system, the distinction between low-wage employment and employment in a decent job with a family-sustaining wage comes into sharp focus. Although members of the target population do not desire a low-wage job, it is often the outcome. At best, low-wage employment is an intermediate step to better jobs; however, too often a low-wage job is another obstacle to an individual's attainment of family-sustaining employment. The low-wage job sector is fraught with disincentives to work—beyond the low wages and lack of benefits. This sector is characterized by high turnover, and individuals in these positions often do not learn the skills needed to improve their marketability. In short, these jobs usually do not lead to better employment.

The employers' participation in the workforce system is governed by their desire to cut costs. Many do see the importance of civic and social responsibility, and may be committed to hiring a certain number of low-income workers. But that number is not sufficient to alter the employment levels in the target communities without a major campaign to bring about change. For the most part, employers, especially those providing decent jobs and jobs that offer room for advancement, obtain their employees through institutions, avenues, and processes that do not access the targeted population, in part by habit and in part by fear of the costs of hiring low-income individuals. Changing this behavior requires a major undertaking that has at its basis a reformation of the perceived incentives facing these employers. Though individual employers may need to move workers into higher-skill positions, business as a whole has little reason to concern itself with the low-wage work problem or involve itself in the shift of workers into higher-wage jobs. In addition, some individual employers see themselves as having a strong need to maintain a pool of low-pay workers.

Government Entities

Federal, state, and local governments are also critical actors. First, they have official agencies that may themselves play a role in providing training or serving as intermediaries, or they may fund the work of these actors. Secondly, the impact that public policy has on the workings of the system cannot be overlooked.

We start from an assumption that policy can make a difference, and therefore must consider how current policies might hinder or facilitate the transformation of local workforce systems. There is a long history of federal government policies purporting to make the workforce system operate more effectively. Even so, local actors have no shortage of recommendations for improving intergovernmental regulations.[3] The most relevant federal policies are welfare reform and the WIA—although policies surrounding student financial aid are also very important). Both seem to have the potential to misdirect efforts that might connect the impoverished to good-paying jobs. The "work first" approach that is at the heart of welfare reform implies that any work will facilitate an individual's transition out of poverty. However, experience suggests that low-wage employment is unlikely to lead to significantly higher income, and it may not even lay a foundation for work habits that would facilitate moving up the job-and-income ladder.

The WIA is being implemented with a "work first" thrust as well, but it also has a potential for progressive change. First, the possibility of aid to employed workers who seek to upgrade their skills could have a positive impact on low-skilled employees. The greatest potential of the WIA lies in the fact that it forces localities to reflect on their system, and to create a set of institutions that could be used to herd the disparate actors together, promoting actions in a unified strategic fashion. This is a potential that reportedly is being overlooked in many, if not most, places. However, some localities are trying to move toward fulfilling this potential.

In the city of Memphis, for example, the local chamber of commerce has been leading an effort to formulate a regional workforce development strategy that encompasses both the business leaders as well as the city agencies and education and training providers—including the school system. Participants in this process believe that they could use their WIB and youth council as part of an initiative that engages various stakeholders in a comprehensive plan for the region's workforce system.

An institutional network is taking shape. In fact, one individual serves as the executive director of the Partnership for Preparing a Regional Workforce (a chamber of commerce initiative to engage local business in discussions around workforce development), chair of the Youth Council (seen as the coordinating body for youth policy), and executive director of the Business and Education Collaboration for the Southwest Tennessee Community College. He also works closely and collaboratively with the school system, in particular the director of career and technical education. These organizations have intertwining boards and significant business involvement and commitment according to a field visit by Donn Worgs conducted on May 9–10, 2001. This network's actors are building the institutions that may bring greater coordination to their local workforce system. At the very least, Memphis is in a position to heighten awareness of the big picture and how its parts fit together.

Overall, two sets of questions present themselves. One concerns the extent to which greater coordination of the actors in the workforce system is possible. Can coordination occur on a regional level, and, if so, how? If not, can coordination be achieved in a more limited segment of the labor market, specifically that part tied most closely to the central city? Again, if so, how? The second set of questions asks whether coordination is enough. Even if coordination can be achieved, is it enough— especially if it occurs in a segment smaller than the metropolitan region?

RELATIONSHIPS

Currently, workforce coordination is limited and key relationships are weak where they need to be the strongest. The relationships among the actors in the system highlight where policy efforts should be aimed. For example, there are often weak linkages between the target population and training providers; thus, at the point of entry into the system, much of the target population is disconnected from training providers and the chain of relationships (training provider to employer or training provider to intermediary to employer) that can lead to employment. Moreover, for individuals who enter the system, the chain of relationships is not likely to yield decent jobs. This is because the training providers who have the strongest links to the target population often have the weakest linkages to the employers, and the employers with whom they have relationships, tend to offer low-wage employment. Without some form of intervention, the target population seems destined to remain disconnected from the decent-paying jobs that can elevate families out of poverty.

The channeling of the target population into low-wage jobs would not be such an unfortunate outcome if there were consistent processes to facilitate the transition from low-wage employment to family-sustaining jobs. This is a transition that occurs too infrequently to make any significant impact on the target population. Fortunately, there are a number of suggestions currently being explored within the training world. Many of these approaches center on the notion of job ladders or "skill supply chains," whereby an individual would have a clear path of advancement, and employers would have a steady, predictable supply of workers. Initiatives that apply this concept are already under way.

For many employers who provide decent jobs, however, the chain of relationships that connects to employees does not lead to low-income individuals. Why is there a disjuncture between the target group and the employers who would employ them? The relationships between institutions, though not necessarily formal, have been constituted by habitual action. When employers want employees, they are likely to call the same "supplier" they called in the past, and these suppliers do not tend to have strong connections to the low-income individuals with whom we are concerned. Without a strong incentive, there will be no change.

Advancements can be made if more members of the target population could be placed in the institutions that have strong connections with employers, and if the link between employers and institutions that have stronger connections to the target population could be strengthened. The overall challenge is to build firm pathways through the system—from training to employment at a family-sustaining wage; these pathways are functions of relationships between the institutions.

These relationships must include awareness of the other actors in the system (i.e., their existence, their needs, abilities, etc.) and trust that these actors can meet the needs of other actors. Awareness and trust operate at different levels of generality. They involve particular individuals and organizations (e.g., a neighborhood leader, the head of the Urban League, a specific workforce intermediary, committee members in the local chamber of commerce, a particular employer, or an official in the state department of labor). A network of such actors can develop the needed level of trust, and support a pathway from the target population to placement in jobs.

Awareness and trust also operate at a very general level. As a category, publicly-funded training programs stand in low regard with the business sector in many cities. In some places, such programs are seen simply as a source of patronage—"a cash cow" for elected officials who seek to use their position to dole out favors. In such a community, business employers might still develop confidence in particular trainers and intermediaries, but still hold the overall system in low regard. Particular actors can form an exception to the general perception and understanding; however, scaling up a successful set of particulars is likely to be extremely difficult if the system as a whole is regarded poorly with only particular exceptions.

Although a small set of actors might demonstrate what is possible, and pave the way to a larger change in relationships, a particular working relationship might also be seen as simply an exception to the general pattern. The looseness of the overall system, and the presence of many autonomous actors may result in small-scale rearrangements of relationships without an overall alteration in the situation. As many have come to realize, what we need is systemic change, but the question is what might leverage such change.

CHANGE

Ultimately, for the system to work effectively, individuals need access to training providers who have access to employers offering decent-wage jobs—directly or through intermediaries or job ladders. As we have mentioned, certain links within this system are weak. The strongest links between the target population, the most job-ready segment of this population, are to the community-based training providers who have the weakest links to good-paying jobs.

Thus, transforming the system becomes a task of transforming relationships on a grand scale. Can it be done? What are the obstacles? One primary obstacle may be inertia. The system is moving steadily along; therefore, to change the system, a reform momentum must emerge. For that to happen, however, the momentum of the status quo must first be redirected. According to Kazis (1998), the momentum of established relationships has begun to slow down, as evidenced by the emergence of many new intermediaries. It does seem that employers felt a slight nudge from the tight labor market of the 1990s and responded by exploring new relationships.

In a recent report released by the Workforce Innovation Networks,[4] the authors argue that employers are, in fact, becoming more concerned about how they get their employees (Jobs for the Future, 2001). Consequently, they have become more willing to "engage the public-funded systems." According to these authors, this willingness results from a tight labor market, rising skills demands, and "the emergence of work-centered social policies at the state and federal levels." In short, the costs of meeting labor needs have risen to a point at which alternative approaches have become more appealing. At the same time, it appears that recent policy initiatives are constructed such that the costs involved with employing an economically disadvantaged individual have been reduced.

The report highlights the centrality of employer organizations to this entire effort. They are the institutions that can broker with the training providers, as well as bear the costs of developing relationships with training providers so that the training that potential employees receive will be reflective of the needs of the employers. These organizations can play five roles: Convening and supporting employers; brokering and providing services to employers and workers; improving the delivery of education, training, and support services; conducting research and development of workforce strategies and products; and helping govern and improve the workforce development system.

One key point that the authors highlight concerning employer organizations is the trust that employers have in these organizations. Trust is central to changing behavior. Even in an optimistic account, however, certain challenges stand out. It is still difficult for employer organizations to get many of their members interested in engaging the publicly-funded workforce development system; it is perceived as too costly an endeavor. Business executives complain that interaction with the public system carries too high a cost—excessive paperwork, turf issues, reporting requirements, inflexible regulations, and restrictions on incumbent workers. They also voice the objection that the system has been detached from employer needs and focuses on the individuals' needs, not the employers'. This disconnection also applies to organizations like the local WIB. Despite the various complaints, change is possible.

> Employers will use the public system if it is easy to navigate, provides consistent quality, and is cost-competitive with other options. If not, they show little loyalty to the publicly funded system and typically have other choices in the labor market. (Jobs for the Future, 2001, 16)

Still many employers believe that working with low-income individuals carries added burdens.

> Employers face higher costs and risks when hiring, training, and upgrading the skills of low-income workers, many of whom have little or poor work histories. Employers often pay a heavy financial and productivity price when they hire less-skilled workers or invest in the development of these workers' skills, because it its difficult to know in advance who will succeed on the job and who will stay long enough to justify the investment. (Jobs for the Future, 2001, 21–22)

Many organizations claimed that such hires required special post-employment support services including child care and transportation. It seems unlikely that employers would willingly increase their costs, or consistently pay what they perceive to be a higher cost, to employ low-income individuals—especially considering the long list of other perceived difficulties.

The challenge is to build confidence throughout the set of employers that hiring low-income individuals will not increase their labor costs or cause any other burden. This, of course, means that at some point this concept must become a reality and then be communicated to employers—no simple task. Making this a reality almost certainly involves significant public subsidy to meet employer expectations about hiring costs. Predictably, then, much of the current discussion centers on employers and what it takes to engage them in the employment of workers from target communities. That is, however, only part of the equation. What about the trust and awareness of the target-community? It is hard to recruit people from target areas to take part in workforce development, and, once participants are placed, retention is an additional complication. What is the nature of that challenge?

THE TWO WORLDS PROBLEM

Progress can be made; inner-city workers can be placed and retained in jobs that provide a family wage. However, this is not easy, and, even with careful planning and design, many workforce participants fall by the wayside at one stage or another. The disconnection between inner-city communities and employers is severe. Neither side of this disconnection seems well positioned to address the problem on its own, and neither employers nor inner-city residents encourage initiatives to reform the system. Hence, it is never easy to build projects to scale.

Race can make this problem particularly complex (see Annie E. Casey Foundation, 2001). Employer prejudice and stereotyping remain as problems (Lafer, 2002, 95–96), but the difficulty runs beyond what most people recognize as discrimination. Diversity training can lower some barriers, but issues of incongruent outlooks and incompatible expectations run deeper than that, particularly when trying to bring the long-term unemployed into the mainstream economy (Wilson, 1996).

It is, of course, important to avoid "blaming the victim," but that need should not lead us to minimize the extent to which disadvantages imposed at one stage can perpetuate themselves and limit life chances, and therefore, alter outlooks at a future time. For the hardest to place, the workforce development challenge starts with the fact that the inner-city labor pool is anchored in a marginal position, historically tied to low-wage work in industries long in decline. Moreover, the nature of inner-city schools and other youth-serving institutions reinforces marginality, thereby making the condition difficult to change.

In some border communities, language looms as a large barrier when, for example, textile plants close and a Spanish-speaking work enclave goes out of existence. Intensive language training might create new opportunities, but that is not a path that middle-aged and older workers find easy to pursue. In other communities, deindustrialization meant that less-skilled jobs disappeared and households lost links to the primary labor market at the same time that inner-city schools had gone into decline. In one survey of participants in a workforce project, applicants were asked to identify barriers; the largest proportion of applicants (30 percent) cited lack of education as a barrier, and another 17 percent of applicants indicated lack of job training (Abt Associates and New School University,

2000, 82). Essential qualifications were often missing, and, as it was, "many of those showing up were simply not ready for training" (Ibid; see also Bernick, 1987).

In accounts of community problem solving, a standard scenario centers on battles over turf, attachment to entrenched procedure, and the difficulties in creating inter-organizational collaboration. We want to suggest an additional dimension of the situation. Current projects do not have a clean slate on which to work. Earlier experiences mean that many employers are "suspicious of subsidized job training programs and reluctant to participate in them" (Abt Associates and New School University, 2000, 9). For their part, inner-city communities also bring significant distrust into the planning process, reflecting their own history of frustrated progress. "Not ready for training" does not emerge from a historical vacuum.

In New Orleans, where community groups played an especially active part in a foundation-funded workforce initiative, major tension surfaced and trust had to be built gradually. Significantly, the project "made a conscious decision to limit the involvement of business and other potentially powerful actors until the initiative had made progress in establishing its voice and agenda" (Abt Associates and New School University, 1997b, 1). Although the New Orleans site managed to keep community-based organizations in a central role and made progress toward increasing trust, all of this came at a cost. The New Orleans site displayed limited ability "to produce detailed strategies, project/prototype descriptions, and action steps" (Ibid).

From another project came the telling observation that it was harder "to change people's world view than they had expected" (Abt Associates and New School University, 2000, 73). Although the report provides no elaboration, there is enough ethnographic research and firsthand reporting for us to know what mindset thrives in poverty and what experiences help form it. It is a view of the world as a place of sparse opportunity. Although employers and even intermediaries often talk about a need to nurture a work ethic, the inner city is not a place of deviant, underclass values. It is, however, a place in which people see the world as ungenerous and, sometimes, openly hostile. Expectations run low, and long-term aspirations are hard to foster.

Both employers and inner-city residents thus bring great wariness to the issue of workforce development. Both sides have histories of disappointment. What, then, to make of site-level observations about motivational barriers and the problem of "cultural competence" that many employers and intermediaries cite? It seems that there is a basis for the divergence between community norms and workplace norms. If so, the urban workforce problem goes beyond such matters as an improved flow of information, better transportation, or decreased misunderstanding in interpersonal relations. It also includes a disconnect between two different worlds—one based in experiences of limited opportunity, economic stagnation and decline, and marginality and the other based in experiences of expanding opportunity, economic growth, and competitive play in the main arena (cf. Bernick, 1987).

Urban workforce development calls for *the reconciliation of these two worlds*. It is not simply about opening up opportunities to an aggregation of individuals. For those at the "hard to employ" end of the spectrum, it is about transformation of a complex situation. It is a circumstance in which one party (i.e., employers) is comfortable with its place and sees little need to change; whatever concessions it makes are minor and involve little loss of status. The other party (i.e., inner-city residents), however, faces a need for major alterations that involve not only a future filled with uncertainties, but also a future that carries with it an implicit acknowledgment of a history of failure—even though the history was not of that party's own creation. In a market-based society, discussions of problems tend to focus on populations of lower socio-economic status and communities, perhaps thereby reinforcing their awareness of their own marginality and the low regard in which they are held.

Given the depth of the challenges to reach the hardest to employ, workforce development needs more than a few incremental steps. Past experience contains few instances of cumulative progress in linking low-income communities with family-wage jobs. Certainly, effective workforce development requires much more than a "jobs first" strategy,[5] and it calls for much more than continuing dependence on the current "system" of human investment to meet the needs of the urban poor.

Seen in its full context, workforce development for the very poor perhaps can be understood best as a problem in modernization (cf. Moses and Cobb, 2001). As such, piecemeal efforts are unlikely to have a lasting effect. Workforce development is an embedded problem, intertwined with a national failure to develop an effective employment policy (Weir, 1992; Mucciaroni, 1990), and a long-standing U.S. attachment to a two-tier system of social policy (Quadagno, 1994; Hamilton and Hamilton, 1997; and Weir, Orloff, and Skocpol, 1988).

Why have inner-city minorities been so closely tied to the economic past? Partly it has been a matter of being confined by race to the central city at the time in which commerce and jobs moved out. Partly it has been a long history of employment in low-wage jobs in industries in decline—labor intensive agriculture in the South and Southwest, manufacturing in what came to be known as the "rust belt," and low-education jobs in textiles and kindred industries in border communities. In short, today's urban youth have inherited a legacy of disconnection from the world of advanced education and economic expansion. As Civil Rights hero Robert Moses cautioned a group of Mississippi students, "Society is prepared to write you off the way sharecroppers up in the Delta have been written off" (quoted in Moses and Cobb, 2001, 150). Historically, many families, both African American and Latino, were moored to faltering economies and the weak schools that typically accompany such economies.

In almost any metropolitan area in the United States, there is talk of two societies—"two Atlantas," "two Chicagos," "two El Pasos," and so on. Talk of two societies is shorthand for one population tied to the economic past, and another population linked to the economic future. Workforce development, then, is a process that faces the challenge of how to break down this divide and shift a population handicapped by a low-wage past to a future economy of decent jobs that pay a family-supporting wage.

The complications of race and class rest on a past not easily overcome. To appreciate the historical depth behind needing a "second chance" is also to understand why even successful demonstrations do not easily scale up, and systemic reform is so elusive. Some observers might argue that the success of a few is evidence that the many could also succeed—if they put real effort into it. *The examples of a successful few may, however, disguise a reality of scarce resources and limited opportunity.* In *A Hope in the Unseen*, an account of how student Cedric Jennings went from an inner-city high school (D.C.'s Ballou) to Brown University, author Ron Suskind describes "a sort of academic triage that is in vogue at tough urban schools across the country." Suskind reports that the idea is: "Save as many kids as you can by separating top students early and putting a lion's share of resources into boosting as many of them as possible to college. *Forget the rest*" (Suskind, 1998, emphasis added).

Special opportunities, whether as part of a first chance or a second chance, do not convey a signal that everyone can succeed. In a context of "triage," scattered examples of success reinforce the view that opportunity is for the few. A "second chance" job at a low wage with few benefits may reinforce the notion that *real* opportunity is for the few. It has little capacity to heighten aspirations.

THINKING ABOUT THE INTRACTABILITY OF THE POVERTY PROBLEM

In their study of antipoverty action, Marris and Rein (1967, 1973) describe social planners and reformers as going through a process of ever widening discovery. They learned that each set of problems linked into others, and the roots of poverty ran deep into the class and racial structures of American society. Moreover, the capacity of public bodies and their civic allies to tackle deeply embedded issues proved to be limited, because concerns about institutional self-interest and turf protection served to sustain the fragmentation of the very entities that had the greatest potential for bringing about social change. Decades after Marris and Rein's initial report, their observations still hold. Problems are linked, poverty has deep roots, and public and nonprofit agencies still find it hard to combine their efforts into a comprehensive approach.

With the federal government largely in the embrace of devolution, unless state governments fill the vacuum, continuing efforts to address problems of poverty and economic disadvantage fall to a scattering of philanthropic institutions and to sporadic surges of activity by local civic and governmental leaders. Such efforts, however, often prove to be two-edged. On the one hand, they show that strategic planning and action intelligently sustained can create opportunities otherwise unavailable for participants. In short, it is possible to do social good. Alternatively, these efforts tend to demonstrate how very difficult it is to make broad advances in social progress.

Although a significant number of people can be helped and moved out of poverty, they make up only a fraction of those in need, and they are not necessarily the neediest. It is a form of social triage. Meanwhile, some underlying set of forces continues to generate "casualties" at a very high rate. Triage gives vital assistance to some, but it leaves many on their own. Indeed, to the many, triage may give rise to the view that opportunity is available only to the few. Of course, we do not know much about how people at the grassroots level judge demonstration projects or even how many are aware of them, but we do know that scaling up is extremely difficult.

We also know that even in an ambitious and multi-city project like the Annie E. Casey Foundation's Jobs Initiative, recruitment of participants from impact (i.e., high-poverty) communities proved to be especially challenging (Abt Associates and New School University, 2000, 46). Although the achievements were significant and the lessons learned were important, the project overall still demonstrates the intractability of the poverty problem. A recurring theme throughout evaluation of the project is the issue of "cultural competence." In some cases, the point was made that employers were simply unaccustomed to the diverse ways of many groups, and sometimes saw job candidates as "too street." But in most cases, the point being made is that the poor were often not "job ready," that they not only needed training in soft skills, but they "were not ready for or committed to the rigor of job training, let alone long term, stable employment" (48). In some sites, staff reported that they learned that wanting a *job* and wanting to *work* were not the same things (48). It was said that much "hinged on a participant's fundamental attitudes and behavior" (Abt Associates and New School University, 2000, 47; cf. Bernick, 1987, 65–79).

Raising the issue of "cultural competence" may simply sound like blaming the poor for their situation. Nevertheless, despite the ideological baggage attached to the phrase, there is a stubborn reality highlighted by the term "cultural competence." Many residents of lower-income neighborhoods appear to be ill equipped to assume work responsibilities in today's economy or pursue upward mobility. Observers on the political right attribute the problem to "welfare" as we knew it before 1996. That, however, is a view that rests more on ideological premises than on historical fact. We need a fresh way of looking at the unyielding character of the poverty problem.

Learned Incompetence

Years ago, sociologist Robert Merton coined the phrase "learned incompetence" to describe the narrow perspective that some administrative specialists acquire from working in an environment pervaded with rules and procedures and with risks and punishments attached to disregard for rules and procedures. People, Merton suggested, cope with the immediate pressures they encounter without much attention to the larger setting within which they operate, and without much regard for the overall or long-term consequences of their actions.

William J. Wilson paints a somewhat similar picture in discussing the consequences of "when work disappears." Wilson suggests that the poor do not possess a different set of values, but that the competencies that they acquire may be largely shaped by the situations they experience. In addition, behavior is driven more by the competencies we possess than by values to which we subscribe. Low expectations undermine the development of job-useful competencies. As Moses and Cobb observe, weak classroom standards can be appealing; they impose no pressure. "If you are a kid. . . , it can be great to go into a classroom and not be required to do any work, a relief not having anything, or not very much, expected of you" (Moses and Cobb, 2001, 171–172). Yet, not placing inner-city and rural students on academic tracks that lead to demanding courses, especially those in advanced math, keeps them out of contention for many of the better jobs in today's economy.

Moses and Cobb see the growth of "serflike communities in our cities today" (2001, 5). As they put it, the shift in the economy "places the need for math literacy front and center" (6). They also note, however, that "math labs in inner-city schools for the most part are used to remediate students about things the technology makes obsolete" (117). Even such basic standards as regular attendance and promptness sometimes are not upheld (Blum, 2001). If schools are lackadaisical about absences and tardiness, then students fail to acquire a vital work competence.

Although there is a substantial body of the working poor who mainly need to have the doors of advancement open to them, there is also a segment of the inner-city poor disconnected from the world of steady, rewarding work. They have little experience with the benefits such work can offer. Their highest exposure is often to low-wage jobs with dead-end futures. This type of work encourages "job-hopping" because it lacks prospects for improvement and imposes no penalties for moving at short intervals. Moreover, as suggested previously, schools and related institutions not only fail to provide needed skills, they may actually teach a form of incompetence for functioning in the work of a modern economy.

Consider the experiences of many children in lower-income families. They grow up in households in which parents have limited education because the parents themselves come from backgrounds in which previous generations were confined mainly to low-wage work that required minimal formal education. Thus, children start with little of the school readiness that middle-class children possess, and, therefore, can easily fall behind. Their parents have little experience or comfort in dealing with school staff. Various subliminal messages are discouraging. Books and equipment may be in short supply. Even when inner-city schools have extra resources and programs, the schools themselves may be old and poorly maintained. Additionally, if schools are maintained and properly equipped, the neighborhood may be filled with dilapidated buildings, abandoned cars, broken windows, and other signs of neglect. Any mix of even some of these conditions conveys a signal that society does not value the students in these neighborhoods, giving them the idea that "they don't count" (King, 2001).[6]

Because these parents are least able and willing to challenge school authorities, schools in lower-income neighborhoods often have the weakest administrators and least-qualified teachers. Schools in lower socioeconomic status neighborhoods also have a long history as places where social control carries a heavy weight, whereas academic advancement carries a lighter weight. Schools focused on social control are least likely to attract and hold highly capable teachers who are in search of professional fulfillment. A bad situation has enormous power to reinforce itself, aggravated by the fact that educators least professionally qualified develop a vested interest in positions that are less accountable. In such schools, educators face a strong temptation to reach a tacit understanding with students that teachers will demand little and overlook much if students will

268 CLARENCE STONE & DONN WORGS

minimize disruptive behavior. Thus, student "competence" encompasses the power to be recalcitrant; it has little to do with academic achievement and even less to do with preparation for the mainstream workplace.

Outside of the classroom, a situation of low-wage work, combined with industries and employment in decline, teaches lessons of pessimism and scarcity. Trust rarely extends beyond a few close friends and family. Organizations and institutions are experienced, not as places of opportunity and recognition, but as places that are indifferent, unresponsive, and perhaps antagonistic. The competencies needed to survive and succeed are those of "fighting," not those associated with fostering cooperation and building forms of collective action. It is not surprising, then, that participants in voluntary job training are often recruited mainly by family and friends, and that even community organizations and churches play an extremely limited role (Abt Associates and New School University, 2000, 44).

"Street" competencies have to do with a combative posture, an ability to defend oneself, and an inclination to define honor and respect in terms of how one is viewed by a small, inner circle. Society generally and its institutions, whether private employers or public agencies, carry little weight in this environment. A recent interview with basketball star Allen Iverson is revealing.

> All I care about is what my family feels about me and my friends, my team-mates, people I care about and know they care about me. Everybody else, I just don't care about them. I wish them well and God bless them, but I don't have time to think about the people who don't give a damn about Allen Iverson, you know?
>
> This is real life. There's nothing easy about life. Nothing easy about being Allen Iverson where everybody's looking at your every move, criticizing you for saying one curse word when you get mad, you know? Feel like you're some kind of villain, the smallest man on the court but the biggest villain in life. I just. . . . I will never put my guard down. I just keep fighting. (quoted in Wilbon, 2001)

Soft skills and employee-appropriate behavior cannot be taught as simply something new to learn. "Street" competencies have to be unlearned or at least knowingly suppressed—which may well entail feelings of disloyalty or perhaps even danger—in order for new competencies to take root. It should not be surprising, therefore, that recruitment from "impact" communities is a difficult challenge, nor that retention of those recruited is also a major challenge.

"Street," like a host of other terms (e.g., cultural competence, culture of poverty, at-risk, disadvantaged, culturally disadvantaged, and ghetto) carries with it a lot of ideological baggage. The connotations of the term even vary depending on who is using it. To describe oneself or one's friends as "street" may be a matter of pride. To be called "street" by others whose motives are in question may be seen as labeling or negative stereotyping.

In some circles, there is a tendency to glorify "street" culture as a form of opposition to mainstream institutions and practices, which are considered exploitive. Understandable as that response might be, it does not serve well to provide entry to the economic mainstream and give access to good, family-supporting jobs. At the same time, employers and their agents need to be wary of the tendency to take forms of dress or manners of speech as signs of an inability to meet work obligations. Some programs seek to educate employers on the matter. Nevertheless, much more needs to be done. It is hard to keep employers engaged in such processes as the welfare-to-work transition. Our point here is simply to underscore how rigorous a challenge it is to reconcile two world views, bearing in mind that employers hold most of the high trump cards.

Overcoming Learned Incompetence

To talk about "learned incompetence" may appear harsh, and it perhaps seems like a version of blaming the victim. However, we use the term to illustrate the point that structural forces in society have shaped a set of experiences that can be self-perpetuating, and these experiences work in profound ways to hinder the entry of the inner-city poor into the mainstream economy. That there are good jobs going unfilled is an indication that social problems are not self-correcting, and that the labor market by itself is unable to bring the inner-city poor into the mainstream economy. To confine efforts to training, placement, and support services may fail to address the impact of structural forces. If workforce development is perceived as benefiting only a few, it does not alter the mindset that opportunities are scarce and unavailable to the vast majority of inner-city residents. The experience of scarcity—of a world in which everyone is out to get what they can today because collectively shared growth is not a reality—will continue to generate people with competencies not suited to the modern economy.

Because ours is a somewhat cynical world, we sometimes talk as if everyone, regardless of race or class, pursues self-interest and little more. This glib view, however, does not account for the varying degrees to which people see their interest linked with the growth and prosperity of institutions and collectivities. One does not have to be an altruist to see that in some situations, one must accommodate to the demands and expectations of an institution or collective in order to succeed. Not everyone, however, brings the same experience to the development of such perceptions. Some may see accommodating to the demands and expectations of others as the necessary price to pay to move ahead. In its benign form, it is a matter of being a team player. In its more cynical form, it is playing the game the way the "powers-that-be" expect. Both forms are different from a world view in which the demands and expectations of others promise no pay-off, but instead hold the risk of exploitation and humiliation. The latter view is more likely to develop in a situation of scarcity and decline, which offers little reason to expect future benefits—especially collective benefits. It matters whether the world is perceived as a zero-sum place in which every gain has to be fought for and taken from someone else, or the world is seen as a positive-sum place, in which team play can improve everyone's situation.

A workforce development initiative perceived as a triage does little to instill an expectation of opportunity expansion. It might reinforce a view that only a few well-connected people can expect to get ahead. If so, workforce programs may well be seen as either futile, or as something to be exploited in a narrow and opportunistic manner. It is hard to ignore the possibility that the many job training and antipoverty programs, including the recent Empowerment Zones caught up in problems of mismanagement and corruption have such a fate because they are surrounded by pessimism and low expectations about collective benefit. Moreover, any occurrence of mismanagement and corruption would serve only to lower expectations and reinforce cynicism. When mismanaged programs are terminated, a zero-sum outlook is reinforced.

Small programs run the risk of being overwhelmed by an environment of scarce opportunity and economic decline. The climate of low expectations is especially hard to turn around in neighborhoods of concentrated poverty. Efforts at change are easily dismissed as token measures rather than as attempts at fundamental reform. In addition, participants—staff and "customers"—are subject to the pessimistic belief that, because nothing matters, everyone is just going through the motions to get what they can, while they can. The seeming exceptions are cases such as the Dudley Street Neighborhood Initiative, in which a large infusion of resources is combined with community organization in order to undertake a comprehensive and sustained approach to community development. That kind of effort holds promise of enlisting residents on a more systematic basis rather than through word-of-mouth from a few friends and family. It holds the possibility of giving people an alternative mindset from the one spawned by a pervasive sense of scarce opportunity.

From Triage to Full Performance

Incremental changes may expand opportunity for a segment of the working poor. For the hard-to-reach population, a more fundamental change seems necessary. For workforce development, the question is whether the centrifugal forces of a loose assemblage can be tamed enough to produce a coherent system capable of moving substantial numbers of low-income people into decent jobs. As described above and amply illustrated across the urban landscape, absent a special intervention, the actors in workforce development are highly independent of one another. There is very little power of command in the workforce arena. Coordination could focus efforts in ways that might be useful. But what would it take to make workforce development a matter of high strategic concern that would bring actors together in a sustained effort?

Consider some lessons from urban regime analysis. How can a city or region build and maintain a stable set of arrangements through which a policy goal can be pursued? First it takes a shared understanding of the task to be accomplished. Cooperation occurs most readily when there is some sense of a common purpose. To engage key actors, this purpose needs timeliness. A sense of urgency is particularly compelling. The purpose needs to be broad enough to encompass the concerns of diverse actors, but also concrete and particular enough to show that it could make a tangible difference. As with any significant cause, framing is important, and it has multiple levels.

At the general level, the purpose expands its appeal if it combines equity concerns with self-interest, as in the manner of San Antonio's Project QUEST. In a quite different example from an earlier era, Atlanta's slogan, "the city too busy to hate," spanned appeals, and Atlanta's business elite talked about "enlightened self-interest." However, Atlanta's ability to combine appeals went deeper than a catchy slogan. Black and white leaders had a very specific agenda of action, developed and negotiated by mid-level staff people. COPS (Communities Organized for Public Service) in San Antonio and other IAF (Industrial Areas Foundation) affiliates also work at multiple levels of specificity.

Framing an agenda is not purely a matter of words. If cooperation is to be maintained, the purpose needs to be a viable one. As noted by a team of education researchers, "it is hard to maintain voluntary participation in organizations that do not sustain significant work" (Bryk et al., 1998). Wishful thinking does not bring people together; therefore, resources are also an important ingredient, and they must be *commensurate with the task to be accomplished* (Stone, 1993). If appropriate resources are not available, the purpose lacks feasibility and will shrink to match the available resources. Triage replaces winning the battle.

Regime analysis uses the term "governing coalition" to describe the actors who cooperate in providing the resources that make pursuit of an agenda feasible. The strength of a regime depends on the resources that the coalition brings to bear on the agenda. An inadequate resource base equals a weak regime. For any policy task, then, a major question becomes: Who can contribute and who is essential? For workforce development this means that employers and potential employees are essential, and both are hard to enlist in efforts to alter existing practices. Intermediaries can be useful in engaging employers and potential employees, but they cannot substitute for them. A chamber of commerce can make a helpful link to employers and promote awareness and trust, but it cannot substitute for employers. A community-based organization can make a beneficial link to potential employees and promote awareness and trust, but it cannot substitute for potential employees. Trainers can provide a useful and perhaps necessary service, but they alone are insufficient as a base for a regime. Labor unions can block access to employment or make it easier, but alone they are also an insufficient base.

The viability of workforce development as a means by which a lower-income target population enters family-supporting jobs, therefore, rests fundamentally on the labor pool and the employer pool. What is characteristic of these two pools if no intentional mobilization occurs? The business sector may have only a scattering of employers who are interested in expanding their local supply of workers for good-paying jobs. The target population of "second chancers" is very large but by all accounts is not inclined to enter en masse into the workforce development process. Training and child care in conjunction with other social supports can increase participation, but the enlistment challenge extends beyond these measures. Yet, when poor neighborhoods are surveyed, jobs emerge as a major concern. Because many residents of poor neighborhoods have experienced mainly low-wage employment, their experience is not a very substantial foundation on which to build expectations about moving into a future of steady work at decent wages. Hence, this population brings a high level of skepticism to the process.

To move beyond a triage regime—that is, beyond using scarce resources to place a small number of disadvantaged people into the mainstream economy—a three-fold approach seems appropriate. One step is to enlist business membership in a coalition aimed at encouraging employer participation in expanding opportunities to an enlarged workforce pool. It needs to be an action coalition that sets tangible goals for both entry-level recruitment and career advancement. The coalition should consist of a wide range of players encompassing the business, the governmental, and the religious and nonprofit sectors. Only in this way can the needed resources be garnered to conduct the kind of coordinated effort that can yield results. Such a coalition needs a professional staff, but of a particular type—one characterized by an unswerving commitment to the coalition's purpose (see the discussion of a "cadre staff" in Rothstein, 1996.). The coalition can carry a message to employers that helps them understand the broad social purposes involved in their commitment, and how the coalition is linked to the long-term interest of business in economic growth (cf. Martin, 2000). The staff could monitor progress, offer technical assistance, and present the overall picture for training providers, intermediaries, and others on the front line, thereby guarding against fragmentation into a scattering of triage projects. Ideally, a high-level civic coalition would be able to involve community colleges, technical centers, and vocational educators in public schools, as well as provide some oversight to proprietary schools. With substantial resources and a guiding structure, a coalition should be able to move workforce development from the margins of city policy into a position of priority; this, at least, should be a primary aim, and it is one to which local government officials could greatly contribute.

Although the civic coalition should incorporate the representation of community groups, coalition membership is not a cure-all. Step two should center on community organization and community development. The skepticism widely embraced in poor neighborhoods can easily outrun the modest gains that even a well-run initiative is likely to produce—at least in the short run. Changing a mindset based on long years of economic, political, and social marginality is no easy task, and it is unlikely to be done from the top down.

Neighborhood-based organizations have the advantage of incorporating workforce development into a larger, grassroots agenda of human development and community improvement. A workforce project standing alone would likely produce modest numbers in relation to overall need; however, if the initiative forms part of a more comprehensive effort, it can contribute to heightened expectations. It is one thing to try to enlist participants in a single activity that *by itself* may affect little change, but it is quite another to enlist participants in an overall movement to alter traditional ways of conducting local affairs.

A bottom-up push aligned with community development, as in the San Antonio example, offers a way of leveraging greater participation by potential employees in a workforce effort. Project QUEST is not a standalone effort, but instead part of an overall strategy of expanding opportunities, developing grassroots leadership, strengthening neighborhood-based networks, and overcoming the isolation of lower-income communities. Workforce development, like school reform and the promotion of youth development, holds the most promise when linked to a multifaceted strategy for attacking disadvantage through community development.

Community development calls for building a different kind of coalition than necessary for workforce development. It defines the task in a different way and, as a result, engages the target population differently. Individuals are not making isolated efforts, but instead become part of a group mobilization. Instead of spotlighting their individual "deficits," shared aims are illuminated. As members of lower-income communities see themselves in a different light, a viewpoint infused by pessimism and a sense of being isolated in an ungenerous world can give way to a more positive view of what is possible. Increasing a sense of efficacy is one of the primary aims of community organization. If achieved, it can serve workforce development as well.

The third step involves an attempt to address the reality that important forces affecting the level of family income are extra-local. State and national policies greatly affect the position of the working poor. Earned Income Tax Credits, the minimum-wage level, support for child care and early childhood development, living-wage agreements, and health care policy are examples of policies that can alter the nature of what is now classified as low-wage work. There are also continuing problems of cumbersome regulations that make it difficult for families to enjoy steady participation in the workforce. A local voice in the national discourse about these issues could provide concrete grounding that is all too often missing. A third step, then, might consist of forming cross-locality coalitions so that the local voice is less easily ignored, and local actors can join with state and national players within the government, the advocacy community, and concerned elements of the business sector. If such a coalition could move toward favorable changes in state and national policy, that movement could contribute to raised expectations. Even an airing of issues relating to employment and the need for decent family incomes could provide evidence that the less affluent sectors of society are not forgotten and ignored. Conventional wisdom holds that those who vote are listened to; however, causal arrows often run in two directions. Moreover, those whose concerns are discussed and debated see a reason to vote. Giving public voice to issues of workforce development and family income has a potential to heighten political interest within lower-income populations, and perhaps even alter the shape of the voting public. That the political climate is unfriendly to the poor may be all the more reason to search for ways of changing that climate. Consequently, we urge pursuing all avenues, hence our call above for a three-step approach.

CONCLUSION

The conventional workforce wisdom dictates that the key goal is finding jobs—any jobs—for lower-income people. In the words of one trio of authors, "The first step is the steepest—the most difficult" (Galster, Glazer, and Wolman, 2001, 41). They go on to suggest that the first step should be followed by additional human investments. This incremental approach may work well for some individuals, and in and of itself poses no harm. Still, we believe it is ineffective in altering the environment in which the problem referred to as "cultural competence" takes shape—the "world view" problem. We think that problem traces back from a multi-generational linkage to low-wage work, especially work in declining industries. Separated from the mainstream of society by color as well as economic situation, the urban poor not only lack material resources, but they also have a heritage of inferior educational opportunity and the experience of social isolation. Consequently, circumstances have fostered an outlook based on marginality not inclusion, on scarcity not growth, and on pessimism not optimism (i.e., expectations of upward mobility). The hard-to-reach poor bring to the labor market a profound skepticism. William J. Wilson and others suggest that people in persistent poverty develop competencies to respond to near-term needs and pressures, but these same competencies are sometimes ill suited to work in jobs in the mainstream economy, especially jobs that possess a long-term potential.

Some advocates of "work first" argue that this approach will at least cause less cynicism than having the poor spend time in superficial, badly-designed, and poorly-managed training programs. The point may apply to some—but not all—job training, but the approach nevertheless assumes that the deficit lies in individuals at the poverty level and that the deficit can be reduced incrementally by measures such as experience in low-wage work. The reality is that low-wage work may reinforce bad work habits rather than inculcate good ones, and usually does not lead to better-paying jobs. Perhaps more important, the "work first" approach assumes that individuals experience economic opportunity as an individual matter, not as a group or community matter. If, however, the collective experiences of the poor are not altered, then skepticism and reluctance may carry the day—their "world view" is unlikely to change. In addition, they may be weakly positioned to receive the kind of preparation needed to secure a stable place in the workforce.

What do we make of this situation? Much of the workforce development effort *on behalf of poor people* takes the form of a triage approach—concentrate on those with relatively few obstacles to entry into the mainstream economy and forget the rest. It is not "creaming"; it is not selecting the easiest cases in order to look good, although that sometimes happens. It is a matter of having the best impact one can have with limited capacity. Consider that many intermediaries working with the "hard-to-reach" poor have few resources in relation to the size and needs of the target population. They aim for positive results by moving a small number of persistently poor into family-supporting jobs. Triage makes sense.

Look at the situation, however, from the perspective of the target population—not from an individual perspective, but from a group perspective. Triage does not end the war. "Incoming wounded" is still the mark of the day. Triage itself does not change the relationship between the target population as a group and the mainstream economy. Systemic reform, after all, is not about increasing the number of individuals moved into jobs; it is about changing relationships.

What does it mean to change relationships? Ultimately this means creating stronger links between potential employers and the target population. This entails overcoming many hurdles, the greatest of which may be establishing strong connections between the target population and the "second chance system" and between that system and employers. The former requires linking low-income individuals to the system in a way that does not reinforce skepticism. We suggest this may be possible by embedding workforce development within broader community development efforts.

Connecting employers to the second chance system, and ultimately to the target population, requires not only exterminating whatever discriminatory practices still exist, but also increasing awareness of the nature of urban poverty and expanding organized, concerted efforts by employers. This is not likely to happen through the actions of individual business executives. It is more likely to happen through the local chamber of commerce or perhaps through an economic development entity. It is also not likely to be a large and far-reaching effort that will change the whole employment system. To attract business involvement requires something specific and concrete, like establishing a One-Stop Center. By themselves, such projects may not amount to much change in the lives of the poor; however, they can provide a basis for involving and informing the business sector in the efforts for change.

What about the sea of wounded who are not likely to be reached by triage measures or One-Stop Centers? Again, we call for a broad approach—an action-oriented civic coalition that includes representatives from business, government, education, nonprofits, and others. The collaborators must aim to encourage employer participation in opening up opportunities to an enlarged workforce pool; promote major efforts in community organization and community development, including workforce development among a broader agenda of human development and community improvement; and influence national and state policies through a cross-locality coalition focused on advancing policies that can transform the context within which those at the local level work.

This broader approach we advocate calls not only for coalition building and a substantial community-based effort, but also for a commitment of resources on a scale that only the public sector can manage. It is important to note that the business sector will be critical to the political alliance necessary to facilitate change. Thus, the sector needs to be educated collectively about the scope of the challenge. Individual business enterprises can and will do little on their own to face the problems of workforce development and poverty. Perhaps, realistically, they see their individual efforts as coming too late in the human investment process to make much difference; however, they can provide valuable political support for needed public policies (Martin, 2000). Business could play the role of catalyst for reform. For example, vocational education needs to face some searching questions, as do those who advocate wide use of the proprietary channel. If these two components of the workforce development system fail to respond effectively to the needs of the poor, then their resources should be diverted to actors who are responsive (e.g., community colleges).

There is a major caveat regarding business involvement, however. The participation of business employers "in workforce development efforts is largely fueled by self-interest" (Annie E. Casey Foundation, n.d.). From this sound conclusion, some observers may be tempted to see the workforce development task as simply one of meeting the labor needs of business. However, we have suggested a different perspective, emphasizing the needs of a hard-to-reach poverty population. The challenge of coalition building takes on a different form from that perspective.

Business has a crucial role to play in workforce development but should not be the partner who calls the tune. Business employers can contribute, but if the problem is defined narrowly as a matter of meeting employment needs, much will go unaddressed. If the engagement of business does not extend to a larger degree, it will be difficult to get beyond a triage approach of helping a small number of the persistently poor. Business often has an immediate stake in keeping wage levels down, and a "work first" approach may only reinforce attachment to low wages. A cycle of low wages and high turnover has a capacity to perpetuate itself, and employers may not see an alternative. Low wages compensate for high turnover, and in business high turnover may result in low wages.

There is, however, more to the picture. Business also has a stake, less immediate but no less real, in social conditions—a point that should not go unexamined. To have a segment of society caught in circumstances that foster concentrations of poverty and an accompanying "world view" is costly. It makes the central city and, to an increasing degree, its older suburbs less attractive for investment. It also generates a high number of social "casualties," only some of which can be treated by triage programs. For human investment programs to work well, business needs to be involved. However, if business participates without awareness of the big picture, we can expect little progress in making urban poverty a more tractable problem.

Overall, if we keep the two-worlds problem in view, we see a need for a multi-pronged effort that is beyond reforming the second chance system discussed here. This effort needs to begin with better schooling for lower-income communities, more responsive vocational training, constricted business reliance on low-wage work, better compensation for jobs at the low end of the skills ladder, and efficient pathways for transitioning from low-wage employment to decent jobs. Each of these efforts requires political mobilization and advocacy. The reformation of the second chance workforce development system will require broad-based coalition building, and community organizing and development. Critical to the task is greater business engagement overall, and enlistment of the poor into work opportunities not as needy individuals but instead as members of neighborhoods that are engaged in a community development process. This is an ambitious agenda, but it holds promise of a cumulative result. If national, state, and local actors addressed all parts of this agenda, we might find that the whole impact is greater than the sum of its parts. If so, it would greatly reduce the distance between the two worlds we now experience.

NOTES

1. But note the critique of that approach by Lafer (2002).

2. GAO's study of twelve states found that in 1995, $273 million in Title IV funds were spent to subsidize the training of over 112,000 proprietary school students who trained for jobs with a projected surplus labor supply in fiscal year 1995. As the labor market tightened in ensuing years, this number may have declined somewhat, but the problem has not disappeared. The occupation with the most such students was Barbering/cosmetology. It is not likely that the economic growth had so strong of an impact on the demand for barbers. As one might expect, students who enter occupations with high surplus, also have high loan default rates.

3. Local actors continue to see rigidities that limit their ability to respond to particular case needs. For example, a low-wage worker who loses her job may also lose her day care assistance even if she could attain new employment within a short period. In the meantime, given the shortage of subsidized day care, she faces a long waiting list to have her child taken care of, thereby limiting the ability to hold a new job and provide for child care.

4. A collaborative effort of Jobs for the Future, the Center for Workforce Preparation of the U.S. Chamber of Commerce, and the Center for Workforce Success of the National Association of Manufacturers.

5. The recent evaluation of welfare-to-work programs found that a mixed strategy of work and expanded human capital was more effective than pursuit of either alone (Hamilton, 2002).

6. The column containing the statement describes the neighborhood setting for Washington, DC's J. C. Nalle Elementary School (King, 2001).

REFERENCES

Abt Associates and New School University. 2000. *AECF Jobs Initiative: Evaluation Report on the Capacity Building Phase (March 1997–March 2000), Cross-Site Report.* Report prepared for Annie E. Casey Foundation. Cambridge, MA: Abt Associates, Inc.

———. 1997a. *Evaluation of the AECF Jobs Initiative (Planning Phase: 1995–1997), Denver.*

———. 1997b. *Evaluation of the AECF Jobs Initiative (Planning Phase: 1995–1997), New Orleans.*

Annie E. Casey Foundation. n.d. "Stronger Links: New Ways to Connect Low-Skilled Workers to Better Jobs." Baltimore: Annie E. Casey Foundation.

Annie E. Casey Foundation. 2001. *Jobs and Race.* Baltimore: Annie E. Casey Foundation.

Bernick, Michael. 1987. *Urban Illusions: New Approaches to Inner City Unemployment.* New York: Praeger.

Blanchette, Cornelia. 1996. *Higher Education: Ensuring Quality Education from Proprietary Institutions.* Washington, DC: General Accounting Office (June).

Blum, Justin. 2001. "At District High Schools, Many Missing the Bell." *Washington Post* (June 11).

Bryk, Anthony S., Penny Sebring, David Kerbow, Sharon Rollow, and John Easton. 1998. *Charting Chicago School Reform.* Boulder, CO: Westview.

Dougherty, Kevin, and Marainne Bakia. 2000. "Community Colleges and Contract Training: Content, Origins, and Impact." *Teachers College Record* 102(1)(February):197–243.

Fung, Archon, and Scott Zdrazil. 2001. "Ecologies of Workforce Development." Paper prepared for the Annie E. Casey Foundation, July 10, 2001. Baltimore, MD: Annie E. Casey Foundation.

Galster, George, Lou Glazer, and Hal Wolman. 2001. "A Regional Approach to Skills Development." Wayne State University, Occasional Paper Series, No. 6.

Hamilton, Dona C., and Charles V. Hamilton. 1997. *The Dual Agenda.* New York: Columbia University Press.

Hamilton, Gayle. 2002. *Moving People from Welfare to Work: Lessons from the National Evaluation of Welfare-to-Work Strategies.* Prepared for the U.S. Department of Health and Human Services and the U.S. Department of Education by the Manpower Research Demonstration Corporation, July 2002.

Jobs for the Future. 2001. *Everybody WINs: Effectively Involving Business in Workforce Development.* A report for Workforce Innovation Networks (June 2001).

Kazis, Richard. 1998. "New Labor Market Intermediaries: What's Driving Them? Where Are They Headed?" A background paper prepared for the Task Force on Reconstructing America's Labor Market Institutions. Cambridge:

Sloan School of Management, Massachusetts Institute of Technology (September).

King, Colbert I. 2001. "A Tour the Mayor Should Make." *Washington Post* (July 28).

Lafer, Gordon. 2002. *The Job Training Charade*. Ithaca, NY: Cornell University Press.

Marris, Peter, and Martin Rein. 1967, 1973. *Dilemmas of Social Reform*. 2d ed. Chicago: University of Chicago Press.

Martin, Cathy. 2000. *Stuck in Neutral*. Princeton, NJ: Princeton University Press.

Medoff, Peter, and Holly Sklar. 1994. *Streets of Hope*. Boston: South End Press.

Mirel, Jeffrey. 1993. *The Rise and Fall of an Urban School System: Detroit, 1907–81*. Ann Arbor: University of Michigan Press.

Moses, Robert P., and Charles E. Cobb. 2001. *Math Literacy and Civil Rights*. Boston: Beacon Press.

Mucciaroni, Gary. 1990. *The Political Failure of Employment Policy, 1945–1982*. Pittsburgh, PA: University of Pittsburgh Press.

Osterman, Paul, and Brenda Lautsch. 1996. *Project QUEST*. A report to the Ford Foundation. New York: Ford Foundation.

Powell, Arthur G., Eleanor Farrar, and David K. Cohen. 1985. *The Shopping Mall High School*. Boston: Houghton Mifflin.

Quadagno, Jill. 1994. *The Color of Welfare*. New York: Oxford University Press.

Rothstein, Bo. 1996. *The Social Democratic State*. Pittsburgh, PA: University of Pittsburgh Press.

Stone, Clarence N. 1993. "Urban Regimes and the Capacity to Govern." *Journal of Urban Affairs* 15(1):1–28.

Suskind, Ron. 1998. *A Hope in the Unseen*. New York: Broadway Books.

U.S. General Accounting Office. 1997a. *Proprietary School: Poorer Student Outcomes at Schools That Rely More on Student Aid*. Washington, DC (June).

———. 1997b. *Proprietary School: Millions Spent to Train Students for Oversupplied Occupations*. Washington, DC (June).

Warren, Mark R. 2001. *Dry Bones Rattling*. Princeton, NJ: Princeton University Press.

Weir, Margaret. 1992. *Politics and Jobs*. Princeton, NJ: Princeton University Press.

Weir, Margaret, Ann Shol Orloff, and Theda Skocpol. 1988. *The Politics of Social Policy in the United States*. Princeton, NJ: Princeton University Press.

Wilbon, Michael. 2001. "The Evolution of Allen Iverson." *Washington Post* (June 8).

Wilson, William J. 1996. *When Work Disappears*. New York: Alfred A. Knopf.

About the Contributors

David W. Bartelt is Professor of Geography and Urban Studies at Temple University, and is the Local Research Liaison for Abt Associates in an assessment of the Annie E. Casey Foundation's Philadelphia Jobs Initiative, a focused eight-year effort to create new job access opportunities for targeted communities and to produce systemic changes in workforce development policy.

Susan E. Clarke is Professor of Political Science and Director of the Center to Advance Research and Teaching in the Social Sciences (CARTSS) at the University of Colorado at Boulder. She is the coauthor, with Gary L. Gaile, of *The Work of Cities* (1998) and author of numerous articles reflecting her research interests, which include local economic development, social policy, and regional governance arrangements.

Scott Cummings is Director of the Midwest Center for Policy Research and Evaluation at St. Louis University. He has published numerous books, articles, and book chapters dealing with urban policy, urban development, and race relations. He has served as the editor of the *Journal of Urban Affairs* since 1987.

Susan Davis is a graduate student at the Evans School of Public Administration in the Non-profit Gateway. Her professional nonprofit administration background includes community outreach/organizing, public information, and fund development.

Robert Flack is Assistant Professor of Public Policy Studies at St. Louis University. He has a Ph.D. in sociology from the University of Washington. His research interests include the demographic and socioeconomic processes involved in city and neighborhood change.

Archon Fung is an Assistant Professor of Public Policy at Harvard's John F. Kennedy School of Government. His recent books and edited collections include *Deepening Democracy: Institutional Innovations in Empowered Participatory Governance* (2002), *Can We Eliminate Sweatshops?* (2001), *Working Capital: The Power of Labor's Pensions* (2001), and *Beyond Backyard Environmentalism* (2000).

281

Robert P. Giloth is the Director of the Family Economic Success area of the Annie E. Casey Foundation, a private philanthropy dedicated to helping build better futures for disadvantaged children in the United States. Before joining the Foundation in December 1993, he managed community development corporations in Baltimore and Chicago and was Deputy Commissioner of Economic Development under Mayor Harold Washington. He has a Ph.D. in City and Regional Planning from Cornell University. He edited *Jobs and Economic Development: Strategies and Practice* (1998) and *Workforce Intermediaries for the Twenty-First Century* (Temple, 2003).

Steven Rathgeb Smith is an Associate Professor at the Daniel J. Evans School of Public Affairs at the University of Washington. Smith is coauthor of *Nonprofits for Hire: The Welfare State in the Age of Contracting* and *Adjusting the Balance: Federal Policy and Victim Services*. He is also coeditor of *Public Policy for Democracy* as well as the editor of *Nonprofit and Voluntary Sector Quarterly (NVSQ)*, the journal of the Association for Research on Nonprofit Organizations and Voluntary Action (ARNOVA).

Clarence Stone is Research Professor of Public Policy and Political Science at George Washington University and Professor Emeritus of Government and Politics at the University of Maryland. His most recent book is *Building Civic Capacity*, co-winner of the Best Book Award by the Urban Politics Section of the American Political Science Association. His current research is on the local politics of setting strategic policy agendas, with particular attention to human-capital issues.

Professor *Allan Tomey* directs the Department of Public Policy Studies' Master of Arts in Urban Affairs degree program. Mr. Tomey's past research includes work for the U.S. Department of Labor and the Brookings Institution. His current research interests are workforce development, economic development incentives, and the economic impacts of gaming.

Donn Worgs is an Assistant Professor of Political Science and Metropolitan Studies at Towson University. His current research focuses on local politics and community engagement in the production of education and workforce development.

Scott Zdrazil is Senior Researcher at UNITE, the Union of Needletrades, Industrial, and Textile Employees, AFL-CIO. He has previously provided technical assistance and evaluated training programs for low-income jobseekers in Milwaukee, Wisconsin, and retraining initiatives for dislocated gold miners around Johannesburg, South Africa.

Index

288   Index